W9-CLH-384

THE
BODY LANGUAGE
OF
DATING

ALSO BY TONYA REIMAN

The Power of Body Language

The Yes Factor

THE
BODY LANGUAGE
OF
DATING

Read His Signals, Send Your Own,
and Get the Guy

TONYA REIMAN

G

GALLERY BOOKS

New York   London   Toronto   Sydney   New Delhi

G

Gallery Books
A Division of Simon & Schuster, Inc.
1230 Avenue of the Americas
New York, NY 10020

First Gallery Books hardcover edition January 2012

GALLERY BOOKS and colophon are registered
trademarks of Simon & Schuster, Inc.

For information about special discounts for bulk purchases,
please contact Simon & Schuster Special Sales at
1-866-506-1949 or business@simonandschuster.com.

The Simon & Schuster Speakers Bureau can bring authors to your
live event. For more information or to book an event contact the
Simon & Schuster Speakers Bureau at 1-866-248-3049 or
visit our website at www.simonspeakers.com.

Designed by Kyoko Watanabe

Manufactured in the United States of America

10 9 8 7 6 5 4 3 2

Library of Congress Cataloging-in-Publication Data

Reiman, Tonya.
   The body language of dating : read his signals, send your own, and
get the guy / Tonya Reiman.
      p. cm.
1. Body language. 2. Dating (Social customs) 3. Nonverbal
communication. I. Title.
   BF637.N66R447 2011
   646.7'7—dc23
                                                    2011020631

ISBN 978-1-4516-2434-2
ISBN 978-1-4516-2436-6 (ebook)

To my wonderful family. You are the core of my life and keep me grounded. I am grateful for you everyday.

Acknowledgments

To Laura Dail, thank you for believing in me. Your professional and sometimes emotional support is appreciated far more than you will ever know.

Thanks to everyone at Simon & Schuster who have been such a pleasure to work with: Anthony Ziccardi, Louise Burke, Parisa Zolfaghari, and Lisa Litwack. A special thank you to Abby Zidle, my editor, for your patience, guidance, and wonderful sense of humor.

A gigantic thank you to Jacinda Little for helping me turn my words and thoughts from meekness to "me"-ness—your word-smithing capabilities have made this book brilliant, delicious, and fun.

Contents

THE
BODY LANGUAGE
OF
DATING

Introduction

ATTRACTION:

> It's biological.
> It's physical.
> It's chemical.
> It's mental.

But it doesn't end there. It's also:

> Detectable
> Manageable
> Maneuverable

Attraction cannot be held in your hand. It can't be displayed in a storefront, nor can it be bottled and sold. In fact, attraction may be one of the last true intangibles left in this world.

But don't let it fool you, it really does exist; and with that existence comes your very own ability to harness its power.

Within these pages, you'll not only discover how to display the body language necessary for making solid dating connections, you'll also learn about man himself: his origins, his evolutionary journey, the purpose of his form, and how he differs from us. In the first half, you'll become acquainted with the human male; in the second, you'll learn how to make the acquaintance of a fine specimen, chosen by you. By learning about the evolutionary background of man, you'll come to understand his nonverbal signals while using your own silent messages to tug on his emotional mindstrings.

––––––––––

Much of my wondering about the workings and nuances of attraction began on a rather nondescript evening at home, the television humming in the background, the babes resting like angels in their beds, and my husband, Kenny, sitting across from me at the kitchen counter, carefully spreading peanut butter onto fresh, soft white bread.

At that moment, as I studied his full head of thick hair, his watchful eyes that traced the knife's path along the edge of his carefully drawn peanut butter line, his sinewy forearms as he pressed the blade of the knife into the sandwich to cut it, the twinkle in his eye as he extended half to me . . . I wondered, *Why did we choose each other?*

Of course, I know why I married Kenny. I found in him the qualities that I knew I wanted in a lifelong mate, a father, a lover, and a companion. But before those qualities were made evident, physical attraction played a significant role in our story.

Whether Kenny realized it or not, I sat across from him that night and dissected every inch of his face: his lightly arched eyebrows; his boyish grin; the angle of his shoulders; the dark, wavy hair that fell haphazardly toward his right eye . . . even his earlobes. All of these things I loved, because I love my husband, but what did these features say to me when we first met? Did I consciously hear their messages, or was the majority of what they said subliminal?

What made his face handsome to me? Why had I passed up faces that were just as handsome, but less . . . something? What was it?

Maybe even more importantly, what drove him to choose me?

––––––––––

The days, months, and years following the dissection of my poor, dear husband have led to this: a book that answers the dozens, maybe hundreds, of questions that I had, and many other women still have, about the intricacies of human attraction.

Because Kenny and I chose to ride the flow of inborn chemical, sensory, and visceral reactions that human evolution had gifted both of us, we found each other. Despite the argument that physical appearance doesn't matter, it was largely responsible for bringing us together. We didn't invent the dance. We simply performed it.

When Kenny and I shook our tail feathers in that ancient, complicated mating dance, which had been choreographed over millions of years, we may not have realized that what we were participating in was an integral part of why the human species has survived for so long, and so hardily. In another time, Kenny could have been wearing nothing but a boar-bone nose ring and a scrap of mammoth hide when he sauntered over to my cave to rustle up some crocodile stew with a side of spicy blonde. I wouldn't have needed to utter a sound, a whistle, or a grunt while I served up a healthy portion of knowing glances, hair tossing, and backside brandishing.

Sure, fashion trends and the inclination toward hair removal may have evolved, but the human mating ritual stopped its transformation when it started succeeding in populating the earth. What *has* changed is the human connection to that mating formula. There are those of us who seem to have been born with an innate "sexual instinct," and those of us who have not.

However, the news is better than good. The formula for dating and mating success can be taught. And it can be learned, rather easily, because every one of you has the ability to dance the dance. It's not difficult. You simply haven't been taught the steps; or maybe you haven't acquired the skills necessary for bridging from one step to the next.

- As we tour the world of dating and mating, you'll learn to define attractiveness. You'll learn to understand why, even though the Situation annoys you like a rattling dashboard, you can't seem to look away when the shirt comes up. You'll get a good handle on why the doctor who's pursuing his degree in massage therapy and holds a propensity for gift giving can't shimmy your shaker like the unemployed semi-amateur wrestler who's been living on your brother's couch for eight months.

- You'll stop for a moment, right between stuffing yourself into skinny jeans and choosing between Cherries Jubilee and Crimson Passion for your lips, to consider the question "Why?" Why do you crush your toes into indiscernible knobs in the name of four-inch heels? Why do you ask your hair to compete for the title of Eighth Wonder of the World?

- Right after you gather answers to those questions, we'll explore the reasons that you want to wrestle with Worthless on your brother's couch, along with the equal, but opposite, reasons that your mother keeps pushing you to accept another invitation from the good doctor. You'll learn to answer questions like "Do men think?" with statements like "Men do think, just differently." You'll learn why you're more concerned with the placement of the TV than what's on it, why you can smell his sweat socks from the kitchen but he hasn't commented on the aroma of your pot roast, and why you can't remember where you parked at the mall, but he can rattle off the location's longitude, latitude, and elevation above sea level.

- You'll uncover the intriguing, and often infuriating, games that a man might play to mark you as a "sure thing" and to grant himself permission to sow sperm like a farmer on speed. You'll creep into his brain and find real answers about why his sex life might be more like the express lane than a stroll through the country market, and why, for some men, the number of women they bed is more important to them than the game score, weight, age, or cholesterol numbers.

- It won't be long before you're discovering the mystery of nonverbal communication. You'll finally have an answer to why two men can say exactly the same thing, but one leaves with a slap mark on his face, while the other leaves with Crimson Passion on his. You'll learn to listen to what his facial expressions, gestures, and posture are saying to you about his state of mind, so that you can turn over some sexually transparent messages of your own.

- You might know that a miniskirt won't complement Father's homily, and that a turtleneck will never get you past the velvet rope. But the real question is this: Is the way that you're presenting yourself directly complementing your dating intentions? If you're dressed like a one-night stand, you probably won't get a second. If you're dressed like June Cleaver, you'll never get a first.

- When you're calculating the amount of time you've spent chasing men, do your eyes spin like a Vegas slot machine? You can save yourself from Not-Interested Nate and Stalker Steve, and carefully land somewhere in the middle, by learning to read some simple verbal and nonverbal cues from men.

- You can use your newfound dating and courtship tactics to play into the preferences you'll uncover to attract his attention. You'll also learn why, and how, staying just out of his reach can drive up your sexual and reproductive price tag, even when other females are falling victim to the bear market.

- If humans could greet every prospective mate the way that Spot greets Rover, we might be able to redefine speed dating. But since armpit and crotch sniffing are generally frowned upon, we can look to science for proof that human pheromones are more than a sideshow at the dating carnival. They are a main "attraction" and should not be discounted in dating chemistry.

By the time you finish reading this book, you will not only be able to firmly grasp the evolutionary reasons for the appearance and ultimate sexiness of the male form, but you'll also be able to grasp the importance of playing up your own assets. You'll grasp the role that touching, conversation, and paralanguage play in making connections. You'll grasp an innate radar that gives you the power to decode men's dating games, while holding a few in your own arsenal. And finally, you'll be able to literally grasp that man in your hands, hold him tight, and use everything you've learned to make him a prisoner of his own free will.

Kenny and I were drawn to each other with magnetic force. Our chemistries and a few well-timed interactions triggered the transformation of basic attraction into something beautiful.

Are you willing to leave your romantic future to fate, or luck, or the stars?

I didn't think so.

Join me. Take the wheel. I'm going to give you the skills that you'll need to drive your love life home.

CHAPTER ONE

The Chiseling of Man

HOW EVOLUTION HAS CARVED THE FAMILIAR FORM OF THE HUMAN MALE

Long ago, the returning sun rose over the horizon to give definition to the grassy plains of a sweeping savannah, to four-legged creatures grazing, chasing, and being chased, to winged beings swooping across the sky in search of insects that swarmed around . . . a vastly different, strangely unique creature.

Like a bird, he stood on two legs. Like an ape's, his musculature was defined and formidable. Like the most cunning of predators, he swept his surroundings with his gaze, his defenses and reflexes sharp. Like the most vulnerable of prey, he stood unprotected upon the harsh, unforgiving plains of what would one day be known as Africa.

But unlike anything else that had ever stamped itself upon that sunrise, he *stood* taller than most of the savannah's four-legged creatures. Two of his feet were not feet at all; in fact, they had long, independent digits. His fur was concentrated, creating a wild and unruly silhouette on his head, above a body that was utterly hairless, and naked. His shoulders were wide, his legs were long, his appendages and extremities unlike any yet supported by this vast bio-network.

As strange as early man must have seemed, a unique characteristic still lay hidden beneath that tuft of unkempt, yet useful, hair on his head. His brain would serve as his largest and most effective weapon, his ally in modernization, and his sexiest of organs. Because his environment would demand more and more of his brain, man's face and stature would change in order to survive.

The changes that have occurred in man's face and body over millions of years make that early man recognizable to us, but far from familiar.

Evolution is a term that's loaded with controversy for some, with answers for others, and with a taboo-type intrigue for the rest. To understand the concept of evolving characteristics, you must first consider the many variations of the human form. There are tall statures and short ones; flat ears and those that seem to fear the head; blue eyes and brown ones; red hair and blond; big noses, broad shoulders, full lips, and skinny hips. Every human face and every body is unique.

Evolution is not something that happened autonomously, or without reason. It wasn't some kind of magical transformation, in which bodies morphed in cut time while the rest of creation stood and watched in awe. Instead, evolution occurred over millions of years as humans effectively eliminated, through mating choices, the bum traits that could have resulted in the extermination of our species.

Clearing Up an Evolutionary Ambiguity

Humans and apes are genetically comparable because they share ancestral similarities.

Your sixteenth cousin, Jethro, isn't the only ape you have little in common with. In a relative sense, even though the genetic similarities between humans and great apes are more stunning than many of us would care to admit (wouldn't any of us pick our noses or throw feces at our enemies if it were socially permissible?),

humans are still vastly different, more complicated, more intelligent, and more spiritual than the animals that may or may not put cousin Jethro's sophistication to shame.

Evolution can be viewed through any number of lenses. It can be perceived as something that occurred to assure our species' survival, as a by-product of sexy mating choices, or as the result of random genetic drift. The facet of the theory on which your beliefs rest can only be determined by you; but no matter your position, the evidence that points toward evolution is difficult, if not impossible, to deny.

Today's men, on average, are 30 percent stronger than their female counterparts. Males generally carry about 12.5 percent body fat, while females (often reluctantly) hold on to percentages right around 25. The typical male's body boasts 56 pounds of muscle, while the female's sports a healthy, but less significant, 30 pounds. A healthy male can lift twice his own body weight, thanks to lungs, a heart, bones, and muscles that outweigh a female's. On average, he's 7 percent taller and 10 percent weightier than a female.

Many of the human male's gifts, aside from the obvious, are evident within the womb, and particularly right after birth. Maternity staff members often note higher hemoglobin counts, longer body measurements, heavier birth weights, higher resting metabolisms, and more lively movements from the little tykes.

Likewise, human male children show a propensity for horseplay, have a seemingly insatiable curiosity, and have a better visual acuteness for snails and puppy dog tails than their sugar-and-spice-and-everything-nice counterparts. It seems that, even from the womb, the human male is being prepared for the tough jobs that his ancestors had assigned him.

Millions of years ago, females, due mostly in part to their childbearing roles, were needed back at the home caves to raise children, to gather berries and other nonviolent foods, and to keep the bedrocks warm. They were simply too indispensable in the raising of future generations to put into the field, for hunting and fighting.

Men could inseminate their women and then move on to provide for the tribe. Men were drawn to the harsh savannahs in search of food and conquests; they were subjected to harsh weather, injury, and stress. The male bodies that were best built to survive these environmental traumas lived to procreate and pass their survival features along to their offspring. This ideal demonstrates Charles Darwin's theory of natural selection. Darwin maintained, as much of the scientific community does today, that features have survived because they offered some benefit to their bearers. Many of the human male's features that we recognize today are in place because they allowed those human males not only to live through a tough day in the field, but to come home and make more babies who would carry on robust survival features.

That's why distinctly male features have survived—because they worked, and they still do.

Let's begin with the feature that not only allowed human males to stand erect and to run from predators that could have easily wiped out mankind, but also now keeps establishments that specialize in everything from wide widths to size fourteens to odor–absorbing insoles in business.

Biological evidence points to the male foot taking a walk on the wild side. If I could name the most neglected portion of the male form, it might be the foot. Why? Because the foot does not contain any major organs, it isn't part of any thought-provoking or sexually stimulating tasks (apart from the foot fetish), and it's generally considered to be unpleasant and merely deserving of being tucked away in a sock with an Odor–Eater and the promise of eventual ventilation.

Big Toes, Big Evolutionary Trade-offs

When you consider the size of humans' feet in comparison to their tall statures and significant weights, any engineer might believe that they would topple over at a mere friendly slap on the back. A clown with long, bulging shoes looks to be in better balance, proportionately, than the standard-footed human—until, of course, you consider the function of the big toe.

Note the difference between the gorilla's big toe and your own.

When humans' predecessors moved from branches to earth, toes that could balance and propel were much more useful than toes that could efficiently peel fruit. Opposable big toes posed serious balance issues for terrestrial walkers, and those with these outward appendages rarely made it out of the starting gate. Early humans needed mobility and speed in order to survive the harsh environments of their nonarboreal (non-tree-dwelling) existence. That's why today's human is able to use nicely aligned big toes to push off every time he or she takes a step—because natural selection effectively weeded out those terrestrial-only bipeds who had no such ability.

Body Watch: The forward-pointing big toe tells us a bit about man's evolution; and now the direction in which his feet point will tell you of his mind's desire. Because he doesn't consciously control the direction in which his feet aim, they're terrific indicators of his subconscious intentions. If his feet are pointing toward you, he's interested.

A man's arch is generally higher than a woman's. This is likely due to early man's need for a spring-loaded step while bounding away from danger and pouncing onto prey and enemies.

Humans are unique in that they walk on their entire foot. Most other mammals use only the toes or balls of their feet (picture a dog's foot). For this reason, the arch was necessary for comfortable walking . . . which inevitably led to longer and more productive walking.

Of course, we can't forget the struggling podiatrist's dream: stinky feet. Because men have larger feet, they also have more sweat glands in those feet. And when those manly boats are in their slips, or shoes, for too long, a bounty of smells, including cabbage, cheese, fish, and sulfur, are summoned. Products of metabolic functions of sweat-loving bacteria, these smells are far from pleasant, but your boyfriend's bouquet is, in fact, the effect of an ancient and useful tracking device.

Consider this: Would you be able to tell, blindfolded, whether it's your brother or your boyfriend who's taken off his Nikes?

That's because each human's chemistry harbors a different concoction of odor-causing bacteria. Though foot smell can be identified in general, it does vary from person to person. For this reason, early males were able to track each other by terrestrial scent. If a soggy-footed man was lost, injured, or being held hostage, his tribal cohorts could sniff out his track and rescue him in a grand display of comradeship (which may actually have had more to do with preserving a tribe member for his hunting or fighting ability). The rescued man then lived to spread his genetic material, which included a propensity for sweaty feet.

However, this nifty scent-tracking ability raises a question: Wouldn't the putrid scent of a man's tracks also draw in predators sporting big noses and empty stomachs? The famed twentieth-century anthropologist Louis Leakey alluded to the fact that human odor was foul enough to make early man repugnant to predators. This was due in large part to man's high-protein diet. If Leakey's theory is correct, and a prehistoric dog was tracking a barefooted man, the dog would know that the creature he was following was a carnivore (because of that putrid, protein-rich stench), a big one, and of an unknown species. Because most animals are xenophobic, or fearful of the unknown, the dog may have backed off in favor of a more familiar smell. As men developed hunting and defense skills they would have fought off many of the predators that tracked them, teaching those predators that the scent of this once-unknown carnivore meant danger. Therefore, the men with the sweatiest of feet were less likely to be pursued by predators that understood how quickly they could be demoted to prey.

Get a Grip, Big Foot

Just as hands have fingerprints, feet also have patterns that vary from person to person. Thick skin, the type found only on the soles of the feet and the palms of the hands, grows no hair (this characteristic is notable in all primates) but has one extraordinary purpose: grip. The ridges on the bottom of the foot did for early humans what a good set of radials can do for your car. Whether man was in pursuit, being pursued, climbing a tree, or bracing during copulation (good reason for today's man to remove his socks during sex), grip was essential for his survival and his procreation.

So let's pay the male foot a bit of respect. It may never enjoy a pedicure. It may never freshen a room. It may be less than alluring in its aesthetics, its feel, and its hygiene, but for goodness' sake, let's give credit where credit is due. Without this complicated machine, one that has deemed itself worthy of an independent discipline, podiatric medicine, the entire human masculine machine may have never progressed far enough to walk into the club, the date, or your life.

A *long* leg up on the competition. Humans are the only bipeds on earth that gain locomotion solely on their "hind" legs, by walking and running. Other primates will walk or run on their hind legs for a short time, and other mammals and birds will hop on their hind legs for their whole lives, but not one could run across the finish line of the New York City Marathon fully erect.

With humans' upright stances had come not only a need to quickly learn to outsmart predators and prey (humans were now down from the trees and enormously vulnerable), but a need to run like hell. Anyone who's watched the Summer Olympics knows that there's no room for stubbiness in the leg department. In fact, most Olympic athletes have legs that range from average to long—usually equating to at least half of their total height.

As early humans spent time outsmarting and outrunning danger, natural selection favored those with longer legs. If you've run the high school mile next to McStretch, you can follow natural selection's virtual thought process. For every two of your running steps, McStretch took one. He could gallop along at a leisurely pace while you had to disengage and dispose of your lower intestine just to make it before Mr. Jim Nasium blew the whistle.

Without a doubt, early humans with longer legs were much better at outrunning danger and overtaking prey. When you consider that men spent much of their time doing just this, you've got a plausible explanation for why men's legs have evolved to be longer and more lean-muscled than women's.

Well-muscled legs are common characteristics of modern humans. They were also necessities for ancient humans. When we made the move to bodily erection, "hind" legs took on twice the workloads they once had. They now had to support twice the weight and aid in twice the balance. The musculature that evolved takes credit for the straight, forward-moving, and smooth operation of today's human legs.

Men's legs are often longer than women's (in relation to height) because boys mature more slowly than girls, which gives their legs more time to grow. This slow growth left boys of millennia past more vulnerable during puberty, but after the gawkiness lifted they were gifted with some advantageous mechanisms on which to escape danger and to run down prey. Stumpy-limbed men were likely left behind to be mauled, consumed, and rendered irreproducible while their taller, leggier companions brought home the goods.

Generally, the male's calf muscle will sit higher on his leg and appear more protrusive thanks to his extra muscle mass and his longer legs.

Body Watch: Often, a man's indecision is made obvious by a leg position known as the *asymmetrical stance*. If one leg is pointed in your direction, as if he's prepared to take a step toward you, but his body weight is resting on the back leg, he wants to come closer, but is hesitant.

The next time you're at the gym and Mr. Athletic saunters in, take notice of the length and the musculature of his legs. If at first glance he seems to have flawless bodily proportions, you'll probably notice, with more scrutiny, that his legs make up at least half of his height. This design contributed to his ancestors' speed in the wilds of the savannahs, and today it serves to speed him right into your line of discriminating vision.

Once he passes, hold on to your free weights. The rear view will hold its own parcel of evolutionary delights.

The male buttocks brilliantly compose the smartest of asses. In comparison to other species, the human male has a more rounded, rather protrusive buttock region. To put it lightly, he's got a bulbous ass. Unlike the female's butt, the male's is composed primarily of muscle, the amount of which determines whether it belongs to an athlete or an accountant.

So, you might ask, why all the bodily exposure for muscles that do their best work on football bleachers? Ah, you've been misled.

Human buttocks are nature's gifts to modern men and women. People that walked the earth only two million years ago had no such features. In fact, their pelvises were less substantial because they were responsible for holding less buttock muscle in place. It wasn't until man learned of the benefits of long-distance running that his butt embarked on a journey of globular proportions. Once again natural selection put in its two cents. The men with bigger, protruding gluteus maximus muscles were not only able to outrun the wild and crazy carnivores of the savannahs, they were also able to continue running for much longer than their pursuers. So while these finely buttocked men enjoyed nights at home, creating more bulbous-butted babies, others had "lost their asses" (which they never really had in the first place) in races with Mother Nature.

The better muscled the buttock region was, the longer a human could stand upright, walk upright, and run upright. Daniel E. Lieberman, professor of anthropology at Harvard's Faculty of Arts and Sciences, put it best when he said, "Your gluteus maximus stabilizes your trunk as you lean forward in a run. A run is like a controlled fall, and your buttocks help to control it."

For early man, the development of well-muscled buttocks may have drawn in the cave chicks (as we'll discuss in detail later), but it also helped him to make great strides in the pursuit of health, food wealth, and dominance. In other words, thanks to the male buttocks, the human race was able to haul ass out of some pretty sticky situations.

That brings us to the body parts that have aided men, throughout history, when those sticky situations were simply unavoidable.

Blue-collar ancestors are responsible for the girth of today's multicolored collars. When you take in the physique of a professional wrestler, an NHL hockey player, a career construction worker, or even your son's phys-ed teacher (*tsk, tsk*), a long, spindly neck probably isn't part of the mix.

Life on the savannah wasn't easy for early man. He frequently had to defend his life against predators and other men. Those men whose heads rested on necks that were shorter and thicker were more likely to survive these wild encounters.

The neck houses food, air, blood, and impulse transportations that are necessary for life, so it only makes sense that encasing these functions in muscle would benefit the physical hunter and the aggressive male.

"Pencil neck" not only refers to an atypical male's lack of girth in the collar department, it also refers to how easily his spine can be shattered. A thin neck is a feminine quality—one that would be of little benefit to the "manly man" while wrestling, human grappling, or animal tackling.

The human male shoulders a great weight, particularly when you consider the rotational abilities of the shoulders themselves. The shoulders are powerful enough to support the human male's muscular arms, but in an inclusively human sense, the shoulders are both versatile and ingeniously engineered.

It's clear that shoulders are the human joints that have ended up with the greatest degrees of rotation and flexibility. Our primate ancestors needed terrific shoulder rotation for hanging from branches, swinging from tree to tree, gathering fruit from limbs, and climbing to escape danger. However, in order for bipedal people to run efficiently, they needed shoulders that would properly balance the movement made by their lower halves. Early humans who possessed shoulders with wide ranges of rotation had better survival rates, and hence carried on to make human babies with those same types of multifunctional shoulders.

As humans started to look more like Tarzan and less like Cheetah the chimp, they also began to stand upright, to walk, and to run. In general, humans maintained the rotational abilities of the shoulder, but more specifically, human males' shoulders grew comparatively larger, because hulky shoulders aided in throwing spears, running, wrestling, and lovemaking, among other important tasks.

Body Watch: A man's shoulders are two of his strongest implements, but that strength can go beyond physical displays of power. Often, a man will use the sheer size of his shoulder to block your view of other men . . . and to block the sight of you from the competition. This is a sure sign that he'd like to apply for a monopoly on you.

Shoulders as Sensory Enhancements

Modern shoulders work in sync with the pelvis to make efficient walking and running possible. When you run, notice how the shoulders and pelvis move in opposite directions. This aids in balance and keeps the head stable, so that your sensory functions, such as hearing, sight, and smell, remain virtually unaffected by your body's locomotion. This would have been helpful throughout our bipedal history: if a human found him- or herself sprinting from a hungry predator, he or she could still smell the pot beast simmering over the open fire, see the smoke rising in a tendril, and hear the bantering of cave gatherers, identifying the way home and to safety.

Without the delicate balancing act that is orchestrated by the pelvis, torso, and shoulders during running, the human head would badly bobble, making precision sight, smell, and hearing shaky at best.

Thanks to the motion of the human shoulder, and specifically the strength of the male shoulder, our ancestors were able to climb down from trees, to hunt, gather, and defend their homes, their food, and their women and children. Men with broad, strong shoulders were better able to defend their possessions and their lives with clubs and spears. They could throw, dig, fight, and hunt with precision and strength.

These lifesaving and life-enhancing traits live on, in today's man's strong, broad shoulders.

A "Humerus" Look at the Human Shoulder

When examining fossils of ancient humans, it becomes clear that the outward-facing shoulder, with shoulder blades situated on the back, is a gift of evolutionary brilliance. When humans' ancestors became bipedal, the backs of their new hands were facing forward, in knuckle-dragging rather than index-finger-dragging fashion. As humans' survival needs grew to include the manufacture and use of tools, the need for a humeral head (top of the upper arm bone) that faced the interior of the body, rather than the back of the body, essentially turned the palms of their hands inward (note the orientation of the palms of your hands when they are resting at your sides, as opposed to the orientation of the soles of your feet).

The reasons that human evolution chose this "humerus" course of action becomes clear with the use of something as simple as a hammer. Try to hold one and use it efficiently with your arm turned inward, and all knuckles facing forward, rather than outward. Don't hit your nose!

Humerus? Actually, it's hilarious.

The human male, "armed" with biceps, could advance beyond other primates because he carried two beefy guns, cocked and ready for bringing down and carrying home the beast. The Neanderthals favored a method of killing prey that involved tackling and stabbing. This required massive strength in the arms. Those men with meager influence in the biceps area likely went without both meat and women.

The strong arms that developed in the Neanderthals, in the first real "arms race," also came in handy when the man invented implements like the javelin. The stronger a hunter's arm, the farther the javelin could be hurled, and the more accurately it would strike the man's prey. This hairpin turn in hunting made the strong male's arm even more important to survival (the farther he could stay from the prey, the more likely he was to retain his life).

The male arm is significantly stronger than the female's. A man's arm is composed of, on average, 13 percent bone, 15 percent fat, and 72 percent muscle, whereas a woman's is 12 percent bone, 29 percent fat, and 59 percent muscle. As you can see, while the bone mass differs little, the female's muscle mass pales in the shadow of a strong man's biceps. A man's extra muscle mass makes it possible for him to throw a javelin a full one-third farther than a woman can (on average).

Body Watch: When a man crosses his arms over his chest, his primary purpose is almost always to make his biceps appear larger. He's displaying dominance, but this also closes him off to interaction. Hand him a drink, a napkin, or your phone number. Unless he takes your offering with his teeth, he'll be forced to open his arms and his mind.

Let's give it up for the strong male's arm—it's borne an enormous weight in the survival of our species, even if its best accomplishments have lately been conducted on armrests.

The function of the bold and beautiful male hand, and its part in helping humankind to "get a grip," can only be denied if you can somehow find a way to overlook its strength and its ingenious design.

There's a reason that your boyfriend can more efficiently crack open the Vlasics. Thanks to the many jobs his male ancestors were responsible for, his hands are twice as strong as yours, or at least they used to be. Now that more of his work is done on a computer rather than a carcass, his hands' strength may begin to dwindle as the need for it decreases.

The male hand is significantly larger than the female's. Because of this, his finger span is also quite a bit wider, once aiding in javelin throwing and large-object grasping, and now aiding in things like advanced piano playing, wrestling, and boxing. This attribute makes the man's hand perfect for the quiet job of strangling beautiful women to death in Lifetime movies.

Despite the fact that his hands are more powerful than yours, they haven't lost any of their sensitivity, as those men who have lost their sight and use Braille can attest.

The skin on the palm of the hand is thick and hairless. This thick, ridged skin of the palms held a noted advantage for early males. It aided in gripping tools when building, weapons when killing, and rocks when climbing. Today it helps to identify the most aggressive of males by offering its uniqueness (in the form of fingerprints) in police booking rooms.

The palm of the hand also holds a nervous tendency to sweat, as any apprehensive job interviewee can attest. This also had an evolutionary advantage: as a man readied to fight other men or beasts, the palm sweat that resulted from his nervousness joined his thick palm skin to aid in gripping.

The fingernails of the hand acted as tiny little helmets of armor for ancient humans. The pain of a blow to the fingertip is greatly lessened with the presence of the nail. Digging with the hands is made easier by the resistance provided by the nails (without them, the bone in the fingertip would take the brunt of the abuse and the fleshy end of the finger would flex too much). A task as simple as picking berries would have been eased by the presence of fingernails, which offered boosts in precision and support.

When you consider the hell that early male hands must have gone through, it can be reliably surmised that fingernails were significant assets—something that evolution chose to retain for both the man and his berry-picking, meat-picking, child-pinching counterpart. Without these handy little finger helmets, humans may have had to endure much more than the occasional hangnail.

Like hair, fingernails are products of the skin and are made from keratin. Differences in strength are more greatly determined by heredity, environmental stresses, and diet than by gender, according to the American Academy of Dermatology. Dated studies have suggested that women's fingernails bear a higher flex-before-breakage strength than men's, and more recently, researchers have determined that they can identify the gender of a fingernail's owner with 90 percent accuracy using the Raman effect (a method in which light is shone through a translucent object to determine its molecular structure), but laypeople will probably never be able to "finger" the perpetrator when clippings are found on the couch.

The next time you visit your favorite juice bar or coffee shop, take special notice of men's hands while they hold up newspapers, send text messages, and grasp coffee cups. Note the girth of the fingers, the ample knuckles, the broad nails, the sprinkling of hair, the pronounced tendons and vascularity . . . and allow yourself to be transported to a time when hands just like theirs were ready to fight at a moment's notice; when those hands could take down and throttle the life from a wild animal; and when they could be brought home, bloody and bludgeoned from the field, to deliver a tender touch.

The lifestyle of the modern man differs greatly from that of his cave-dwelling ancestors, but thanks to necessities born long ago, we still get to reap the benefits of the versatile and handsomely appointed male hand.

The male chest is a sexy wrap for a sacred cavity. Like most of the human male's body, the chest is sizable because past occupations demanded it to be. Encased within a man's chest are organs that helped him to sustain himself amid the harshness of the savannahs. As early man switched from foraging to hunting as a means of sustenance, he found himself having to sprint to keep up with the fastest of prey and outrun the most vicious of predators; and he also had to demand endurance running of his body, because hunts often turned into the equivalents of today's full-blown marathons. It was a significant departure from his days of wandering in search of vegetation.

As man's lungs expanded to accommodate this new, more physically demanding lifestyle, his chest cavity expanded to house them. Those men with broader chests were, understandably, the prime cuts when it came to athleticism, hunting, and fighting.

Body Watch: A man knows that a large chest is both attractive and domineering, so he may choose to use the *arms akimbo stance,* in which he places his hands on his hips and stands tall. This will enlarge his chest, make his presence known to other men, and mark him as masculine in your eyes.

The Great Nipple Probe

Maybe you've heard the expression "as useless as tits on a boar hog." Though crude, it applies to the questions surrounding the presence of human male nipples as well.

Why do men have nipples, anyway? The first part of the answer is developmental. When in the womb, all fetuses begin their lives as females. Before the fourteenth week of pregnancy, when testosterone shows up to make those fetuses with a Y chromosome into boys, nipples are already in place. Human nipples are not aftermarket options, but rather, standard features for all models.

This raises the question of resulting function. Can any reason be cited for evolution allowing the nipple to prevail? Deep inquiry might assign the male nipple responsibilities that are similar to that of a pacifier (sucking satiation without lactation)—and in reality, that comparison flirts with accuracy.

The function of the male nipple is erogenous. Just one male nipple holds within its quarter-sized breadth 3,000 to 6,000 touch-sensitive nerve endings and 2,000 to 4,000 erogenous, or sexually stimulating, nerve endings.

I don't know about boar hogs, but the male nipple is certainly not useless. In fact, in our studies of evolutionary holdovers, it has proven to be quite responsive.

The belly of the beast, also known as the male abdomen, differs from the female belly in that it grows thicker hair (including the yellow brick road of sensuality—the treasure trail); the distance between the navel and the pubic region is shorter; and it is, putting aside any extra junk in the core trunk, generally flatter and harder than a female's.

A smaller percentage of body fat along with a higher percentage of muscle makes the display of the coveted six-pack abs an ubermasculine trait. Female bodybuilders aspire to, and often achieve, this rutted and rugged look, but it was coined by the men of yester-century, when core strength determined the likelihood of a tackled beast being either dinner or diner.

Next time you're at the public pool, take notice of the variety of abdomen sizes that are unveiled. Imagine that the pool is a crystal lake where fish dive and crocodiles lurk; that the diving boards are cliffs from which waterfalls, men, and beasts tumble; that the towels spread on the grass are animal hides; that the magazines being read are loincloths being sewn; that the walking taco salads from the snack bar are buzzard legs from the community fire. Now imagine the different jobs that you might assign to each man, depending on the size of his abdomen.

If you're like many women of today, as well as women of millennia past, you'll likely call on the flat-abbed, athletic men to wrestle your children from the jaws of the crocodiles, to bring down prey for your next meal, and to fight members of enemy tribes while you wait with anticipation to see who will plummet from the top of the cliff. However, this doesn't mean that you should discount the ability of the potbellied men to provide; it's unlikely the women of long ago did, either. The front-heavy men might not get the job done with brute strength or raw courage, but they will do it with resources that they have acquired. A potbelly is seen as a side effect of a hedonistic lifestyle, and if a man has the resources to promote that lifestyle for himself, there's probably enough to share with a woman and her children. In the faux pool scenario, the hedonistic man might grant younger, stronger men pardon for rescuing children, bribe the enemy with animal hides or food, and fetch dinner from the food stores that classified him as rich.

Today rich men are thin and athletic, while men without adequate resources are overweight because junk food is cheap, blurring the lines that once spoke of a man's route to success. However, there are still clear messages sent by a man's midsection, and we will, at least for the duration of our own lifetimes, be influenced by them.

Some Males Have a Gut and Some Are Well Cut

As Arnold Schwarzenegger asserted in the film *Kindergarten Cop*, "It's *not* a tuma'." And as Arnold Schwarzenegger asserted in *The Terminator*, "I'll be bock." These two scenes provide us with gleaming examples of two different males' abdomens: the gut and the cut.

As the human male ages, it's common for his belly to grow. Often a "pregnant male" look might develop, in which the majority of the body is thin while the belly protrudes as if it's flirting with maternity. This, in fact, is an evolutionary holdover.

The majority of early men were probably fit, stacked, and generally hard-bodied, but there were those members of early tribes who were considered to be wealthy, in that they had enough food stored in their caves, or enough fat stored in their bellies, to survive a famine. Women had their choice: a fit man or a wealthy man.

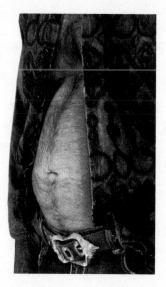

Today's potbellied specimens are not helpless in their midsections' growth, but they might be predisposed to this strange profile.

Some men's bellies are so large that one might wonder about the last time they've seen their feet . . . or the family jewels. These men's bodies, not surprisingly, are comparatively famine-proof, thanks to their fat-wealthy ancestors.

Evolutionary evidence supports modern man's back. When ancestors of the modern human stood up, on their journey to becoming what we know today as *Homo erectus,* there were incredible amounts of pressure placed on the back.

From lifting heavy kills to climbing to wrestling, a well-muscled back went the mile in supporting man's ancestors' physical lifestyle.

When all male work was blue-collar, the back muscles were worked often, keeping them strong and able to support his upright stature. But in modern times, back muscles have been permitted to dwindle to weak bundles of shrinking tissue, which leave the mechanisms of the back without the support they need to withstand the persecution of daily life. Between the ages of thirty-five and fifty-five, 90 percent of men will have some type of problem with their backs, ranging from annoying aches to "my back's out . . . I can't get up" maladies.

We've all heard the piece of advice "Lift with your legs, not your back." This same warning would never have been grunted or whistled within an early human settlement. Legs were for running. Backs were for lifting. It seems that since we, as a species, don't do much running or lifting anymore, the legs have picked up the back's slack, while the back has been demoted to stress management.

Don't we all envy prehistoric woman just a little bit? How romantic it must have been when a man lifted his lady over the threshold of their cave to carry her to an evening of crazy love, without first bracing himself, lifting with his legs, and mumbling to himself, "Now don't throw out your back."

A "hippy" male is not the norm. Male hips aren't given a lot of attention; and rightly so. The more minimal the hip, the more masculine its appearance is considered to be.

The average width of the human male's pelvis is 14 inches, while the average female's hips measure 15.3 inches. A man's torso generally fades into his pelvis without much fanfare in the curve department.

The reason for this dissimilarity is simple: the human male will not be pushing an object the size of a Thanksgiving turkey through his pelvis anytime soon.

If you've ever wondered why some men look great in jeans and others look more like your aunt Edna, conduct this visual experiment the next time you're in the grocery store or at the county fair:

Isolate the rear view of a fine denim example. With your eyes, follow the line that his hips make. You'll probably find that there's very little contour and no indentation at the waistline. Now find Aunt Edna's fraternal twin and I'll bet that his jeans fit tightly over his rump, that his hips are as wide as his chest, and that his waistline has a cinched appearance.

Often, the Aunt Edna's Jeans Condition is simply a case of bad dressing. Men's jeans should be cut to minimize the hips and deemphasize the waist, while leaving plenty of room in the legs. There's been a lot of talk lately, in the realm of feminine fashion, about the horror of "mom jeans." This might be a crime against what some call "good taste," but its seriousness pales in comparison to the silhouette that results from a man's decision to don these archaic, tight-waisted style specimens.

So don't discount the hippy male when he's just out of the gate. It could be his clothing. With a good pair of jeans, he might have all the potential of Mr. Denim Dream.

Male head hair remains nearly as mysterious as the mullet. The preservation of humans' head hair, and the ultimate loss of much of our body hair, would be the stuff of a Sherlock Holmes novel, had Sherlock Holmes dabbled in evolutionary biology. During earth's earlier days, the appearance of humans must have been met with some double takes by the rest of creation— similar to the stare that dogs like the Chinese crested receive today.

Today's human hair is identical to that sported by our ancient ancestors. The fact that human hair's structure has remained unchanged for a colossal stretch of history tells us that it has served its purpose well. But that raises one all-important question: What was, and is, the purpose of human head hair?

Head hair has become such a part of our daily routines and our views of other humans that we may have never asked, "Why do we have head hair?" The existence of the genetic condition known as congenital hypertrichosis lanuginosa gives credence to the idea that the bodies of our ancient ancestors may have been nearly completely covered in hair. Reasons for our losing the majority of that hair include the thermoregulatory one hypothesized by Dr. Peter Wheeler, who surmises that early people were subjected to extreme heat on the savannahs, causing profuse sweating, and that dense body hair interfered with sweat's cooling ability. The hypothesis goes on to say that this cooling mechanism, along with the discovery of fire to compensate for hair's insulating properties, caused bodily hair to be largely lost while head hair was maintained to protect the head, one of the few horizontal surfaces on the human body, from the sun. In other words, the seats of men's and women's most indispensable organs, their brains, were protected from adjacent infection. Humans with somewhat hairless bodies could promote the efficient evaporation of sweat while protecting their most functional organs beneath head hair. Ergo, they survived to pass on genes to me and you.

Another speculation on the loss of full body hair comes from Helen E. Fisher, a biological anthropologist at the Center for Human Evolution Studies at Rutgers University. She maintains that humans lost their hairy coats because bare skin was more sensual and more able to convey sexual signals like blushing, engorgement, and nipple erection. Our ancient predecessors who could send sexual signals and be more effectively stimulated by those of the opposite sex produced more children. Of course, hairy predecessors got by well enough to send their genes trekking through the centuries, but those with ready-to-heat sexual communications became more successful, and took over the copulation . . . and the population.

Long head hair also may have served early humans as camouflage. Picture this: Two men are hiding amid a clump of brush. One man's naked cranium is highly visible, reflecting the noonday sun. It might even be pink or red, thanks to burning from previous noons. Alongside him is a man with a mass of tangled hair that covers his head and neck. It falls over part of his face and camouflages most of his throat. Which man makes the better target? Which man's physiology is protecting some of his most vulnerable parts, as well as helping his crouched figure to visually melt into his surroundings?

Early humans with copious amounts of head hair likely had higher chances of survival because their heads, necks, faces, and jugulars were largely hidden, transforming all of these essential elements into indefinite targets.

Another reason that head hair may have taken root through the ages aligns with another Charles Darwin theory, that of sexual selection. Put simply, sexual selection is based on choice— the choice by one animal of another animal based on characteristics deemed attractive for producing healthy offspring. For instance, if an ancient woman were faced with a mating choice between two men, one with thick, long head hair, and another with sparse, patchy head hair, she would likely choose the former. Today it's known that malnutrition and disease can lead to excessive hair loss. This was also likely known millions of years ago, when early humans witnessed others of their species fall victim to hair loss (among other symptoms) and then death. Therefore, thin, sparse, or nonexistent head hair was not a quality that women looked for in otherwise virile men. Even if those unhairy men had inherited terminal growth hair on their heads (like chest hair), or their hair was healthy but sparse, they were unlikely to be chosen as prime candidates for procreation.

Long hair signified past and present good health.

It could be assumed that a man with long hair had been healthy for a long period of time (at least long enough to grow the wild bush on his head), and he would therefore score more often, propagating his bushy-hair genes across the savannah.

Caution should be taken in comparing the evolution of the head hair (as related to the elimination of terminal growth and patchy hair, or to nonexistent hair, on the head) to male-pattern baldness. The receding hairline has not been bred out of the human species because it was not only seen as a sign of wisdom (as a result of age) and a propensity for settling down, but also as a clear indicator of raw manliness.

The survival of male-pattern baldness today could also be a product of sexual selection. Long ago, women recognized a balding man as more mature, less aggressive, and less likely to take risks that could profoundly affect a family. As a result, men who displayed baldness were likely older and more ready to stick around once their seeds were sown—at least that's what those women believed. We all know young men who are prematurely bald. And likewise, we know some ripe old men who have kicked the bucket with full, beautiful heads of hair intact. In either case, the perception of age is almost always affected by the man's balding, or lack thereof. Many guys curse this affliction without realizing that women have likely chosen this characteristic for them, because they once considered it a good quality to have in a mate.

The ancient balding man's sexual dominance didn't stop there. Testosterone, the hormone responsible for everything male, is at the "root" of male-pattern baldness. Once a human male comes into sexual maturity at puberty, his genetics will determine the amounts of testosterone that flood his body, and where those doses are directed. For a young man who is destined to sport the chrome dome, testosterone will rush to his follicles to deactivate, and essentially destroy, the papillae responsible for hair production. By the age of thirty, it will take either a Hair Club for Men scout or a common passerby to diagnose his looming baldness, but no matter how obvious, his shedding will have begun. By the age of fifty, he will join more than half of all men who can expertly reflect both the sun and the fluorescent lights in Costco. By the age of sixty, he will no longer be stuck in a recession; he will find himself slumped into a hair depression.

But really, there's no need for the baldest of our men to fret. The same hormone that's responsible for deep voices, large testicles, and virile insemination practices is responsible for the condition that many men call a malady. There's no shortage of women

Bald can be sexy.

who consider bald men to be sexy. That's because a man who owns his baldness, or even takes matters (and razors) into his own hands, establishes an air of dominance by owning that cue ball.

Finally, heads of hair, aside from the propensity to male-pattern baldness, are not genderlicious. The human male and human female heads of hair are identical in their constructions. Differences in appearances don't arise until anthropological, social, and religious aspects "head" in.

Foreheads are man's "temples," designed for the new, highbrow intellectual. As man learned to rely more heavily on his brainpower, his frontal lobe grew to accommodate his new brainy qualities. As a result of his expanding gray matter (which would ultimately more than triple), man's forehead expanded up and out. One look at the skull of a Neanderthal man will reveal prominent bony ridges above the eyes, without the forehead that we're familiar with today; his skull sloped back, rather than up from his eyes. The bony ridges above the eyes didn't disappear through the evolution of the brain, but were swallowed by man's new feature: the forehead.

Now that the savannahs were teeming with brainiacs, life should have been simpler for humans. But there was a noted complication that arose from the newly restructured face. Rain, sweat, and other falling debris could now make downward paths straight into the eyes.

One theory as to why the entire upper portion of the human face lost hair, but the eyebrows remained, is that the eyebrows served our ancestors by channeling the sweat and water that now streamed down the face from the forehead out and away from the eyes (note the direction of the hairs in the eyebrows).

Another theory for the retention of hair above the eyes relates to signaling. The eyebrows are keepers of emotion, easily conveying sadness, grief, puzzlement, greetings, sarcasm, eroticism, and much more with their contrasting properties. Most eyebrows stand out dramatically from facial skin tones (even chimps' eyebrows are light on dark faces), making them good emotional indicators, even at a distance. If an ancient human possessed eyebrows that contrasted significantly with his or her facial color, that human could have easily signaled a "mean no harm" message from far off, preventing an injurious or deadly enemy attack.

This communicatory theory might also help to explain why a man's eyebrows are bushier than his female counterpart's. In the wilds of the savannahs, ancient man's needs to communicate at a distance were likely greater than a woman's. Creating peace among tribes, or creating havoc, was usually left to the brawnier of the sexes. This evolutionary holdover can also loosely be used to explain nature's propensity for creating unibrows on men more often than on women.

There are noted gender differences in the human brow. The human male's brow is heavier, creating more of a shelf over the eyes. The eyebrows are less arched, generating a plane that is often nearly horizontal. These differences likely served two purposes. First, the human male's brow has a more aggressive appearance. The more testosterone coursing through a male's system at puberty, the more likely he is to display a heavier brow (but only within his genome—someone could have injected Pee-wee Herman with buckets of testosterone at puberty and he would still look, for the most part, like Pee-wee Herman). Therefore, heavy-browed men generally (and rightly) gained a reputation for being domineering, aggressive, and fertile. These men likely won many battles, as well as sired many children.

Second, a heavy forehead with big, bushy eyebrows gave early man some distinct advantages in the field. He had a screen from the sun, diversion for rain and sweat that ran down his brow, and better protection for his eyes in the case of a blow. For these reasons, a heavy-browed man was more likely to make it home at the end of the day with meat, to a mate ready to create plenty of heavy-browed, hardy sons.

The waxing chair will never host as many males as it does females. Though some men feel compelled to tame their eyebrows into neatly trimmed facial decorations, most will continue to view them as they were meant to be: masculine implements that served a purpose in the ultimate survival of our species.

The outer ridges of the ear are as unique as fingerprints, but with no significant difference in construction between males and females. Though the outer ear is considered to be vestigial, because it cannot move to home in on sounds like other animals' ears can, it does hold value in helping humans to hear. The human ear can zero in on a sound's location to the accuracy of three degrees, thanks to its design and to the neck's impressive rotational ability.

Earlobes serve no protection or hearing purpose. They seem to have been maintained by the human body for two purposes: erogenous satisfaction and beautification. When humans are engaged in foreplay, the earlobes become engorged, responding nicely to kissing and other such activity. When humans are engaged in the spending of copious amounts of money, these same bulbs of fleshy tissue make perfect seats for diamonds, and emeralds, and rubies, oh my!

The male eye: "All the better to see you with, my pretty." Human beings gather 80 percent of all information with their eyes—that's 400 percent more than is gathered with all of our other senses combined. The function of the eye itself is so complicated that even Charles Darwin, evolution's guru, tripped and blundered over how such a complex machine could have been a product of natural selection.

The eyeball of the human male differs little anatomically from that of the human female (it may be a bit larger); however, the presentation of the eyeball on the masculine face shows some notable differences.

A man's eyes usually seem to be smaller, more sunken, narrower, closer together, and deeper set than a female's eyes. These differences are not due to the construction of the eyeballs themselves, but rather to the masculine, testosterone-crafted features that surround them. A man's eyes will most always appear to be smaller than a woman's. This isn't because the eye itself is smaller, but because his lids are lower, creating a more squinted or drawn-blinds look.

Whatchoo Lookin' At?

The human eye is distinct from other mammalian eyes in that it shows more of the white. This characteristic likely survived because of its invaluable signaling ability. To illustrate, a chimpanzee's eyes are fully brown. From any significant distance, it can be difficult to determine if the chimp is looking at you, your child, or the man in the Bermudas and straw hat to your right. Without the zoo fence separating you from the chimp, you could fear attack at any moment, because his gaze, and his intentions, are significantly veiled. Conversely, when you encounter a man, you can pinpoint the object of his intentions by determining the direction of his gaze or the nervous movements of his eyes.

Back in the day, when words still eluded humans, a look that was ill perceived could have meant the difference between life and death. Without visible whites, any man, at any time, could have been met with the grunting or pummeling equivalent of

"Whatchoo lookin' at?" when in fact he wasn't looking at anything but a rock, a tree, or another man's cavewoman...

Okay, maybe sometimes he deserved what he got.

Body Watch: The whites of man's eyes make it simple to determine the direction of his gaze, but they also make it easy to pinpoint the best way to communicate with him. If he looks up while talking to you, he'll respond best to visual words from you ("I see" or "Picture this"). If he looks to the side while thinking, he'll value auditory cues ("I've heard" or "Listen"). And if he looks down when searching for his responses, he's a tactile sort, who likes hands-on references ("Touch on the subject" or "I sense").

The human male bats an eyelash *for*, not *at*, evolution. How many times have you envied the length and fullness of a man's eyelashes? They're not supposed to have features of beautification, right? Well, all that would be a great argument if eyelashes were meant to beautify.

Eyelashes are actually the curb feelers, the whiskers, and the awnings of the eye. The eye deserves such protection, since it is a direct connection to the brain and the most exposed portion of the central nervous system. Such a dynamic, sensitive, and exposed device as the eye might be more widely insured if famous artists, golfers, and interior decorators weren't gifted by nature with the small but powerful implements known as eyelashes.

Humans didn't wake up one morning on piles of molted hair, shivering under the weight of Jack Frost. It happened gradually, over generations. Furthermore, humans didn't really lose that hair at all. Instead the hairs evolved to be smaller, giving men and women the illusion of being hairless. While in the midst of this transformation, humans who maintained eyelashes had the use of eyes that were shielded from sunlight and were better able to focus on important tasks like defense and hunting. Those humans who had tiny hair triggers on their eyes that would snap the blinds shut, quickly enough to put any Venus flytrap to shame, effectively saved their eyes from dust, sand, dirt, and insect irritation and trauma.

Eyelashes: Not Products of Your Ordinary Follicles

At the point where the standard human skin of the eyelids joins the conjunctiva (the mucous membrane that lies on the underside of the eyelid), eyelashes sprout. But what is an eyelash, really?

Under a microscope, the human eyelash looks much like a human hair, until you make your way to the image of the very tip. There you'll find evidence that the eyelash is actually a sensitive feeler encased in material that's similar to the covering of other hairs.

Give your arm hair a quick brush with your fingers. Now do the same to your eyelashes. Eyelashes carry a definitive sensation, which promotes the quick closing of the eyelid when anything brushes against the lashes.

Magnification of a human eyelash. Note the detectors, or feelers, on the tip, which are extensions of the core of the lash.

Nosing around in a big way: one of man's biggest and best endowments. The human nose is unique compared to other creatures' snouts. It's not a muzzle; it's not a beak (although in some cases it has been referred to as such). Generally, the human male's nose is more prominent than a female's, and there are a number of theories that strive to explain this difference.

Our primate cousins' noses are flat with upturned nostrils, so why is the human nose so prominent, with nostrils that face the ground? It can be helpful to picture our ancestors as having a variety of nose shapes—like those you might find in a rhinoplasty catalog, plus some more, upturned, less contemporary noses. When hand-to-hand combat became part of tribal life, injuries were common. The bony bridge of the nose, in conjunction with the heavy brow and cheekbones of the typical male, protected the eyes against blows from blunt objects. You know today that if you were to smack your boyfriend in the face with a two-by-four (this is allegory, not relationship advice), his eyeballs would be minimally affected. This is in part thanks to the bony protection provided by the prominent male nose. Those human ancestors with flat, minimally protrusive noses would have been more susceptible to soft tissue injury (and a blind man on the savannah would have had the same chances of survival as a blind man walking on the D.C. beltway).

Another factor that contributed to the shape of the modern human nose was our ancestors' descent from the treetops. On the ground they had to swim; and if you've ever snorted a schnoz-ful of water, you know how difficult an upturned nose would have made a simple dip or a lifesaving dive. Additionally, the closer to the ground a human found him- or herself, the more dust, sand, and other wind-driven materials they would be exposed to. Downturned nostrils were likely aids in keeping such debris out of the nasal passages and sinuses, as were mucus and nostril hair.

Humans' first words were far from soliloquy, they in no way mimicked the Gettysburg Address, and they were far from profound. In fact, they weren't words at all; they were grunts and whistles. As vocal cords developed to give humans a wider range of vocal capabilities, there was a greater need for resonance within the sinuses. A larger nose gave them this ability. Speaking with less of a nose would result in everyhuman sounding more like anyhuman-with-a-nose-pinched-shut.

Body Watch: We all know about the wooden puppet whose nose grew when he told a lie. But, believe it or not, little cartoon boys aren't the only victims of this malady, known in the biological realm as the *Pinocchio Effect*. When a man is aroused, anxious, or being deceptive, the capillaries in his nose will become engorged, causing it to grow by up to one millimeter. This change is imperceptible to the human eye, but it will cause him to swipe or scratch at his nose.

Though the human nose is larger than those of other primates, it claims a sense of smell that is significantly deficient. This might seem counterintuitive at first, but it can be helpful to focus on your nose's other important function: air temperature and humidity regulation. Sure, noses smell (a sense that was lessened as sight evolved to be a human's primary sense), but they also serve to police the air that enters and exits the nostrils, sinuses, and lungs. The ideal temperature for air that's inhaled is 95 degrees, and the ideal humidity is 95 percent. The nose ensures that these ideal factors are reached. This explains why peoples of arid climates (Middle Eastern peoples, for example) have large-bridged, more prominent noses—the greater surface area

Note the prominent bridge of this man's nose. His ancestors found this necessary for humidifying dry desert air.

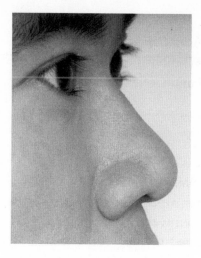

This man's nose is relatively flat, a characteristic that would have protected his ancestors' noses from frostbite.

of the mucous membrane is needed to add the proper humidity to the inhaled air. Flatter noses, such as those of Eskimos and Mongolian peoples, didn't need such adaptations; moreover, longer noses would have been more susceptible to frostbite.

One Man's Stench Is Another Creature's Chanel No. 5

Though today's human's nose doesn't detect smell as well as our ancestors' noses did (just ask the sneering sommelier), we cannot discount the ability that it has retained. Long ago, human noses transmitted information to brains about the safety of potential food items. Our scent receptors' qualities are species-specific, thanks to evolution's weeding out of those humans whose receptors weren't matched to their dietary needs and weren't capable of sending alarm messages to the brain. If humans weren't repulsed by something that could harm them, they might eat it and die, effectively cutting off their reproductive abilities and leaving those with better sensitivity to dangerous smells to procreate.

An example: Rotting flesh smells putrid to a human, but is beak-watering to a turkey vulture. Human feces repulse humans, but rabbits eat certain types of their own pellets for nutritional reasons.

If a rabbit and his nose didn't find his own turd appetizing, he might become nutritionally deficient. If a human found his own feces enticing, he could end up seriously ill or dead. Herein lies the importance, and the fascination, of evolutionary scent tweaking.

Why are men's noses larger and hairier than women's? When you consider all of the evolutionary factors covered above, this can be reliably explained. First, a man would have needed more facial protection, because he belonged to the gender that most often found itself embroiled in brawny battles with trappings like clubs and fists (if women fought, they likely used fingernails and teeth). Men needed more nose hair to filter the dust and dirt that they encountered on the open plains while hunting and exploring. Men's nostrils had to be larger—to supply the higher hemoglobin counts noted at the beginning of this chapter, and to ultimately feed their larger organs and muscle masses with a plenitude of oxygen (particularly while men were running from bloodthirsty predators). Women spent lots of time in cool caves and by warm fires in times of extreme temperatures, but not the men. They relied on their inborn cooling and heating devices, their noses, to regulate the air that was permitted to enter their bodies. Men's noses also needed to be larger to cool them after taxing, lifesaving sprints.

Finally, I would be remiss if I didn't mention the human male nose's ability to perceive pheromonal messages from the opposite sex, without the male's conscious awareness. In this sense, man's nose has maintained its reputation as one of the sexiest (and most phallic) of organs.

Rhinoplasty used to be the stuff women's noses were made of, but men are joining the ranks. Because large noses are not viewed as the prominent, proud phallic symbols that they once were, the American Society for Aesthetic Plastic Surgery reports that men now account for 24 percent of all nose job patients. I suppose the mantra "Big feet, big Pete" took over for the old fifteenth-century one, "Big nose, big hose."

This doesn't mean that "outstanding" noses will remove themselves from our evolutionary future. It simply means that mothers might be taken aback by the topographical profiles of their children.

The "cheeky" male is robust, bold, and brimming with testosterone. Probably the most notable difference between the male cheeks and the female cheeks (not those cheeks . . . move northward, ladies) is the absence of fat deposits in the male face, as well as the higher and more forward positioning of the male's cheekbones.

Modern man's very early ancestor *Paranthropus robustus* sported a pair of humongous cheeks. These things gave new meaning to a "heart-shaped face" in that they generally protruded in both the profile and the margins of the mug. As discussed in the brow and nose sections earlier, they probably served to protect the eyes from blows, but their real functions stepped in at dinnertime.

Robustus's diet consisted of a lot of fibrous, tough vegetation (as evidenced by this species' flat, herbivore-like teeth, with canine teeth conspicuously absent). Their massive cheekbones were necessary for supporting the large jaws and big ol' teeth that they needed to chew what we, today, would consider a diet fit for a giraffe. Since then, humans took to eating raw meat, then cooked meat, then chicken wings, and then nachos. As you can surmise, a large chewing machine, like that sported by *robustus,* was no longer necessary.

A man's facial cheeks have a more chiseled appearance than a woman's. They're also set higher on the face, with higher arches on the lower sides of the bones (more "rainbow" shaped). These anatomical differences are the results of genetics, of course, but more interestingly, they also come from an influx of testosterone at puberty. Male cheekbones send messages of aggression and strength, unlike soft, rounded, feminine cheekbones, which are more childlike.

Body Watch: The cheeks are terrific indicators of genuine happiness. When a man smiles, watch his cheeks. If they rise, his smile is genuine. If they remain in place, he's a big faker.

Throughout history, man's cheekbones have served three main purposes: they have adjusted to accommodate the latest in diet trends, they have made implications of aggression toward would-be attackers, and they have sent testosterone-laden messages to those females who were most interested in fertility. With all those things going for them, it's no wonder that man's cheekiness has persevered.

You'll get more than lip service from the human male's lips, but that doesn't mean they get the appreciation they deserve. A man's lips get little attention. That could be because most of those lips' best work is accomplished at the breast—his mother's, that is.

Humans' lips are far more everted, or rolled outward, than those of other primates. Evolutionarily speaking, that's because they need to be. Human breasts are more convex (round and bulbous) than those of other mammals, and our nipples are notably shorter and more difficult to grasp than the average mammalian teat. Grasping and suckling become simpler when the feeding mechanism matches the food source.

Long ago, those babies whose mouths' mucous membranes were more significantly everted could better suckle from their mothers. Therefore, those babies grew faster, stronger, and healthier, and in turn had better chances of living to propagate their stout-lip genes.

A contributing factor to the endurance of humans' everted lips is the evolutionary growth of the human female's breast. As men chose women with larger breasts in a display of sexual selection, those round-breast genes were passed on more widely than flat-breast genes, making the survival of those babies with better-grasping lips more likely.

Because human lips are essentially the mucous membranes of the mouth turned outward, they are cunningly sensitive to touch. This aided in nursing (finding the breast) as well as in lovemaking (again, finding the breast).

Body Watch: If a man enjoys the sight of you, his jaw will drop at the moment he sees you—but it won't be dramatic. This physiological response will manifest only as a slight parting of his lips.

A man's lips are generally thinner than a woman's for one notable reason: lack of estrogen. We'll discuss this point in more detail in chapter 3, but for now you can operate on the evidence that a man sporting lips as bulbous as Angelina Jolie's would likely get less sack action than one whose lips more closely resemble those of Brad Pitt.

There's a reason men don't wear lipstick, or even sheer lip gloss: women don't dig it. Men covet the red, shiny nature of lip dressing on women because it helps plump, feminine lips to mimic the appearance of aroused labia. Since women aren't (usually) into this likeness, the idea of bulbous, pink, shiny lips on a masculine face is a turnoff—right up there with food in the teeth.

The human male gets mouthy; well, sort of. Human mouths are actually much smaller than they used to be, due in large part to an evolving diet. Anthropologists can make deductions as to a mammal's eating habits by studying fossils—namely their body, teeth, muscle, and mouth shapes and sizes.

Along the timeline of human development, there is a significant increase in body size that corresponds with a noteworthy reduction in the sizes of the teeth. This seems to be counterintuitive, because more growth should call for more food, which should call for more chewing and more capable teeth; that is, until you consider that both of these changes came about around the time fire was discovered, and meat had begun to be cooked.

As humans moved from the fibrous vegetation that had once sustained them to cooked protein, their mouths shrank and the rest of them ballooned.

The human male's teeth are larger than the female's. He has a larger jaw, so it makes sense that his teeth would follow. It also makes sense that he would have evolved to carry a bigger set of choppers because his caloric requirements are higher than those of the average female.

The next time you eat a steak dinner with a date, take note of the size of the bites he cuts and the speed with which he chews each one. You'll probably discover that he can devour a slice of meat more efficiently than you can, thanks to his larger teeth, larger mouth, and more powerful jaw . . . and be finished before you're past the T in your T-bone. Caveat: I'm not suggesting that you instigate an eating contest, nor am I predicting the same results when dessert is served.

He is human male, hear him roar. There's no arguing that the average human male's voice is deeper than a female's. The "Pledge Drive" episode of *Seinfeld* does a good job of demonstrating just how perplexing a male with a high voice can be to the human ear, with the introduction of Dan, a male "high talker."

By now, you're probably down with the fact that testosterone is responsible for many male features. The depth of a man's voice is no different. The male's larynx is approximately 30 percent larger than the average female's, as evidenced by the very manly Adam's apple. Ask any transvestite or cross-dresser about the "hardest" part of his anatomy to hide, and he'll likely testify that his larynx will give away his true identity quicker than anything duct tape can harness.

When a boy's system is flooded with the almighty T, the pitch of his voice drops significantly. This would have come in handy in the bush, when men who weren't yet skilled in hunting had to scavenge meat from other predators. A mighty "roar" would have benefited man in scaring the real killers from their prey. The "high talker" hunter may have been left with nothing to eat, or may have ended his day, and his life, as the main course.

Watch a televised political debate between two male candidates and take note of the pitch of each contender. Try to tune out their actual words. Which one would you assign the most credibility to? Which one would you want leading and protecting your town, state, or country? A deep voice isn't just sexy and indicative of a generous testosterone level, it represents authority and protective tendencies.

The bearded male speaks for his ancestral "roots." There has been plenty of passing conversation about why the human male grows a beard, while the female face remains smooth (and plenty of tête-à-tête about certain females whose natures have "gifted" them with the carpeted look).

There are a few theories that have been raised as to the purpose of a human male's unique facial hair.

One theory rides the same wave as a head hair retention theory: that the human male's beard's main purpose was for protection. While early man traversed the battlefields of the savannahs, a beard not only kept his face and neck warm (by shielding him from wind) and cool (by trapping cooling sweat), it also hid some of his most vulnerable attack points, such as the jugular.

It also showed a level of masculinity, strength, and aggression to enemies. Even without a beard, the male's jaw is heavier than the female's. The beard might have served to exaggerate this feature, staving off punks who might have otherwise contemplated stirring the pot.

Another hypothesis sees the beard as merely ornamental, in a sexual sense. It marked males as males, even at a distance. It carried scents emitted by the sebaceous glands of the face, which were, and still are, more active in males with high levels of testosterone. It also spoke to a man's maturity. A kid with a peach-fuzz face might be strong enough to shoulder the weight of a lover, but not a family that needs his support.

Species identification could have also been a significant task undertaken by the male beard. When we see a large cat with a mane, there's no question what type of animal it is. Like the lion, man must have been easily identifiable by other species because of his dramatic, interminable beard growth.

No matter the evolutionary purpose of the beard, there's no denying that the presence of facial hair is distinctly male. Women likely chose to copulate with men who showed this feature, for many of the same reasons men chose not to copulate with women who maintained mug rugs of their own.

What's your male facial decoration preference? Do you go for an area rug (goatee), a toilet rug (mustache), wall-to-wall carpeting (full beard), shag carpet (long beard), or hardwood (clean-shaven)? No rule is rigid, but chances are that if you covet the carpet, you also value a man with lofty testosterone levels and all of the "perks" that come with it.

From Bare to Beard, in a Blink

For a departure from the facial same-old-same-old, in a matter of seconds, take a peek at the video created by Christoph Rehage, who in 2007 set out to hike from Beijing to Germany without shaving. Take note of how your impression of him is affected, particularly when the "rug" is pulled out from under you. You can find the video at www.thelongestway.com/extra/thevideo.

Men's pubic hair used to be more of a public sight. At least that's one of the theories for why it exists. Some anthropologists believe that pubic hair's purpose is to signal sexual maturity. When an ancient woman of the bush (pun intended) saw a man whose bird nest was plentiful, she automatically knew that he was sexually mature enough to treat her right in the bedrock, and that he was chronologically mature enough to provide for her potential family. This hypothesis is supported by the fact that when a boy enters puberty, hair begins to grow on his most hormonally sensitive areas first. And since the influx of testosterone kicks off sexual maturity, the pubic hair acts as a flag for this momentous event. Additionally, among many races, the pubic hair's color dramatically contrasts with the skin color, assuring that members of the opposite sex couldn't miss the small, but striking, billboard of ripeness.

Speaking of ripeness, another theory surrounding the retention of human hair in the pubic region involves the preservation of the scents that are excreted from apocrine glands in the pubic area. When humans roamed the savannahs in a bare naked state, scents were easily swept away by the uninhibited wind. A tuft of hair in the most sensual area probably helped to capture and maintain some of that scent, which would subliminally speak to prospective mates (even if those prospective mates were unaware of the true power of a crotch's bouquet).

Since early humans were unique in that they copulated face-to-face, a third premise teeters on the idea that pubic hair served to protect the delicate genital region from abrasion. Since a large number of today's people remove pubic hair, this theory holds less weight than the ones mentioned previously. Unless, of course, we're having a lot less sex than the "people of the bush."

Playing with the idea of the penis brings evolutionary evidence. The penis has long been veiled under a sheath of taboo, and I'm not talking about the foreskin. Maybe if Adam hadn't eaten the fruit, his own fruits would be enjoying the same freedom that the rest of his body enjoys today. Nevertheless, just like every other part of the human male's anatomy, the penis endured its own climb up the evolutionary mountain.

Probably the most striking facet of the human penis is its size. In relative and actual terms, it's the largest among all primates. For example, the average male gorilla's body mass is triple that of a human male's, yet the human male's penis is grander, more majestic, and downright bigger than the gorilla's.

Because the penis itself has no function outside of the sexual (John Bobbit could still urinate), this must mean that women of yesteryear possessed noted inclinations toward larger male sex organs, resulting in today's average erection size of six inches in length and five inches in circumference.

The length of the organ may have some evolutionary reproductive function, in that when ejaculation occurs, the closer to the cervix (at the top of the vagina) seminal fluid can be deposited, the closer to egg fertilization the sperm will be.

Because of its design the penis acts like a suction piston, sweeping the seminal fluid and sperm of other males from the vaginal canal with its coronal ridge (the margin at the base of the glans, near the end of the penis) during thrusting. Because sperm can loiter around a woman's cervical door and lounge in a seminal pool for up to five days following insemination (waiting for arrival of the egg), this function of the penis can be instrumental in removing another inseminator's sperm and crowning the most recent inseminator as the winner of a sperm war.

It's unclear whether women chose men with larger penises because their performances were worthier of standing "O's," because larger penises made frontal copulation easier and more pleasurable, or because (unknown to women) men with larger penises were more capable of planting their seeds. But what is clear is that it would be hard to find a penis today that isn't capable of getting the job done—thanks to the choices of our ancient sisterhood of hard-to-please vixens.

Man's source of procreation is housed in his precious, vulnerable testicles. This raises the question of why, if man's testicles have the ability to curl his toes and cross his eyes with pain, they're situated where, and how, they are. Though women cannot have empathy for this pain, not a single one of us would want to give wrestling with a wild animal a shot while a pair of highly sensitized, flailing testicles dangled between our legs. One might surmise that something as accommodating as evolution might have given man a more secure way of transporting the sperm that hold the key to future generations.

The orientation of man's testicles has long haunted him. Early on, before clothing was the norm, a running man was surely assaulted by the pelting of his own testicles. In likely response, the loincloth was invented, opening the barn door for sweating, chafing, irritation, and what today's man affectionately refers to as "bat wings" (adhesion of the scrotal skin to the interior of the thighs).

It seems that internal testicles, like those of many mammals, would be more convenient, more comfortable, and more easily controlled for the human male. But, as with every feature, there's an evolutionary reason for why traits are the way they are.

We've all heard of shrinkage (thanks to George's keen demonstration on *Seinfeld*), and this phenomenon actually helps to explain why the testicles are stored on the exterior of the human male's body. When he's cold (George: "I was in the pool!"), a muscle at the top of the scrotal sack will draw the testicles up, closer to the body to warm them. If he's hot, the muscle will relax, allowing them to fall away from the body, to catch a breeze and cool them down. If the testicles were housed inside the body, the sperm might cook inside their own seminal fluids.

The cremaster muscle in a male's abdomen and the dartos fascia in the scrotum are responsible for raising and lowering the disco balls that get the reproduction party started. But they're also responsible for protecting man's most precious jewels in times of conflict. When a man is stressed, these same muscles pull the testes upward. This is considered to be an evolutionary tactic devised to save the male gonads during conflict (in other words, less flailing equals fewer chances of injury).

Another theory that strives to explain the testicles' outdoor lifestyle is that internal placement would cause undue loss of seminal fluid and sperm. After studying the urine test results of rowing athletes, the late British ethologist Michael Chance learned that seminal fluid was present in their urine. This was reportedly a result of the sphincterless male reproductive system allowing pressure in the lower abdomen (affected while rowing) to expel seminal fluid into the urinary tract. As a result of his findings, Chance came to believe that if human testes were housed internally, the percussiveness of an aggressive lifestyle would make this an everyday problem.

Though in size the male penis towers over those of other primates, the human male's testicles are smaller. This can be attributed to the human male's comparatively monogamous lifestyle. Chimps and bonobos have testicles that resemble anything from grapefruits to melons, but these animals are highly promiscuous, using sex for everything from procreation to friend-making to food attainment. They need more sperm to fuel their bedding and bargaining behaviors.

The larger the demand, the larger the factory must be. This helps to explain why men with a penchant for infidelity are more likely to break the marriage chain and take their gigantic balls elsewhere.

Evolution also recognized a problem with the growing musculature of the human male in relation to his testicles. Bigger thighs equaled less room for the family jewels. This explains why one testicle hangs lower than the other. Thanks to this neat design, they only take up the half the room that they would if both testes were placed precisely side by side.

The evolution of the male form is remarkable. Not one part of a handsome specimen looks the way that it does without reason. The men of today may have given up boar brawling and tribal attacks, but their bodies bear the evidence that these lifesaving activities were once a major part of their ancestors' daily lives.

Every man is evidence of the hardiness that preceded him. He's living proof that his ancestors had what it took to rise above, to go beyond, and to survive an environment that was out to eliminate the weak. That being said, there are very few men out there who don't have the ability to pass praiseworthy genes on to your children. Still, you're left with a hefty challenge: to choose from a plethora of viable options (good, better, and best).

In the next chapter, we'll discuss why certain male features are considered to be more attractive than others, and how those attractive characteristics can help you to choose from an embarrassment of options. Thankfully, in general, we no longer have to ask ourselves if a man will survive to help raise our children or if he's healthy enough to pass along hardy characteristics to our offspring. Evolution has taken care of that.

Now that we've effectively dismembered and examined the entirety of today's beefcake's body, let's move on to why each male body part, when well constructed, captures the attention of the female eye and heart and other girly parts.

CHAPTER TWO

The Male Form's Magnetism

THE ATTRACTIVENESS OF A FINE MALE SPECIMEN, DEFINED

Ladies, we've all been there: you're making copies at the shipping store, you're choosing the perfect mango at the market, or you're jogging off your lunch at the park, when you see Him. You may not know him, may have never seen him before in your life, and you may determine that backflips wouldn't get him to notice you. But none of that matters. The man oozes physical perfection. He moves with a fluid motion that throws you into a virtual hypnotic trance. If you could get closer without being arrested, you just know that he would reek of sexual aptitude. You can't put your finger on the reason, but he's captivating.

With all the talk about how looks don't matter—that attraction is more about chemistry, compatibility, trust, honesty—many of us have only enjoyed our lust for the male form behind the curtains of our own minds (close to the places where we stash memories of half-gallon ice cream indulgences and insurance fraud), when in fact we're just as smitten with the male form as men are with ours. A study out of Northwestern University found that no matter what women said (that they valued high earners above hot tamales, for instance), their first choices in speed-dating scenarios still rested on good looks. In fact, there was no discernible variation between men's and women's preferences for attractive mates.

You don't have to squelch your admiration of the male form for a moment longer. In fact, it should be celebrated. Your sisters who lived millions of years ago

No matter what we say, women are swayed by good looks.

were much like you. Maybe they could have used a good depilatory service and a few sticks of deodorant, but they had many of the same tastes in men as you do. In fact, they're the reason that men look the way they do today. You see, they also thought men were incredibly sexy—particularly those men who could best help them create healthy, strong babies.

Ninety-nine percent of human evolution occurred in the midst of a harsh environment that had the capacity to claim human lives without remorse. For this reason, women chose men who sported the features that would give their children the best chances of surviving the climes, illnesses, and killing fields in which they lived. Because they chose the hardiest of features in their men, those features proliferated to become the standards of sexiness, as well as of survival.

In the primeval landscape mentioned above, there were no condoms. Because there was no contraception, women had to choose mates very carefully. They had limited supplies of eggs and each pregnancy could put them out of commission for up to several years. So if a woman did the wild thing with a man whom she deemed less than fit for churning out hardy little ones, she risked devoting three years of her life to carrying, birthing, and raising a child that might not survive anyway.

For these reasons, ancient women chose their men with discrimination. If their choices were good, they built their family tree. If they were bad, their genealogy withered like a seasonal weed. Which leads us to modern-day definitions of male attractiveness . . .

Are you a butt girl?

Or does your boat float on washboard abs?

Are you a sucker for Rock of Gibraltar shoulders?

We all have our beefcake ingredient preferences, but few of us can put a definition on that attraction. Is there any practical purpose to an ass that can deflect a quarter? It's simply decorative, right? Wrong.

Each typically attractive feature of the male body was chosen by the ancient sisterhood of insatiates, and each one is still considered to be as hot as a ripe habanero.

But how can these measures of attraction remain intact when so much else has changed? Modern humans have established civilizations, instituted marriage and family models, marked adultery and coveting as unacceptable, and given judiciary systems the power to prosecute and jail those who engage in activities that were once everyday occurrences; and still, we lust after the same male characteristics that our long-gone sisters did. Will our biology ever catch up to our civilization?

Peruse any newspaper and you'll bear virtual witness to the struggle that exists between biology and civilization. Helen E. Fisher of Rutgers teaches that today's instances of adultery, stalking, battery, sexual jealousy, and divorce can all be attributed to the conflict that ensues between our old mating styles and our new restrictive, civilized ways of living.

Long ago, sex drive evolved into a formula that worked in the most efficient and effective manner for proliferation of prehuman species. That process preceded our abilities to make decisions. When our ancestors descended from the trees and their prefrontal cortexes grew, causing their foreheads to expand to present-day form (as discussed in chapter 1), they adopted what we affectionately call "the psyche." They were no longer animals driven only by estrus and a primordial need to procreate; they were thinking beings that could make commonsense mating decisions as we do today.

As hypothesized by Fisher, we are still subject to the mastery of our primordial brain. When you spot a male specimen to whom you're attracted, your "old brain's" hypothalamus snaps into action, signaling the pituitary gland to call in dopamine and norepinephrine and to suppress serotonin: a mixture that will cause your thoughts to be dominated by Him, energy levels to be amplified, feelings of happiness and well-being to be intensified, heart rate to elevate, perspiration to turn on, and thoughts to turn toward the great giddy-up. Not only is this the same reaction that the members of your ancient sisterhood underwent, it is also still activated by the same male characteristics.

Civilized living has not yet overridden this primeval reaction. Our old mating formula is still rooted deeply in our brains along with temperature regulation, hunger, thirst, and bodily growth. Attempting to disengage the attraction to certain male features would be like trying to elongate your legs with meditation or like turning off your need for water while crossing the Sahara.

As mentioned earlier, the difference between our mating choices and those of our ancestral sisters lies in our prefrontal cortexes. Our superior decision-making abilities allow us to move above initial attraction levels to make long-term choices, which are greatly influenced by civilized living, our cultures, and our childhood experiences. This could be the big delineation between lust and love. But just for now, at least for the duration of this chapter, let's sink into the ancient easy chair of biological attraction. Let's take a break from reasoning and just enjoy the view.

For an overwhelming majority of women, lean musculature is the first and greatest "seefood." Most women agree: the male form that sports lean musculature has it all over the muscle-bound bodybuilder form. In a survey conducted by *Psychology Today*, women chose the muscle-bound look only as a last resort. Their first choice was "medium with moderate muscle mass."

Why would this be? With all of the talk until now about evolution valuing the stronger men, why would more muscle mass be a bad thing? I think it's relatively safe to assume that women see the overgrown silhouette as largely unnatural, and believe that excess muscle mass requires a large amount of protein to maintain (at least that's what ancient women probably believed). Remember, there were no energy bars or protein shakes many thousands of years ago, so in order to preserve huge musculature, a man would have had to spend day and night rounding up meat to feed to his pet muscles, leaving little or no time for protecting his family. Additionally, humongous muscle mass is indicative of skyrocketed testosterone levels, and since too much of this male hormone can compromise an already weak immune system by inhibiting the response of T cells (that's why women's immune responses are snappier), a hulking male might speak to our subconscious wimpiness detectors. Even if an übermuscular man is perfectly healthy, with normal testosterone levels, his mere appearance says, "Whoa there, girlfriend" to our inborn mating sensibilities.

Surely, a moderate-to-high level of testosterone can be a good thing, but when it comes to men who "lift things up and put them down," like the meathead from Planet Fitness commercials, women are bound to say, "Enough is enough."

Really, can a man be expected to run to rescue someone, chase down the bad guy, or tackle the family's next meal if he can't even walk without his gym pants hanging up between his thighs?

Sexy or scary? You decide.

The ABCs of male attractiveness begin with a V. At least that's what seven hundred women like you, ranging in age from nineteen to sixty-five, said in a Cambridge University zoology department study when they were presented with an assortment of mannish photos, ranging from beefcakes to sponge cakes.

Quickly eliminated were the male forms that resembled pears (wider at the hips than anywhere else) and those figures that made toothpicks look curvaceous.

The women's preferences lay with the men whose shoulders were the widest portions of their bodies, resulting in an upright V shape. Fitness experts claim that the ideal shoulder-to-waist ratio for men is one in which the shoulders are 25 percent wider than the waist, but any ratio sharper than that (a differential higher than 25 percent) is even more desirable.

Though a man who is in good physical shape is more likely to sport the V shape than a recliner radish is, this desirable quality should not be confused with the muscle-bound look. A V shape that's accompanied by lean, compact musculature, often referred to as the "wrestler's V," is a combination that gets plenty of glassy-eyed looks. It speaks of strength (broad shoulders) and endurance capabilities (no fat in the abdominal area).

Notice how the wide shoulders and narrower waist and pelvis form a V shape.

A sexy man's treasure chest holds many riches. Along the line of the V-shaped man, a chest that is wider and more barrel-shaped than the waist contributes to a man's attractiveness factor. In the spirit of the V shape, the chest is most attractive when it's a bit narrower than the shoulders and wider than the waistline and hips. This design speaks of a large lung capacity, which carries men through rigorous activities, including running, fighting, and yes, sex.

The great chest question might be, "To airbrush or to hairbrush?" Women seem to be deeply divided on the question of whether an area rug or a bare floor is better for male exterior design in the chest area. Much of the preference is cultural, with European people preferring a full chest of hair and American westerners loving the smooth, youthful appearance of a hairless chest.

However, the hairy tide may be sweeping to the west. The opening of the twenty-first century saw a surge in the demand for "real men" who boast a healthy smattering of chest hair.

In the Cambridge study referenced above, the women who found the V-shaped men most appealing found them even more appealing once chest hair was added to the images. Additionally, chest hair seems to have marked itself as an indicator of maturity. A significant number of those who preferred it were over the age of thirty. Considering these results, chest hair could have been viewed as a desirable quality by the women of the wild, wild past. A man with a healthy coat of chest hair was likely more mature and better prepared for supporting a family.

The sexiest of men's waist-to-hip ratios are tight races between numbers. The ideal waist-to-hip ratio for men is 9:10 (the hips should be no more than one-tenth larger than the waist). If a man's hips compete with his shoulders, his figure will receive few other honors.

In an evolutionary sense, the shoulders and arms were important to a man's survival and success in the bush. However, wide male hips would have been deemed unnecessary after the smartest of cave people ruled out men as childbearing candidates. This followed evolutionary suit: maintain the beneficial, and reduce or eliminate the pointless.

A man's buttocks are his seat of influence. Few ladies would argue: a study surrounding the attractiveness of male buttocks would only be complete if we could act as hands-on judges. There's just something about a set of perfectly hemispherical, globular cheeks that transform to bulges of hard, seizing muscle when he's running, lifting, or thrusting . . . excuse me, I got sidetracked there.

We talked in chapter 1 about how the human buttocks work to hold the human body in its upright position. But ultrastrong, prominent buttocks go beyond that. They make great contributions to a man's athleticism, speed, and agility by supporting the center of gravity: the pelvis. And coincidentally, a man's well-muscled buttock region is more attractive than the typical accountant or truck driver butt because an impeccably constructed ass sends visual clues to our brains about his ability in the sack. It tells us that he's more than capable of driving his sperm home, to "eggcellent" reception, with maximum thrusting power.

A human face is attractively male, when presented in the correct proportions.

Raise your hand if you think Will Smith or Brad Pitt is incredibly sexy.

That could be the breeze felt around the world. These two men's faces do possess some major sex appeal, but to define the details of that sex appeal would be difficult for most of us. Maybe this would be a good place to interject the cliché "We can't see the forest for the trees."

According to Dr. Eleanor Weston, a paleontologist with the Natural History Museum in London, a man's face largely defines both his survival strength and his attractiveness to the opposite sex. Men whose faces feature a shorter-than-average distance between brow and lip, creating somewhat of a short, broad face, are considered to look more masculine. As an attractive young man's face develops during puberty, the distance between the mouth and the brow remains short, while the jaw, forehead, and the width of the face grow large, proportionately.

This feature has survived into this century because women of past centuries regarded this facial recipe to be mouthwatering.

Testosterone Proves Itself to Be a Capable, yet Aggressive, Artist

In order to understand why prehistoric women may have chosen the beefiest of faces, it can be helpful to grasp the caustic nature of testosterone. When a young man who's destined to wear the features we recognize as most masculine (strong jaw, heavy brow, high and forward cheekbones) embarks upon puberty, his body is flooded with a generous amount of testosterone.

This all seems harmless enough, until you consider that testosterone can be detrimental to the human immune system. When a young man's immunity is robust enough to retain operation despite a system onslaught by testosterone, that man can be said to have a hardy resistance against disease.

Whether early women realized the advantages of their predilections or not, what they effectively accomplished, by choosing faces that were chiseled in the most masculine of ways, was to incorporate the most resilient of genes into their own children and the children of future generations.

It turns out that manly faces aren't just candy for present-day eyes; they're also like orange juice for future immune systems.

Symmetrical men have passed geometrical endurance tests. Without realizing it, one glance at a man's form tells you of his past health and of any interruptions in that health. Bilateral symmetry of the face and body is often touted as a prerequisite for beauty, but in a biological sense, it tells potential mates of reproductive fitness. A man whose features are balanced and symmetrical possesses a hardiness that protected him against the ravages of testosterone and other stresses while in the womb. You see, when an egg is fertilized, cell division begins soon thereafter. If nothing shows up to throw a stone in the process of this cell replication, the resulting child will be bilaterally symmetrical because his cells split without interruption or disorder from predetermined genetic glitches or other external factors. When testosterone shows up to transform an essentially female fetus into a boy, it can be dubbed the "D-day before the birthday." If a baby boy comes out of the T-bombing without being catawampus or otherwise crooked, it can be assumed that his little system was robust enough to endure the onslaught while still maintaining growth order. When marinated in testosterone, a body's immune system, it is believed, is weakened. So a body's ability to go on in spite of the testosterone bath means it must have some immunity to spare (and to pass on to offspring), making the resulting symmetry quite sexy. It can also be assumed that a symmetrical adult male's immune system protected him from growth-interrupting illness during adolescence and young adulthood, since growth is essentially the replicating (splitting) of cells.

Illustrating the attraction to the symmetrical male form, a

recent study captured the dance movements of 183 Jamaican teenagers on digital software that reproduced their moves with faceless, invariable figures, and then asked women to rate the attractiveness of their dancing. Results showed that those young men with the highest degrees of body symmetry were deemed the best dancers.

To translate this study to evolutionary terms, it can be said that dancing is a form of athleticism, and that early men were judged to be sowers of good seeds if their performances in the wilds of the savannahs were noteworthy. Scientists now believe that bilateral symmetry (between legs, arms, feet, etc.) promotes better coordination between nerves and muscles, resulting in more fluid, controlled movements and better athleticism.

This could explain why dance clubs and jukebox bars, despite the best advice of dating experts, are still top-notch choices for making dating, and mating, choices.

Often the detection of the asymmetrical man will be subconscious. You may find his appearance or movements to be somewhat awkward. This is your evolutionary reproductive sense telling you that his genes are not adequate for your high reproduction standards (healthy, fertile children).

The theory of balance in body and in countenance has been proven a number of times in studies showing that symmetrical men need to invest less time in courtship and less money on dates than their cockeyed (and cockbodied) cohorts.

If tall drinks of water are on the menu, women have proven to be quite thirsty. The average man is 5'9", but if you were to survey a group of women, you would probably get a preference average of about 6'.

Why do women prefer men who tower over them? A few theories are worth mentioning.

Because a man's underarms are rich in apocrine glands, which emit subliminal scent messages to a woman's nose about compatibility, a 6'-tall man's pit would fall right at about face level for the

Notice how her nose aligns with his armpit.

average female, making the idea of "crying on his shoulder" akin to "sniffing from his armpit."

In an evolutionary sense, a taller man could use his long legs to run faster, both to escape danger and to tackle that elusive meal.

Also in an evolutionary sense (feminists, look away), women have, for the majority of recorded and unrecorded history, looked for protection. A bigger, more formidable mate could supply the defense that a woman and her children needed to boost their chances of survival.

And finally, and most interestingly, taller men, on average, are the proud owners of larger penises.

So whether women are looking to scratch-and-sniff, to eat, to be protected, or to take pleasure in the top-of-the-line playground equipment that tall men have to offer, there's no denying that Josh Duhamel (6'3") has it all over Danny DeVito (4'10").

Swagger Improves the Stuff He Struts

When T.I., Kanye West, Jay-Z, and Lil Wayne collaborated to perform "Swagger Like Us," they weren't far from the mark when they declared their collective "swagga." I'd venture to say that not one of these guys has trouble in the sack department, and

much of that might have to do with their natural style of locomo-tion: the swagger.

Professors Louis G. Tassinary and Kerri Johnson, of Texas A&M University and New York University, respectively, conducted a study to determine if body movement when walking could con-tribute to, or detract from, a person's perceived attractiveness. The foursome above wouldn't be surprised at the professors' findings: a man's attractiveness, according to female participants, more than doubled when he added a shoulder swagger to his normal walking style.

When T.I. declares, "No one on the corner have swagga like us," he must be referring to the corner reserved for reproductive winners.

One glance at the male form sends a speedy message to a woman's psyche: he's either attractive or he's not. But ask her to articulate the specific qualities that elicit this attraction and it poses a notable challenge.

Every male feature's attractiveness (or lack thereof) gives a woman's brain clues about his ability to survive and to pass along strong genes to his offspring. This is not accomplished through ra-tional thought, but rather through an ancient, subconscious path-way that makes the preselection of mates effortless. Most male features that women consider attractive offer something to indi-cate health, longevity, and the ability to reproduce well.

So what does this mean for your dating game? It means that when you're attracted to someone, there's a biological reason for it and it's probably worth pursuing. Later in the book, we'll discuss variables that can affect attraction, but for now, you can rest as-sured that when all of you is loving all of him, that's a good place to start.

Now that you know why the male form looks the way that it

does, and why certain male features are considered more attractive than others, we can move to the vantage point of the male. He loves the feminine form. He has for millions of years. But why?

In the next two chapters, we'll explore the evolutionary purpose of every feature of the feminine form, and define, in detail, what makes a fox a fox.

CHAPTER THREE

The Fashioning of Woman

HOW EVOLUTION HAS CRAFTED THE SWEET AND CURVACEOUS FEMALE FORM

When you consider how much the male face has changed to adapt to the harsh environments of the wild, the female face's journey pales in comparison. The woman's face has changed little, except that its features have evolved to become a bit more dainty, thanks to man's choosing of mates with small, ultrafeminine features.

However, there are other female features that have grown larger over millennia; and every one of them was essentially built by the men who chose them, because they spoke of fertility and child-rearing potential.

Generally speaking, women didn't evolve into the hulks that we recognize as men because they weren't in the field, being pounded by the brutal environment and its perils. Women were too reproductively valuable to lose in the wilds of the savannahs, so they were left behind at the homestead, where evolution left them largely unchanged, except for the traits that made them better baby producers. A tribe could lose a number of men in the field without its birth numbers being affected, but if it lost even a few women, the birthrate would suffer. This concept leads us to the human tradition of protection of women by men, and why our bodies and the majority of our minds have evolved to accept it as the norm. For millions of years, the survival of our species has relied on adventurous and athletic males facing the dangers of the wilds, while protecting the women who were so important to the production of future generations.

Women's appearance is largely babylike. The maintenance of facial fat, higher voices, and childlike hairlines provokes the same protective tendencies in males that the faces of children do. This could essentially be the reason that evolution has favored women that look as we do today: because the way that we look and the way that we sound makes men want to guard us.

Because we covered the general evolution of humankind in chapter 1, there will be no redundancy here. Instead we'll simply cover the unique features of the woman.

Paul Bunyan or Big Foot, she isn't. The female foot is generally smaller than the man's. Of course, there are exceptions, particularly where tall females and short males meet, but on average, the human female's foot measures 9.5" long, while the male's measures 10.5". The woman's foot is almost always more narrow than the man's, and her heel is more slender is relation to the ball of her foot. On a man's foot, the differential between the ball of the foot and the heel isn't as dramatic. This is why many cross-dressers have difficulty finding Manolos that don't rub their heels.

Evolutionarily speaking, as nature demanded that the male foot expand in all directions to withstand the burdens that cruel environments placed on men while they were hunting, exploring, and fighting for territory, women's feet remained largely unchanged in size. They simply didn't need clodhoppers to complete their all-important jobs, which were carried out close to the home cave.

She's got legs; she knows how to use them.
ZZ Top knew that a woman's legs aren't like your garden-variety set of male, utilitarian implements. During puberty, a girl's legs experience a rapid growth spurt, resulting in a "leggy" look

that is rarely duplicated in an adult woman's form (an exception being Nicole Kidman); but this look is fleeting. It won't take long for her upper body to catch up, resulting in high-school-senior-year legs that are proportionately shorter than her eighth-grade classmates may have predicted.

Generous muscle size requires a lot of protein to maintain and was only required for the hard, manual labor that was generally assigned to males of long ago. For this reason female calves evolved little from their pubescent forms. However, this doesn't mean that female legs are weak. According to a study conducted by the fitness researcher Wayne L. Westcott, PhD, men can lift, on average, 50 percent more weight with their legs than women can, but when the weight lifted was compared to the performer's body weight, it was found that both sexes could lift 75 percent of their own body mass. The evolutionary reason for this parallel? Supporting the burden of pregnancy, of course.

The rest of a woman's leg also contributes to a successful pregnancy, but this next evolutionary holdover has little to do with muscle and everything to do with fat. The chubby cells that like to congregate in female thighs are beneficial to the babies that we carry: they host the fatty acids that are essential for proper fetal development. This is monumental. Move over, thunder thighs; welcome, wonder thighs.

"Does my butt look big in this?" Who among us hasn't asked this question? Even though a butt that contains more fat than muscle is distinctly feminine, that doesn't stop us from stressing over the girth of our derrieres.

If the evolutionary purpose of a woman's buttocks was simply to hold her erect while standing, walking, and running, her rear would differ little from that of her male counterparts.

But since the feminine backside has taken on more of a gelatinous quality, the reason must be rooted in reproduction (as most every feminine feature is).

Other female primates' rear ends only protrude from their bodies when they're ovulating and ready to give conception a shot. When their posteriors swell and redden in anticipation of mating, they'll put their gears in reverse regularly, backing up to every potential mate they meet. This advertises their condition and their desire for copulation.

When compared to other primates, the human female's rump is rather constant in its protuberant display (fluctuations can only be attributed to extra sets of leg lifts and distinctly separate stretches of cheesecake eating). This points to the human female's propensity for disguising her estrus. She is different from other creatures in that she mates all through her cycle, at times of fertility and infertility. This is a method that women have been using for millennia to control which males father their children. When females stood up alongside their male tribe members, their labial regions were suddenly more hidden than they once had been. With this came a degree of liberation for women. Females could choose to conceal ovulation from those suitors who were less than desirable, and display it to those men whom they found irresistible.

Maybe Sir Mix-a-Lot's hit "Baby Got Back" should have been titled "Healthy Baby Got a Momma with Back." It seems that the extra baggage on a woman's rear carriage could have a lot to do with fetal nurturing. You'd be hard-pressed to flip through any parenting magazine without seeing an ad or article that doesn't tout the benefits of DHA (docosahexaenoic acid) for babies. For every 100 mg daily allowance increase of DHA, the average baby's brain will take on an extra 0.13 IQ point (that applies to the little tykes and princesses who are still swimming in the amniotic lagoon, too). We know that DHA, an omega-3 fatty acid, comes from certain fish, olive oil, prenatal vitamins, and baby formula, but would you have ever guessed that it's also housed in your factory-supplied seat cushion? The fat that's housed in a woman's butt is rich in long–chain polyunsaturated fatty acids and omega-3 fatty acids (including DHA), which, as mentioned here, are both important for fetal brain development and enhancement.

Now, whether or not early man made the connection between big-assed women and bright-ass kids is unclear. What we can surmise, however, is that those babies who had the nutrients necessary to pass the many tests that were thrown at them daily were the ones who were most likely to survive to procreate (and to pass on the genes that contributed to butts that grew and grew . . . no brownies involved).

Think Your Butt Is Too Big?
You Must Be Stoned

Women of the Stone Age had a lot of junk in their trunks. In fact, they had the whole darn flea market in there.

Though you still may enjoy the occasional canine-style romp, your prehistoric ancestors considered it the norm for reproductive activity. Long before *Homo erectus* erected himself, people were doing just about everything on all fours (not excluding sexual relations). As time on two feet passed and the human buttocks developed in both males and females, the female buttocks "grew" to be clear signals for sexual selection; and because males were partial to the pear shape, butts grew and grew and grew . . . until a line of Stone Age women could be mistaken for the line outside a liposuction clinic.

This continued until it became clear that men had created some problems for themselves. Those extra-large and in-charge buttocks were interfering with rear copulation (which at this point in time was still the equivalent of our standard missionary position). This condition, complemented by the male's evolving penis and the gradual forward tilting of the labia, all pointed to a shift to frontal copulation. It made sense. It was simpler. It served to bond pairs and to make the sexual act a more intimate and loving achievement.

This shift left big butts in the dust. Now that frontal contact was the norm, men's sexual focus shifted from the buttocks to the breasts. As a result of this newfangled sexual selection, women's backsides became less significant and their breasts began to take over as hemispherical equivalents.

Go ahead—put on a top that flaunts some cleavage, look into a mirror, and try to put the image of another dual-hemispherical part of your body out of your mind. Can't you just see the Stone Age fashion advertisement now? "Breasts are the new asses— nipples are just a perk."

A hippy chick is a reproductively fit chick. The average human female's hips measure 15.3" across, while the average male's only measure 14". The most obvious reason for this difference lies in the female's main occupation throughout history: childbearing and child rearing. Not only does a wider pelvis make births easier (especially important for those babies who are plump and healthy), but it also aids a mother in hauling children around after they've been fired from the amniotic lagoon. When people stood up, it was no longer simple for babies to hitch rides on moms' backs. The back had gone vertical. Hips (with the help of arms) were swiftly taking over as the primary resting places for those infants and toddlers who needed transportation.

Before the age of episiotomies, C-sections, forceps, and pain meds that didn't come from a root or a leaf, women with narrower-than-average pelvises were more susceptible to death during childbirth. If an otherwise healthy child became lodged in an insufficient pelvis, there was no turning back. The mother or the baby, or both, would eventually die.

It's also interesting to note that as the human brain grew, so did the human head. Therefore, human babies were born with bigger noggins. Bigger pelvises were needed to accommodate this new design, and those women who sported the hippy look were more successful at bearing these new pumpkin heads.

Primeval men were likely to select mates with pelvises that they deemed wide enough to bear the healthy babies that they wished for. Thanks to modern birthing methods, string-bean figures have made a resurgence in recent centuries, but that doesn't mean that they have anything on the curvaceous babe. More on that in chapter 4.

The female's spine is well conceived for pregnancy. You know that the human male's back is generally wider at the shoulders and narrower at the hips, creating that V shape that's so appealing. Though the female back doesn't invert the V, it does reduce those manly proportions to more feminine ones.

The lower back of the female is wider than the male's, and her upper back is narrower, proportionate to her body size. In evolutionary terms, this can be explained by both her lack of lifting with the arms and shoulders and her propensity for spewing tiny humans from her loins.

The back is the hardest-working part of the human female body. Not only did it have to adapt to supporting an upright stature, but it then had to adapt to supporting an extra fifteen to thirty pounds of weight during pregnancy, which made females rather front-heavy and quite unstable.

The female's back is wider at the bottom than the man's, but narrower at the waist.

The arch in the female's lower back, which is more prominent than the male's, can be attributed to a need for better stability during pregnancy (the tendency of pregnant women to lean backward when standing "supports" this theory).

A Lady's Spine: Prim, Proper, and Poised for Pregnancy

When a woman's pregnancy is nearly at full term, her center of gravity shifts forward significantly. Because of this, she feels an inclination to lean backward, to essentially keep herself from falling on her face.

Researchers from Harvard and the University of Texas got together and examined the spines of some long-deceased men and women and determined that a human female's lumbar curve spans three vertebrae, while the male's only spans two. This provides for better flexibility in the lower spine of the female. Additionally, the larger connection points between each of the lumbar vertebrae in her back provide for more stability and better protection against breakage when she is under stress from the extra weight of pregnancy.

In order to assign an evolutionary value to this variance, it's important to understand that a woman without this lumbar flexibility may have been in significantly more pain than a woman who boasted this feminine design. Pain would have meant lack of mobility. This would have translated to less food being gathered, and a reduced ability to escape from danger.

This change may have never taken place in the human female spine if our ancestors hadn't stood up. The spines of female chimps (which are not true bipeds) do not bear this distinction.

Her belly is nothing like his. It's an abdo*women*. Like many other parts of a woman's body, her belly is shapelier than that of her male counterpart. And, as you've probably learned to accept as the norm, it has to do with her body of work: conception and pregnancy.

The average female's abdomen is more rounded below the belly button (particularly in the case of the dreaded "pooch"), has a more deeply buried navel, and advertises a longer distance between the navel and the pubic bone than a man's abdomen. In short, she's got more equipment in there, stores more fat for pregnancy there, and must have enough square footage to accommodate an occasional tenant.

On an hourglass figure, everything goes to waist. A distinctly human female attribute is a waist measurement that pales in comparison to those of the chest and the hips. This is not a

trend that was started on a runway, on a magazine cover, or in a liposuction office; nor was it proposed by a mathematician with a penchant for the number sequence 36, 24, 36. In fact, it's older than any single one of these mediums.

The small, feminine waist is an evolutionary holdover from our ancestral fathers' desire to have and to hold a virgin. Considering that the average woman's waistline increases by six to eight inches after childbirth, a narrow waist often speaks to inexperience in the "having and holding" department (at least that which has been reproductively successful). Because pregnancy drains a body's resources (cite brittle hair, decaying teeth, and anemic blood as evidence), a virgin (or at least a previously unoccupied uterus) is often the most nurturing place for a baby to be planted.

To take that concept one step further, the narrow waist combined with the larger chest and hips indicates that the subject is not only virginal, but also sexually mature (as opposed to the string-bean, prepubescent girl).

The average woman's waist measures 28" (unless you're a run-way model, in which case it's a wispy 24"), but the true appeal of a feminine waistline might not be its hard-and-fast measure-ment, but its size relative to the hips. In order to appear virginal, the waist should be only 70 percent the circumference of the hips (at least that's what the average man says). More about that in chapter 4.

Feminine shoulders are more aesthetic than utilitarian; unless, of course, you're a gymnast. A woman's shoulders are, on average, only seven-eighths the width of the average man's. But the real variance comes in the depth of the shoulders. There the man's musculature takes the evolutionary cake.

Historically, women have needed less muscle in the arms and shoulders, because their tasks required less physical strength. Like much of the rest of the body, the female's shoulders are blanketed in a layer of fat, giving them a more rounded, elegant look than those of the male. Bet you've never heard the words *fat* and *elegant* used in the same sentence before, but it makes perfect sense when you consider that much of the feminine shoulders' appeal comes from their imitation of the breasts' form. There goes evolution with those bilateral hemispheres again.

A woman won't get caught up in arms races. That's because her arms are slighter than a man's for the same reasons that her shoulders are smaller than his. Her ancestral mothers simply didn't need power to do their jobs—they needed tender touches. The average female's arms are shorter, are thinner, and have less muscle mass than the average male's.

Though the feminine arm is smaller than the masculine one, that isn't the only characteristic that makes the two distinguishable from each other; there's also the carriage of those arms. Women

sport elbow angles that are 6 percent greater than males'. This results in women's arms being carried closer to their rib cages. A man's arms, when at rest, usually fall directly from his wider shoulders without touching his sides.

Knitting, embroidery, or microsculpting, anywoman? Women might not be cracking walnuts with their sheer paw power, but they do enjoy a better precision grip, more flexibility, and superior fine motor control with their smaller hands. This can hardly be considered a deficiency when you ponder the many things that the hands of women have accomplished, the first of which may have been efficiently picking berries and other fruits from the bushes and trees of the savannahs (or a pomegranate from the forbidden tree in the Garden of Eden).

If you think you've had some bad hair days, imagine how "tressful" life must have been on the savannahs, where brushes, mousse, and stylists were as unrealized as bathing and tooth brushing. Nevertheless, long head hair must have held some type of appeal, or it wouldn't have made it to the twenty-first century.

Today, our bodies are homes to two types of hair growth: terminal (like arm hair) and long (like head hair). When our ancestors' bodies were covered in hair, it was mostly the terminal type (otherwise we would have be tripping over our calf and ankle ponytails), but there was a point in time in which long hair made its appearance. And when it did, it probably served as a signal of health. Just as women were choosy about their mates' manes, if a prehistoric man spotted a cave babe with long tresses, that meant she had been healthy for quite a long time (long enough for that head of hair to grow) and that her body was currently healthy enough to support her own life as well as another's. When long head hair was complemented by quality reproductive signals, she was considered to be good mothering material. These days, a sensible bob might speak more to a woman's willingness to settle down, but millions of years ago, the long, tornado-blown look was all the rage.

Which leaves only one point to cover in relation to the woman's head of hair: Why is female-pattern baldness not the subject of late-night infomercials? The easy answer would come from the reference to testosterone and how it deactivates a man's papillae during puberty. The anthropological answer is that men simply didn't choose to procreate with bald women. Men were interested in youthfulness, and nothing said "scratch" like a knocked-up cue ball.

Though waning, feminine eyebrows are still subject to waxing. A woman's eyebrows didn't evolve to look the way that they do. Instead they stayed largely static throughout unrecorded history, and from her own childhood through to adulthood. She didn't need protection from the elements like her male equivalents did. Instead she needed two devices that would signal her emotions before spoken words were all the rage.

The classic feminine eyebrow is higher, more arched, less bushy, and thinner than a male's. Put a pair of caterpillars on a woman's face, and she'll be in the waxing chair quicker than you can say, "Depilatory."

**Her windows to the soul are also the windows to millen-
nia past.** The female's eyes are more expressive than those of
males. This is due in large part to the fact that the construction of
her brow, nose, and cheekbones opens up her eye sockets, making her eyes appear larger. Because her eyelids are generally open
wider than men's, her eyes show more white than males'. This was
likely very valuable before the spoken word was stylish, sending
clear signals to others about the subjects of her thoughts and her
intentions.

Again, her face remained more unchanged from childhood
than the male's. She didn't need the bony protection for her eyes
that men did. Therefore, her large-looking, childlike eyes (which
are actually anatomically smaller than her male counterparts')
spoke to men's protective impulses.

Women are nosy . . . not in form, but in function. The typical human female's nose is smaller than that of the human male
(and it has nothing to do with rhinoplasty trends). When ancient
men went into the wilderness to hunt, they needed their large
noses to deliver enough temperature and humidity-controlled air
to their lungs for the supply of oxygen to their aerobically working bodies. Because women didn't engage in this type of pastime,
their noses remained smaller: again, more childlike.

Though a woman's nose is more diminutive than a man's, her
sense of smell towers over his. How many times has this conversation gone on between you and a man?

"What's that smell?" you ask.

"What smell?"

"That rancid reek of death times ten."

Gruff sniffing sound. "Can't smell anything," he replies. "Is dinner ready?"

She's a Baby Olfactory

Psychologist Marsha Kaitz conducted an experiment that included a panel of forty-two postpartum mothers who had spent a minimum of one hour holding their newborn babies. Kaitz then presented each mother with three T-shirts, one of which belonged to her baby. In every instance ... in the case of every one of the forty-two mothers ... the correct T-shirt was identified by smell alone.

Prominent cheekbones are not classically feminine, no matter what European runways say. The typical cheek of a woman is soft, rounded . . . even childlike. It has very little bony protrusion, if any.

High-fashion models generally sport cheekbones that are prominent, bony, and situated high on their faces. As you've learned in chapter 1, this look is widely accepted by the anthropological and biological community as a masculine feature. So why are models in women's clothing celebrated for having masculine traits? Because an androgynous figure looks better wearing a lampshade dress and a checkerboard hat and carrying a dingo skull purse than a highly feminized character does. Masculine cheekbones are terrific complements to these twiggy, prepubescent figures, and are perfect unrealistic matches for the unrealistic outfits they're wearing.

Traditionally, men have chosen mates with more rounded cheeks, because they echo the look of childhood, thanks to the typical layer of subcutaneous fat that the average woman carries over her cheekbones.

Pouting lips are spoiled. They get what they want, especially if what they want has to do with procreation.

That's a sentiment that has been shared by men for millennia. Babies' lips are plump as a standard, but as puberty hits, boys' lips cower into their mouths. Females' lips follow an entirely different narrative. When a young woman enters puberty, the influx of estrogen causes fat to accumulate in her girliest of parts, including her lips.

The inflated condition of the human female's lips has survived for millennia because of its erotic signaling purpose. Not only do the texture, color, and shape of the facial lips mimic the appearance of the labial lips; the facial lips also flush when aroused and experience an increased level of sensitivity, just as the labial lips do.

The human species' finest communicators are its female members, by far. In the early years of the human species, they were the organizing communicators, the planners, the equivalents of today's personal assistants, life coaches, and meddling mothers-in-law. When speech replaced grunts and whistles, women were the majorettes of linguistics parades, leading their gender to today's daily spoken average of twenty thousand words (men speak roughly one-third of that amount per day).

Due in large part to the reduced size of a woman's jaw, her teeth are smaller, more curved, and less angular than those of a man.

Licking Man's Biggest Muscles

Did you know that you have a muscle that's stronger than any single muscle in a man's arms, legs, back, or neck? If you've ever been told that you talk too much, or that your best work is done with your mouth open, you can take that as a compliment to your gender.

The muscle in question is your tongue, and its well-deserved accolades are long overdue. Not only is it your strongest muscle, but it's also the only one that originates at one end and terminates in midair. Every tongue is unique—like a fingerprint.

Thanks in large part to the feminine tongue's better vowel sound sustenance and the 11 percent less distance that it needs to travel to produce sound, female humans are the best communicators on all the earth.

High-necked shirts should be left to their reptile namesakes, because the human female's neck is simply too graceful to bury under a shell.

We've already discussed why early men needed short, strong necks: if they were long and spindly, they could easily be broken in the line of duty. A woman's collarbone is situated lower in relationship to her backbone than a man's. Additionally, the lesser musculature of the female neck gives it a tapered look, rather than a columnar appearance, like the man's. This length and girth vulnerability has been exploited throughout history, with strangulation being a murder method of choice for many crimes against women. Since women weren't in the prehistoric line of duty, their necks evolved little from their childhood forms.

As with many sexual dimorphisms, the opposite of "masculine" is "feminine." Where the neck is concerned, long, thin, and delicate are definitely not masculine, so must be uberfeminine.

Within a woman's neck is housed the supporting partner for her tongue—the larynx. It contains

A woman's neck is finer and more contoured than a man's.

vocal cords that are shorter than a man's. It is also 30 percent smaller than the male's and is situated higher in the throat. This leaves the Adam's apple to Adam. It also leaves the higher voice to Eve, who would have elicited protectiveness from Adam with her voice's high-pitched, childlike quality.

The explanation of the dual purposes of your dual mammaries is "breast" left to evolutionary science. One of the most puzzling portions of a woman's body is her breasts—puzzling in that they seem to have been constructed more for sexual signaling purposes than for feeding children.

We covered the human's everted lips earlier, and how they're necessary for grasping on to the globular shape of the human female's breast. Though evolution has gifted us with these adaptive lips, it is still fairly difficult for human babies to suckle from the hemispherical human breast, especially when compared to the ease with which other mammals nurse. When human infants nurse, their noses are often blocked by the fat of large breasts. Additionally, babies must learn to grasp the entire areola in their mouths, rather than just the teat (as other mammal babies do).

It seems that as men and women stood to explore the earth on two feet, the men's sexual attentions shifted from the derrieres of the ladies to their new, frontal equivalents—the breasts. Even though large breasts are no more capable of delivering ample amounts of milk to hungry mouths, men seemed to have developed a propensity for choosing mates with swollen mammary glands, or breasts. This departs from other primates' preferences. For apes and the like, swollen mammary glands act as sexual turn-offs, because they tell males that the melons belong to a nursing mother, who cannot conceive.

Another evolutionary theory involves female identification. If a figure could be spotted from a distance, and that figure's profile displayed large breasts, the viewer could reliably determine that the far-off figure was female, and he could approach to entreat for sex. Flat-chested chicks could have been mistaken for men who could pummel the snot out of a horny, approaching male. Therefore, bosomy ladies got more cave invitations.

Another theory involves our old friend estrogen. Estrogen is responsible for the fat accumulation in the breasts, so in supposition, more e-vage would mean more cleavage. A study conducted by Polish biological anthropologist Grazyna Jasienska supports this hypothesis: Jasienska found that women whose chests were 20 percent larger than their upper torsos were 300 percent more likely to conceive.

Unbalanced Breasts, Unbalanced Fertility

During puberty, estrogen acts like Miracle-Gro for breasts. Because the breasts' eruption takes place over such a short period of time, any disruption of estrogen flow can cause one breast to rocket ahead of the other. The other will never "catch up."

Though a large part of the female population is a bit lopsided (always putting their best breast forward), a much smaller portion is noticeably partisan, requiring corrective surgery or removable implants in order to appear balanced. Because asymmetrical breasts are products of estrogen glitches, conception has been proven to be more difficult for our sisters with biased breast development.

Unless You're Nursing a Litter, Two's Enough

The typical human female has two breasts. In an evolutionary sense, this can be attributed to our small birth numbers. But, as if there's a recessive "litter bearing" gene floating around in the gene pool, up to 6 percent of the population has an additional superfluous nipple or operational breast. Usually appearing under the armpit, these tag-alongs have also been recorded as being found on the genitals, breastbone, thigh, hip, shoulder, buttock, face, back, and foot.

And "an extra" is an understatement in some cases; a physician in 1886 recorded the case of a woman who proved to have eight auxiliary breasts on her body (the original Octomom?).

These extra mammary features, which are sometimes functioning glands, other times only nipples, other times only areolas, and other times just bundles of extra breast tissue that become tender during premenstrual syndrome, could (and can) be found on at least a few familiar personalities. Among them are Anne Boleyn, the Greek goddess Artemis, Lily Allen, Tilda Swinton, and Moms Mabley (Moms? . . . isn't that appropriately plural?).

And one more thing: this condition, known as polythelia or polymastia, isn't reserved for those of the female persuasion. Mark Wahlberg, Jackson Browne, Brian Jones, and Frank Langella are (or were) all "triple-nipplin' it."

Her private parts have journeyed from posterior placement to full frontal. When females got around on all fours, a nice conversation of grunts, whistles, and facial expressions could be had without sexual connotation creeping in. After our ancestors stood up, a woman's girly parts were brought front and center, as complements (or distractions) to human interaction. But in a true paradox, or maybe as an evolutionary balancing act, this stance also served to conceal her fluctuating fertility.

Now that the female's genitals were both frontal and more hidden, ovulation became less obvious to other members of her tribe. The swelling, reddening, and sweet smell of ovulation were no longer broadcast from her protruding, on-all-fours, posterior billboard. Only close contact could determine her fertility factor, and even that paled in comparison to the signals sent forth by other primates. The evolutionary reason for this concealed ovulation was likely to promote pair bonding and intimacy—both of which provided subsequent children with more stable family lives that came with male protection as part of the package.

Another speculation as to the reasoning for concealed ovulation is that a female could better steer sexual selection if she could control who fathered her children. If only she knew when she was fertile, she could choose the father(s) of her children inside the confines of her own private mind, resulting in male paternity confusion, or even trickery.

———————

There you have it: the evolutionary reasons for the appearance of just about every part of your body. Most of the changes that occurred (or didn't occur) were rooted in reasons that either flirted with or shouted about reproduction. In chapter 4, I'll decipher the characteristics that make those parts desirable to the opposite sex . . . and explain why they have been perpetuated into this, the twenty-first century.

CHAPTER FOUR

Fascination with the Feminine Form

UNCOVERING FEATURES THAT BELONG TO THE SEXIEST OF WOMEN

Some women may define a sexy female form as a thin (or skinny) figure with high cheekbones and as few curves as femininely possible. It seems that we've been persuaded to believe that all forms of fat are evil, ranking right up there with extortion and illegal fur trading.

But ask a man what's sexy, and his primeval mind will turn immediately to a completely different vision. I don't want to give it all away, but his sugarplum visions have a lot to do with curves, strategically placed fat, and childlike features. That's because at his primordial brain's core, he's looking to make a good reproductive investment. His reactions to your most attractive features are not results of cognitive thought, but of subconscious responses to characteristics that his ancestors deemed irresistible.

Millions of years ago, initial attraction was man's single motivator, but today, thanks to a more recent design, the prefrontal cortex or "thinking" brain, he can also make decisions that will land him a woman who is not only a prolific reproducer, but also a good long-term partner. Men didn't always think in futuristic terms when it came to mating. Most often they chose women whom they deemed to be fertile virgins capable of producing neurologically and immunologically sound children, hit it, and moved on. But with modern civilization have come morals and women's disinclination toward sex without commitment. This means man must now make choices that he can live with, not just sleep with.

Despite the modern world's morphing of sexual behavior, men are still wildly propelled by initial physical attraction, and that raises the question "What is attractive?" We know what we consider to be sexy, but we should turn to research that tells us what the experts (men) are saying.

Included here is a virtual interview with the human male on one of his favorite subjects: the ideal female form.

Let's start with hair, since it's the subject on which most of your days start. You roll out of bed, you stare into the mirror at an unkempt bundle of kinkiness, and wonder, "Why? Why not just shave my head and spend the extra hour every day feeding the poor or doing leg lifts?"

The answer is simple. Hair is sexy. It's symbolic of your good health. It identifies you as female. It pegs you as a good reproductive risk. A head of long, thick, lustrous, shoulder-length hair tells males that you've eaten well for at least the last four years, and have been free from major disease. It also tells them that you've likely not borne any children yet, since carrying a fetus is one of the worst things you can do for the shine and condition of your hair.

Do Blondes Have More Fun?

I can't commit to their relative fun factors, but I can say that blondes do get more attention from the opposite sex. There are two distinct reasons for this: the first is youth and the other is rarity.

For many people of Nordic descent, their hair gets its start on the blond side and gradually fades to a shade of brown. Others remain blond, but only to the tune of 2 percent of the world's population. Considering this, blond hair must equal youth. And as we've discussed, youth is a valuable reproductive trait if you're of the female persuasion.

Another reason that blond hair is considered to be more attractive by a generous portion of men is that, put simply, it's different. Lighter colors draw the human eye. Blond hair reflects light and is therefore more attention-catching. Since males are highly vision-oriented creatures, it goes without saying that blond hair stimulates the visual portions of their brains.

High estrogen and low androgen make a pretty face. Though many factors contribute to the femininity of the human face, a good place to start is with those chemicals that make us male or female: hormones.

As discussed in chapters 1 and 2, testosterone gives men their prominent brow ridges, short faces, and heavy jaws. So logic would lead us to believe that these traits, if present on a woman's face, would detract from her beauty . . . and this logic would be correct. The model of a feminine face exhibits a smooth forehead, high and arched eyebrows, large eyes, a small nose, rounded cheeks, plump lips, a face that grows narrower near the bottom, and a small, pointed chin. These features display a perfect hormonal storm: one in which testosterone is overshadowed by estrogen. For example, a small chin and large eyes look the way that they do because the face *has not* been affected by high levels of testosterone, while lips that are plump and cheeks that are padded with a layer of subcutaneous fat appear so because they *have* been affected by estrogen.

Visual Preferences Give New Meaning to "Girly Girl"

Ask a man and a woman to select the prettiest female face, and the likelihood that you'll get conflicting opinions is high. Studies have shown that women will most often choose the face with moderately feminine features (e.g., Jennifer Aniston), while men will choose the face with ultrafeminine traits (e.g., Angelina Jolie).

The cover candies for fashion magazines generally have ultrafeminine features, with larger-than-average eyes and lips, and smaller-than-average noses. When their photos are presented to a computer aging program, it will generally guess their ages to be between six and seven years.

So, why would men choose women who, from the neck up, could be their daughters? Are they perverted? Not usually.

Historically, men have chosen women with feminine traits because those traits spoke of a woman's fertility. Those men generally operate on the assumption that "more is better." If plump lips indicate high estrogen, resulting in an enhanced ability to conceive, then lips the size of travel pillows must mean she's Fertile Myrtle, right?

Such is the thought process of the man's oat-sowing brain.

There is much to be said for the average face. If you were to take one hundred transparent images of different females' faces and stack them on top of each other, the resulting image would probably be beautiful. Why? Because familiar faces are beautiful, and features that are not too extreme in any proportion are considered to be aesthetically pleasing. These factors make the Goldilocks face (not too big, not too small, not too soft, not too hard) nearly perfect. This theory is so foolproof that even babies reach for the average face over one with extreme features.

Body Watch: For an entertaining exhibit of the average phenomenon, visit www.MorphThing.com, upload different combinations of photos, and watch the beauty multiply.

From Average to Stunning with Just a Tweak

Psychologist David Perrett wanted to know what would happen if he took an average-featured, beautiful face and gave it a bit of personality. So he did just that.

He started with a good-looking, average-featured feminine face and made a few digital adjustments. He made her eyes larger, lifted her cheeks, and carved down her chin. The result was a model of superior beauty. If the first face would have stopped traffic, this one would have caused a pileup on the beltway.

A beautiful geometry lesson can be found in feminine facial symmetry. In chapter 2, we discussed how symmetry tells us of a man's resistance against testosterone's negative effects. Symmetry in the female face can also tell us of her hardiness. If her cell division's smooth operation was disrupted by glitches in nutrition, congenital defects, or environmental stresses, her face will be asymmetrical and thus detract from her reproductive charm.

At the University of New Mexico, the reproductive importance of facial symmetry was confirmed when the facial measurements of more than four hundred men and women were studied.
The findings showed that those humans with the greatest levels of
facial symmetry also boasted the best health records and the few-
est instances in which antibiotics were needed to fight infection.

Gwyneth Paltrow is a classic example of how symmetry works
to a face's advantage. Even though her eyes are wider-set than
average, and her mouth is broader than average, her face's symmetry works to classify her as beautiful.

Cate Blanchett, Kate Moss, and Christy Turlington also possess famously symmetrical faces.

Just How Warped Are You?

Curious about your own facial symmetry? Or the symmetry of your
love interest(s)? Visit www.symmeter.com, upload a photo, and
discover how organized, or untidy, the features in question are.

If you find that you're a bit off-kilter, don't fret—the majority of
the population wears faces that are asymmetrical to some degree.
You can utilize these beauty tips to enhance your facial symmetry:

If your **eyebrows** don't mirror each other, pluck hairs from the
top of the high one and the bottom of the low one to cajole them
into a good average. An eyebrow pencil can help to balance your
brows' symmetry, but please, steer clear of coloring yourself right
into Looney Tunes.

You can balance an asymmetrical **nose** by applying a touch of
shade to your face next to the side that's smaller. This will create
the illusion of a nose shadow that matches the larger side's.

If your **eyes** are asymmetrical, avoid the sharp, defined lines of
liquid liner. Soft, smudged looks will make the unevenness less obvious. To balance the look of the eyes, use a white kohl liner on the
mucous membranes of both eyes, but apply it more heavily to the

smaller eye (this will work to expand the white of the smaller eye). When you're applying dark liner on the upper lid, a heavier line on the larger eye, coupled with a thinner line on the smaller eye, will help to balance the look of the eyes when they're open. On the lower lid, a liner that reaches farther into the inner corner will make an eye look smaller, so you can move the line inward, just a bit, on the larger eye. A touch less mascara should be applied to the outer corner of the larger eye. Any type of illumination will make an eye seem larger, so using a foundation that's one shade lighter than the rest of the face around the smaller eye will help it to "pop" like the other one.

The best way to highlight **cheeks** is to apply a contouring powder (two shades darker than your skin tone) under the diagonal line of the cheekbones, use a highlighter on the top of the bones, and color the apples of the cheeks with a bronzer or blush. If your cheekbones are asymmetrical, you can follow this same procedure, but adjust the height of your artistry as needed (move contouring, etc. higher for a lower cheekbone).

The upper **lip** can be made to appear symmetrical by applying concealer onto the high side and using a lip pencil that closely matches your natural lip shade to trace the lip line that you long for.

If your **jawline** isn't a symmetrical superstar, brighten depressed areas with highlighter and darken protruding areas with contour powder. By doing this, you're essentially creating the illusion of symmetrical shadow and light.

It's true what they say: practice makes perfect . . . or at least symmetrical. Remember, your face is your canvas. Even professional artists ball up and toss first attempts, so get your color palette and your makeup remover ready: you've been given permission to play.

Body Watch: Some believe that the divine proportion of 1:1.618 is a ratio that is universally attractive, for everything from architecture to facial features. If you're ready to see just how well you stack up to faces around the world, grab your ruler and a mirror, and go to www.measureyourlooks.com to redefine your impression of perfection.

Wide-eyed and *naive,* though seemingly insulting, are two adjectives that can be used to describe a pretty, feminine face. Though women's eyeballs are slightly smaller than those of men, their daintier facial structures make those eyes seem much larger than the hooded male versions.

Because women's foreheads, cheekbones, and noses weren't designed by evolution to protect eyes in battle and while hunting, women's eyes have more room to shine. Generally speaking, a beautiful female face is both youthful and feminine. Big eyes speak to both of these requirements.

The Blue Eye Paternity Test

If the guy across the bar can't keep his blue eyes off you, it could have something to do with your own set of baby blues.

Bruno Laeng, a psychologist now at the University of Oslo in Norway, conducted a study regarding the eye color choices of men who themselves had blue eyes. Most chose women with blue eyes. At the root of their choices were desires for paternity certainty.

When the men in Laeng's study chose blue-eyed women, they were guaranteeing that their babies would have blue eyes. If their kids were born with dark eyes, the fathers would automatically know that their women were doing the horizontal polka with dark-eyed dancers.

Likewise, blondes can conduct the same type of paternity test. If the yellow-haired dream across the beach likes how your blue bikini complements your blond hair, he might be considering conducting a biology lesson of his own.

Full lips are all the rage, but this is nothing new. For millennia, males have recognized a set of full, pouting lips as signs of arousal, fertility, and eroticism.

When a woman is sexually aroused, her lips' capillaries fill with blood, making them appear dark and swollen. Because a woman who is already in an aroused state is an obvious turn-on for any man, this look gets lots of looks. Red lipstick exaggerates this effect and has been popular for this reason for centuries.

A woman with full lips is considered to be fertile for one main reason: estrogen is responsible for naturally plumping the lips during puberty; and women whose systems are rich in estrogen are generally more fertile.

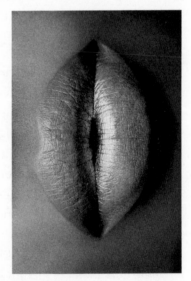

And last but not least, a woman's full lips look like, feel like, and respond like the labia. For men, there couldn't be better news.

And we wonder why they like wet kisses.

A woman's face is no place for a big nose. Whether you consider the evolutionary reasons for men's prominent noses (oxygen delivery,

A woman's facial lips are attractive to men because they mimic the labial lips.

cooling, humidification) or the phallic symbolism that they carry, a woman's face had no need for a supersized schnoz.

Because her lack of testosterone generally leaves the nose alone, a small nose is considered to be a feminine trait, and an ultrasmall nose to be an ultrafeminine trait.

For evolutionary reasons, this nose would look better on a male face.

The Deceptive Beauty of Rhinoplasty Screws with Evolution

The average size of the human female's nose is the result of sexual selection, while the size of the male's nose is chiefly a product of natural selection (in other words, men chose women with smaller noses because those small noses signaled low testosterone levels, while nature chose men with larger noses because of their good cooling and respiration abilities).

What will happen to the noses that we know if people continue to renovate their given facial landscapes with nose jobs . . . essentially tricking the opposite sex into believing they're choosing desirable nose genes? First off, when the teenagers in a family start to sprout some serious facial topography, the man of the house might wonder what big-nosed son of a gun had gotten into his bed, and women might be prompted to conduct an ancestry search for a recessive gene of monstrous proportions. Second, more big-nosed children will be born to spread the nosy genes around. This raises a ponderous question: Will big noses come back in vogue, since the average size of the male nose is bound to increase? Or will plastic surgery become the next big "in demand" career as we attempt to cover up something that we (evolution's vehicles) have created?

Now, there's absolutely nothing wrong with an ample nose. If we weren't talking about beauty standards, it wouldn't even be brought up. However, the fact that rhinoplasty lays down a speed bump on the evolutionary road cannot be denied.

A healthy BMI makes men say, "Oh my . . ." Men, in general, prefer that women have an average body mass index; that is, not skinny and not overweight (somewhere between Calista Flockhart and Roseanne Barr . . . more like Marilyn Monroe or Jennifer Lopez).

This preference would come as no shock to an evolutionary biologist or anthropologist. Sure, partialities vary from culture to culture (Westerners tend to value thinness more than those who live in other geographic areas), but a healthy weight does just what its name suggests: it indicates health.

Extra body weight (a BMI of 25 or more) affects fertility because the excess fat triggers overabundant estrogen production, making ovulation unpredictable. Additionally, obesity can cause vaginal collapse, which can block sperm from reaching the cervix. Once pregnant, obese women run higher risks of gestational diabetes, and their children will be prone to diabetes during adulthood.

On the other end of the spectrum, a woman who is underweight by 10 to 15 percent (a BMI of 18 or less) may stop menstruating and ovulating—and we all know what that means: no place for Mr. Sperm to rest his little head. A skinny body often has difficulty hosting a healthy fetus, in that the child needs nutrients from a healthful diet as well as the complexes contained within a healthy woman's butt and hip fat. Fat-lack can result in under-weight babies, premature babies, or babies with complications from vitamin, mineral, folic acid, or DHA deficiencies.

Today's Western obsession with thinness is likely a result of the elite being thin. In the past, when food was scarcer, the wealthy were chunkier because they had more food to eat and they enjoyed sedentary lifestyles—everyone wanted to be like them. Thin people were looked down upon. Now everyone tries to imitate the weights of the upper crust, by avoiding things like piecrust.

In past millennia, men weren't concerned with the size of a woman's tiger hide dress, but rather with a healthy weight—just enough fat to support his offspring, but not so much that it would chop down his family tree.

The Male Masses Prefer an Average Feminine Body Mass

It seems that, at least in the United States, women are a bit confused about feminine BMI as related to the preferences of the masculine sector. Because we use our body mass indexes, or BMIs, or skinniness, to practically compete with one another, with the size zero or size two jeans as the pies in the sky, we tend to impose those inclinations onto men.

An American study asked women to choose both their ideal body type and the body type that they believe their mates, or prospective mates, would prefer. In both instances, the body type choices were thinner than normal.

When a group of men were asked to weigh in on their ideal feminine BMIs, they overwhelmingly chose those bodies that were curvy and of medium weights (BMIs ranging from 18.25 to 24.9), proving that men do prefer "real" women.

Waist-hip ratio is the ultimate measurement of attractiveness. If you haven't heard of WHR, surely you've heard of the hourglass figure. It's the silhouette that makes our forms uniquely feminine, and utterly irresistible, to the opposite sex.

Keep in mind that WHR is a ratio, not a measurement. In other words, the circumference of your waist isn't as important as its relative relationship to the measurement of your hips. The ideal WHR is .7 or 7:10. That means if your waist measures 30", and your hips measure 43", your WHR is ideal (at least under the verdict of an all-male jury). If your WHR is even lower (e.g., 30" waist and 45" hips), consider yourself the lucky recipient of a sexy bonus. If your WHR is higher (e.g., 30" waist and 34" hips), don't fret . . . they make sit-ups, torso twists, booty implants, and low-rider jeans with pocket embellishments to counteract your figure's boyish tendencies.

It's not the weight, but the waist, that matters.

Waist-Hip Ratio, Like a Drug

In a study conducted by Steven M. Platek and Devendra Singh, fourteen men were presented with before and after photos of women whose figures were altered with corrective surgery. Though the body masses of the women remained fairly constant, the postsurgical waist-hip ratios were brought to the ideal .7.

When the men looked at the pictures of the .7 WHR figures, an MRI showed that the reward centers of their brains were activated (the same areas activated by drugs and alcohol).

Weight changes alone register only in the visual brain substrates, making changes merely observable, but do not qualify them as stimulating or repelling. However, when the optimum WHR bodies were presented in this study, the anterior cingulate cortex, the portion of the brain responsible for making decisions and processing rewards, lit up in all the men studied.

Whether you believe in sexual addiction or not, this study makes it hard to deny the existence of the "casual user."

Hold the Fries, Order Two Shakes

Shape is crucial to the attractiveness of the feminine form, but it turns out that the way that shape moves through space is also central to flipping some lids.

In a study headed by Kerri Johnson of New York University, more than 50 percent of male participants declared that any woman could boost her own attractiveness by adding a notable hip sway to her walk, regardless of her body shape.

Johnson found that the jiggle can be taught, but many movers and shakers need no coaching. Her conclusion came after observing young college women's behaviors in various situations, with the most hip sway surfacing while the women were in the presence of young men. Their carriages were most relaxed in situations that didn't involve the opposite sex. In the immortal lyrics of Kelis, their "milkshake[s] [brought] all the boys to the yard."

However groundbreaking this study may be, the hip sway is no new concept. In fact, Marilyn Monroe was known to shave some heel from one of her shoes to make it shorter than the other, purportedly to stir up her own shake.

Long legs equal longevity. Richard Gere loved Julia Roberts's 88" of legs in *Pretty Woman;* Ralphie's dad was obsessed with the long, single extremity in his living room window in *A Christmas Story*. In general, men love long legs, and as I'm sure you can guess, it has nothing to do with marrying someone who can reach the top shelf, and everything to do with reaching into the most optimal of gene pools.

Women with legs that are 3 to 5 percent longer than average (average being 45 percent of their total height) are the lucky bearers of sexy pegs, according to the male participants in a study out of Poland's Wroclaw University. This isn't surprising, when you consider that women with shorter-than-average legs experience higher instances of cardiovascular disease, high blood pressure, type II diabetes, heart disease, high triglycerides, and strokes.

Body Watch: To determine your leg length percentage, divide the length of your leg by your total height, in inches. If the result is .48 to .50, you've got it goin' on in the leg department. For example, if you're 5'8" and your legs measure 34", divide 34" by 68" and you'll find that your resulting leg length percentage is 50 percent.

It's no wonder that men are more likely to choose the leggier variety of female—she'll be around longer, and in better health, to raise their children.

Women with longer legs also give birth to larger babies, on

average. A study out at the University of Bristol found that for every half inch of female leg length (over the average), her baby would pack on one additional ounce. This is noteworthy because bigger babies are celebrated for their abilities to stave off maladies such as diabetes and heart disease, and they don't fall victim to the health risks that come with low birth weight. Historically, men would choose women who could bear substantial babies for them, because healthy butterballs had better chances of survival.

But how does a woman end up with the legs with which to catch the eye of the opposite sex? Genetics plays a role, as it often does, but there is another important factor involved. It's childhood nutrition. Between the ages of two and four, a girl's diet is critical. If she doesn't absorb the nutrition she needs, her resulting physique will be out of proportion (long torso, short legs). Because proper nutrition during her formative years is important to overall health, a girl with proportionate legs (in other words, average or longer) has had a healthy past, and a good chance at a healthy future.

One last thing should be mentioned. It has to do with fertility (surprise, surprise). Because a girl's legs' growth is finished at the end of puberty (a male's legs keep growing after puberty has ended), her nutrition throughout her adolescence is important to that growth. Because much of her reproductive future is mapped out during her pubescent years, long leg growth during this time is a good indicator of future reproductive success, according to Newcastle University's Martin Tovee.

In conclusion, "she's got legs" isn't a sentiment that's reserved for the wolf men of ZZ Top. It's shared by a wide range and large number of men, for reasons that contribute to wide ranges and large numbers of gene proliferation.

The feminine form is one that boasts symmetrical, yet average, features; full lips; a long torso with a narrow waist; full breasts that are placed high on the torso; breasts and hips that are wider in proportion to the waist; a wide pelvic floor (distance between upper thighs); long legs; and a notable shake in her shimmy.

Every one of these features can be attributed to good fertility, carrying and birthing capabilities, child-rearing potential . . . and each one will contribute to his initial attraction to you. Of course there is a part of every woman that wants to believe that looks don't matter, but the evolutionary system that has been laid out before us dictates that this just isn't so (at least not yet). Illustrating this point, *Psychological Science* recently reported on the importance of beauty in the conveyance of personality traits. Researchers at the University of British Columbia set up interactions among volunteers and asked them, following face-to-face communications, to evaluate the other person's beauty as well as personality traits in the areas of openness, conscientiousness, extroversion, agreeableness, and neuroticism. Those being rated were also asked to rate themselves in these areas. Results showed that not only did raters give people with higher levels of perceived beauty higher scores in each personality area, but they were also highly accurate in rating each trait in order of impact, when compared with the subjects' own ratings of themselves.

This study proves not only that people pay more attention to beautiful people, but that people who are perceived as beautiful can more effectively convey the traits they wish to convey (or that they believe to be their best ones). For you this means that by recognizing the role of a man's primeval brain in his mate search, you're opening up opportunities for yourself to reach his more logical and decisive prefrontal cortex.

The primal choices that men make while searching for mates are products of their innate needs to propagate their genes. Even if a man doesn't realize why he is attracted to you, the most ancient part of his brain is telling him that you look like a promising procreator and therefore deserve deeper investigation. Being conscious of the features that flip a man's instinctual switches can help you to get past the first elimination round, where you'll win over his primitive brain, so you can move on to other conquests—like his prefrontal cortex.

CHAPTER FIVE

The Long Haul or a Short Ride?

THE PHYSICAL CHARACTERISTICS THAT TELL OF HIS CAPACITY FOR COMMITMENT

Now that you've established a more intimate relationship with man's evolutionary timeline, you're probably ready to assign a label to your very own dating timeline. If you're willing to commit to no more than coffee (or a caffeinated romp), your choice of a male companion *should* differ from the choice you'll make if the dress is already altered, the veil is steamed, and the tricolored tulips are en route from the Netherlands.

I stress *should* because women's choices in mates don't always align with their inner intentions. Too often, women who want real commitment (the picket fence, the golden retriever, the joint checking account) choose men who are unable to commit to anything that doesn't have a day, a time, and a seat number printed on it. Likewise, today's independent woman might think she's cornered the market on casual relationships, only to find that her "casual fling" already has the minivan lease drawn up.

There's hope. Dating doesn't have to be a crapshoot. If you're clear about your own romantic intentions, you can use some shortcuts to help you identify the right guy with moderate to high accuracy.

As cruel as pigeonholing can be, we're going to engage in a lively game of it right now. You can twist it, you can magnify it, you can dilute it, but when there's no more manipulation left, you can't deny that there always have been, and probably always will be, two general categories of men: long-term mates and short-term dates. They've been playfully referred to as Mr. Right and Mr. Right Now, and these terms have been used in highly subjective ways. For example, Ken might be right for Barbie to marry, but not for Christie, Barbie's British friend. He's Barbie's Mr. Right and Christie's Mr. Right Now. This is accurate to an extent, but it's also important to understand that most men are either built for the dream house or the hot tub. Instead of being right for Barbie or Christie, some men are right for commitment and some are right for flings. If Ken's willing to commit to a dip, and nothing else, he's going to struggle if caged into the dream house. If his aspiration is to settle into the dream house, he's going to feel left out in the cold no matter how hot the Jacuzzi is.

That's why it's important to match your dating choice to your mating voice. Disqualifying the five days surrounding ovulation, when your choices will usually lean toward the "one-night stand" type of man, your dating goals should align with your dating choices.

Expecting to get orange juice from a lemon might be more probable than getting commitment from Mr. Right Now, so let's delve into how a man's appearance can give you clues that could affect the rest of the night or the rest of your life.

The structure of a man's face does give some insight into his testosterone levels and the resulting strength of his libido. Enter testosterone once again. Women have a love-hate relationship with this hormone, and it's no wonder. It gives men the valor and the vigor to fight for our honor but it also fuels those actions that dishonor us.

When you first meet a man you can assess his level of testosterone by looking at his facial structure. If his brow ridge protrudes far out from his face, making a straight, bony ridge over his eyes; if his cheeks are high and bony, constructing a sort of shelf under his eyes; and if his jaw is large and forward-jutting, you're in the presence of a man with high testosterone levels. Additionally, if his eyebrows are bushy and his beard is heavy (the five o'clock shadow may need to be consulted), his testosterone levels have probably been kept elevated by plenty of sex and masculine competition.

If you're up for a noncommittal-type fling or a long-term thing with plenty of action, this guy will probably be easily convinced to play along. High testosterone increases the human libido as well as the desired volume of sexual activity. If managed (that is, satisfied), this can be great for the health of a relationship. However, his super-libido might also prompt him to want to spread his seed elsewhere the first time your field isn't open for plowing.

This man's very masculine face tells of his high testosterone level.

If you're looking for more of a commitment, you might do better seeking out men with faces that are slightly feminized. Foreheads, cheeks, and jaws that aren't as prominent; eyes that are a bit wider; and facial hair that will hide out for more than six hours are all reliable indicators of testosterone levels conducive to fidelity.

This man's slightly feminized features tell of his relatively low testosterone level.

Tiger's Testosterone Loop

If you're a golf fan, you may have drawn a parallel between Tiger Woods's loss of the World Golf Championships and his spending more time at home with his pregnant wife and two-year-old daughter. When Tiger was out romping with his mistresses, his performances on the green skyrocketed. If this wasn't a direct result of the testosterone surge that comes from sex, competition, and winning, it's certainly a good example of what one looks like.

When he was at home nurturing his family, Tiger's testosterone levels probably dipped, as most men's do once they settle down. But when he hit the golf circuit again, and started winning on the greens and in the sheets, he was on top of every one of his games.

A face a child could love is one that's probably good marrying material, as well as good fatherhood material. If you're in the market for a long-term provider for your brood, you have the instinct and the decision-making power to choose a face that will naturally align pretty closely with your goals, according to the University of California, Santa Barbara's James Roney.

A team of researchers led by Roney conducted a preliminary survey of a group of men to determine how interested they were in interacting with children. Then those researchers measured the testosterone levels of those same men.

When presented with photos of the men's faces, 70 percent of women polled were correct in determining which faces belonged to men who were most likely to be more interactive fathers.

Though the women in the study probably would have had difficulty pinpointing how they knew, they just knew. That's because the female brain is tuned to pick out testosterone cues in the male face, such as a strong jaw, a heavy brow, and generous facial hair growth. Because testosterone isn't a prerequisite (it could be a deterrent) in the calm, rational, and loving rearing of children, she'll likely pass over testosterone-laden faces when she's interested in a committed mate and father. This doesn't mean that a very masculine male cannot be a good father; it simply means that his interest in interaction with those kids will likely be lower. In fact, a higher testosterone level does hold an advantage in rearing kids—the man will be more willing to physically defend his family (though this ability was more likely to be needed when babies were living in caves, not bi-levels).

Studies related to this topic are particularly interesting because they join the primordial feminine brain with the more modern ability to make rational decisions. Millennia ago, a brawny protector was more necessary because of the dangerous situations in which our ancestors lived. Now we're more interested in interactive parenting partners. The research results show that we can use our primordial brains as detection systems, and then our modern, thinking brains to make decisions.

Regardless of women's innate ability to detect walking fatherhood material, it never hurts to have a bit of practical knowledge in this area—just in case you're like the 30 percent who got it wrong.

Symmetry is a double-edged sword. Men whose features are symmetrical are considered to be more attractive, as we discussed earlier, but that's only the beginning of the list of talents that these geometrically sound hunks possess.

Besides harboring the quality genes that future mothers are looking for, men with symmetrical features of the body and face hold the ability to bring their partners to orgasm more often. In a University of Albuquerque study, eighty-six couples who had been in committed relationships for two years or more were questioned independently of each other. Then the men's features were measured for symmetry. The findings showed the female mates of the most symmetrical men were the most satisfied sexually (that is, if you equate orgasmic bliss with sexual satisfaction).

On the surface, these results look simple—as if the men were so steaming hot, the females' eggs were poached at the mere sight of them. This is partially accurate, but oversimplified. Because the female orgasm increases the chances of conception by softening the cervix and by suctioning sperm to the site where her egg will make its grand entrance, her body is virtually crying out, "I want his genes!"

Symmetry has this type of effect on our psyches because our evolutionary learning curves take over, steering us toward the best genes and ensuring the ultimate survival of our ever-beautifying and ever-strengthening species.

This doesn't mean, however, that symmetry, the best genes, and the best orgasms make the best, most faithful marriages. Sometimes they simply make good flings. This is where a woman must make a conscious decision (fidelity or good genes?) before her primordial brain or her menstrual cycle makes it for her. If monogamy were not a way of life (and morality) for many of us, there would be no question. We could simply harvest the genes that we desired from various, symmetrical sources, and then settle down with cockeyed Pete. This can be done, as we'll discuss later in the book, but it's not always practical or widely accepted by the poor Petes of the world.

Still on the fence? Consider these points: Symmetrical men not only boast the shortest periods of pre-sex courtship, and the smallest investment of time and money on dating, but they're also known to cheat more often.

"Nice to meet you. I'm going to need a saliva sample."

If this were an acceptable way to greet potential mates, you could have your long-term and short-term relationship questions answered in the time it took the laboratory to mail the results. But until dating services find a way to artfully work this into the application process, we're simply going to have to entertain ourselves with the prospect.

As is best demonstrated in the behavior of the male prairie vole, a hormone called vasopressin has a profound effect on dopamine (a feel-good chemical) in the brain. In studies, those male voles with longer vasopressin receptor genes groomed their pups more attentively, were more monogamous, and were more likely to choose their current mates over any other vole-uptuous hotties that might scamper past.

The human variation of this feature, the RS3 334 gene, comes in seventeen different lengths and also acts as a receptor for vasopressin. The longer the gene, the more likely a man is to feel satisfied and contented in a long-term relationship.

Since we've already established that measurement of a man's genes isn't possible (at least on the first date), and we can assume that quizzing him about his father's and grandfather's sexual trysts won't fly well, we'll have to just keep this scientific information in our own "gene" pockets for now.

If you wonder if he'll have the balls to cheat, just look. Though views differ in this area, Robin Baker, author of *Sperm Wars,* hypothesizes that men with larger testicles have them because their testosterone levels pre-incline them to sow more seed (and they need bigger factories to keep up with the demand). He also maintains that men with larger-than-average testicles are more prone to frequent ejaculation—even if that ejaculation doesn't happen with their committed partners (in other words, they're more likely to stray).

According to Baker, men with smaller-than-average testicles are more likely to guard their chosen mates and practice fidelity. Their smaller sperm factories don't need to top the market on production, because their genetics predispose them to having no reason to compete with other sperm donors.

Though neither large testicles nor small testicles are more successful in the procreation department, their existence does give us some clues about genetic predispositions, according to Baker.

An obvious question follows: How can you determine, upon first meeting, or laying eyes on a man, if his testicles are of the peanut or PayDay persuasion? You can't, really. Consider this method to be only a secondary factor in determining his promiscuity potential.

Of course, if you're bolder than the average woman, you could ask for a look at his boys. His responsive action ("No way" or "Hell yeah") could provide the short-term or long-term answer you're looking for.

Your fickle preferences, as viewed through a hormonal cloud, can often distort what you think you're looking for in a man. During the few days that precede your monthly ovulation, your desire for sex is higher than usual. This is your evolutionary urge to procreate. Your body is telling you that the egg is on its way, and you'd better go find someone to take a shot at it.

During this time, you may find yourself attracted to the more virile, testosterone-laden men we've talked about. It makes perfect sense, really. Your body wants to conceive, so it's identifying the men with whom that can most reliably happen. Maybe you truly want to marry your fiancé, the attentive and romantic medical student, but you can't seem to get the college quarterback out of your head. Wait a few days. It's likely that once the hormonal cloud lifts, your view will become clearer.

Depending on where your intentions lie, this can cause plenty of romantic and reproductive confusion. Keep tabs on your own schedule and you'll know whether your attraction is purely hormonal or a product of your lifestyle choice.

The Fickle Phases of You

Why do you sometimes find yourself trashing your female friends' big breasts, only hours after donning your own push-up bra?

Why do you sometimes ignore the brawny bag boy at the supermarket, and other times sweetly request that he push your cart (while you contemplate the best way to throw him in the trunk and take him home)?

Why does the attention you receive from the opposite sex always seem to take on either a feast or famine characteristic?

Every one of these questions can be answered simply: hormonal fluctuations.

In order to gain a better understanding of how your hormonal fluctuations (particularly of estrogen, testosterone, and progesterone) affect your thoughts and actions, consider keeping a calendar of your menstrual cycle.

DAYS 1–8: On the first day of your period, you might feel like your body's out of commission, but your brain is revving up for some serious hormonal spikes. During the next five days, your estrogen levels will begin to climb, making you keenly interested in interaction with others, relaxed and fulfilled by conversation, and talented in verbal and memory skills. As testosterone begins its ascent, your libido will gradually increase.

DAYS 9–13: Testosterone and estrogen are on dramatic upswings. By day 10, your testosterone levels will bring sexual thoughts to the forefront, so throwing that bag boy into your trunk with the eggs and escarole becomes a real possibility.

Estrogen will firm and plump your skin; make your digits, ears, and breasts more symmetrical; clear up your complexion; and brighten your lip color. It will sweeten the taste and smell of you and will prompt you to choose more feminine, frilly clothing that might show a bit more skin than is your norm. Your dreams and daydreams might be dominated by visions of sugarhunks dancing on you, and you'll notice that you'll get more glances and advances from men.

Other women, particularly beautiful ones, might receive some glares from your direction. You might find yourself trashing other females to male suitors and craving the company of guys over gals.

DAYS 14–20: On day 14, your egg will enter the fertilization zone, prompting the drop-off of estrogen and testosterone, along with an increase of progesterone. Your mind-set will shift from that of a sex-crazed vixen to that of a doting mother. Your verbal skills and clarity of thought might plummet, while your affinity for babies increases. You might feel more comfortable being alone than surrounded by people. A general sense of well-being will remain, while your desire to compete with other females decreases.

DAYS 21–28: As your brain experiences withdrawal from estrogen and testosterone, the sense of well-being you enjoyed for most of your cycle is not only a distant memory, but 1 in 25 of you will turn into depressed, even psychotic, versions of yourselves. You'll be more likely to schedule consultations with astrologers, counselors, and psychologists, and your propensity for committing crimes and getting into car accidents will skyrocket. Sex will likely be the furthest thing from your mind, though a good romp could soften the irritability that causes men, children, and woodland creatures to scamper for their lives at the sight of you.

When you *know* what you want, you're more likely to *get* what you want. You've probably heard the phrase "You can't have it all." In many ways, this concept applies to the search for a mate. Do you want financial security or the feeling of a hard body next to you? Do you want long-term commitment or hot, orgasmic sex? Do you want upstanding genes or an upstanding, faithful man?

If you were a character from *Sex and the City,* would you be Charlotte or Samantha? If you're like Charlotte, your goal is long-term: love, marriage, and kids. If you're more like Samantha, your goals are short-term: sex, sex, and more sex. But if you're more like Carrie or Miranda—torn between a stable relationship and a fling, undecided, unsatisfied, always questioning your current choices—then you're going to have difficulty choosing the right mate because even you don't know what you want.

To be fair, there are an infinite number of characteristic combinations that work to create men who are as different as their fingerprints. But you will greatly increase your chances of satisfying your highest criteria if you can answer some tough questions about your desired romantic direction.

Again, know what you want and get out there. Use what you've learned here to target the type of man that best fits your goals. You can determine within a fraction of a second, and with a high level of accuracy, whether a man is genetically built for the fling or the long-term thing. The method isn't foolproof, but when combined with other elements of biological attraction, it offers some clues that simply shouldn't be ignored.

Use the studies and information contained here to add to your bank of knowledge, but don't believe for a moment that husbands don't come in steamy varieties or that short-term flings can't involve sensitive, caring people. They do exist, but in order to increase your odds, it's helpful to think in averages.

Stereotypes persist for a reason—many of them ring true. This awareness will shave time, effort, and heartbreak from your quest.

CHAPTER SIX

The Sex-Biased Brain

PARALLEL PARKING, NAGGING, EMOTION ...
FROM WOMB TO TOMB

In the dark recesses of two different mothers' wombs, two fetuses are undergoing the treatments that will shape their futures. It's been six to eight weeks since conception.

The fetus that bears dual X chromosomes, the one that will be female, stays constant in its development, maintaining the labia and the nipples that have already been placed. But the other, the one with X and Y chromosomes, will be flooded with a nearly injurious dose of testosterone (remember how it can affect symmetry). The outer labia will grow to become the scrotum. The clitoris will grow into a penis. The male's nipples will remain—it's too late to wipe them from the bodily slate.

Though genitals will be the first markers the babies' parents use for gender identification, it won't be long before physical characteristics seem to be lesser distinguishers of gender than other factors, like emotional, social, and sexual behaviors. You see, while testosterone is going to work changing a blank slate (girl) into more of a topographical version (boy), it's also wiring the male fetus, beginning at around six to seven weeks following conception, creating the neurological connections that will make his brain distinctly male.

Decades later, when these "babies" meet, their learning styles, problem-solving abilities, verbal skills, and expression of emotions will prove that the biggest gender gaps are housed within humans' skulls. Both types of brains propel their users through this world quite effectively. But the operation of each is vastly different.

In truth, the differences in the sexes' bodies pale in comparison to the differences in their brains. Less than a century ago, it was believed that a child's brain could be conditioned into behaving like a boy's or a girl's. The way a child was dressed, the toys that were provided, and the type of language used were all believed to affect a child's gender future. If a boy grew up to be gay, it was assumed that his mother must have dressed him in taffeta and forced him to play with Barbie. This thinking has been revolutionized thanks to research that proves that brains are not blank slates but in fact are born in one of two forms: either female or male. Of course, some men have brains that tilt toward emotional disclosure, while some women excel in masculine professions like engineering. Some men can tell the difference between maroon and magenta, and some women can parallel park a pickup truck on the first try. But for our purposes, we'll speak in generalities. We'll cover the ninetieth percentiles, the majorities . . . the typical male and the typical female brain.

When we break off and couple up, in mating, dating, and marriage, it's easy to believe that our inborn differences can be "learned away." But just as a brain's gender tendency cannot be changed during childhood, it cannot be changed during adulthood, when its connections are further reinforced by daily and monthly hormonal influxes and withdrawals.

If every woman and man could claim to have an intimate understanding of how their mates' minds process information, we could all feel more enlightened within our interpersonal relationships. In the spirit of this ideal, we'll travel through a collection of stories that demonstrate a man's (Bob's) and a woman's (Jan's) difficulties in understanding each other's thinking patterns. Within each story, you'll find a *Gender Enlightenment* portion, which will include the information you'll need to move toward your own sense of opposite sex enlightenment.

It's the night of Jan and Bob's first date. When Bob arrives at the pub, he parallel parks in the closest space, slipping easily into the curbside spot.

Meanwhile, Jan is walking from three blocks away. She would have taken the tight spot out front, but past parking blunders have prompted her to steer clear of it.

Once inside, the two meet at the bar and proceed to a table in an adjoining room. Bob pulls out the closest chair for Jan and then proceeds to take the seat against the wall, facing the door. Music blares from the connecting barroom. Couples at neighboring tables are speaking loudly, in order to be heard over the music.

Jan and Bob cover the basic first-date protocol: jobs, hobbies, good books, favorite movies . . . with the information exchange largely being headed by Jan. She listens to his story about how he landed his job and asks him questions about its travel requirements while she decides on shepherd's pie. She tells him about her childhood cat, Cinnamon, while she points to her favorite dishes on his menu. Bob finds it difficult to concentrate on what she's saying: not only is she speaking quickly, with lots of facial expressions, and jumping from one subject to another, but she also stops occasionally to make reference to the conversations going on around them. Bob is exhausted, and he's barely said a word.

GENDER ENLIGHTENMENT: Parallel parking has posed a hurdle for women since the dawn of the steering wheel. Because the portion of Bob's brain assigned to spatial tasks is not only larger but is contained and specialized for three-dimensional rotations, this is simple for him. Since he was a boy, the spatial manipulation portion of his brain has been turned on and never turned off. When he first learned to read the word *jump*, for instance, his brain wanted to make his muscles jump. He may have even twitched in his kindergarten seat. His word-to-action brain is always ready to go to work, and operates without being specifically called upon. Bob can picture his car in relation to the other cars and adjust his motor movements to match placements in space because his brain has been specially designed, through his ancestors' historical "jobs," to do so. But, to the contrary, Jan's spatial ability is only contained within one side of her brain, and is often flipped to the "off" position. For her to imagine her car in relation to the other cars, she might have to literally talk herself into deciding just how far her bumper is from another car's fender, and even then she'll resist taking the chance of going a few inches farther, because her brain is programmed to take fewer risks than Bob's. For Jan, it's easier to find head-in parking and then walk.

A British study has shown that 71 percent of men can parallel park, accurately, on the first attempt. The same study showed that only 23 percent of women could do so. Women often perform better at this spatially challenging task after they've had plenty of chances to practice, but since the initial learning proves to be difficult, and must often be carried out in the midst of blaring horns and other impatient and judgmental drivers, Jan may never invest in this course of learning therapy.

Bob sits with his back to the wall. This is protective in nature, because he can see and anticipate any problems from fellow pubgoers or outsiders coming in the door. Because Bob's ancestors were built to protect their families (when they weren't in the wilderness downing the next meal), one of testosterone's jobs is to promote defensiveness. This is the same protection factor that will probably prompt him to take the side of the bed closest to the door when he and Jan wed.

In the areas of speech and auditory skills, Jan excels. By the time she reached the age of twenty months, she probably knew and used two to three times as many words as Bob did. This was due in large part to the corpus callosum, a bundle of fibers that connects Jan's right brain to her left brain. Jan's corpus callosum is 30 percent larger than Bob's. What this means is that her left brain and right brain can communicate more efficiently with each other. Additionally, more information can be transferred more efficiently.

The functions of the left brain include reading, speaking, writing, and logic. The right brain is largely responsible for visual processing, space, and emotion, though the sexes differ somewhat in the placement and concentrations of these abilities. Because Bob has less connectivity between the hemispheres, he's better at concentrating on one aspect at a time: reading the menu, then talking to Jan about her job, then eavesdropping on the neighboring couple's conversation. A brain scan would reveal that Bob is practically deaf while reading his menu. But Jan's brain's circuitry is designed a bit differently. Because her speech and listening capabilities are held in both sides of the brain, and because Jan's interconnectivity is superb, she can speak and listen, or listen and read, or speak and read, at the same time.

Stark reality tells us that Jan and Bob are ill-suited for conversation. It also explains why women spend time together talking for hours, and why men spend time together saying very little for hours. The term *scatterbrain,* no matter how insulting, is a rather appropriate descriptor for a fast-talking female. Her speech is "scattered" across her brain grid, and her mouth is "scattering" everything that registers on that grid. The prescription for remedying this problem is simple: women need to slow down and concentrate on one topic at a time. When Bob is subjected to Jan's verbal acrobatics, it's as if he's been placed in front of a three-ring circus and told to report the happenings of each arena in tomorrow's early edition. He'll panic, know he's incapable of doing it, and shut down from the stress of it all. It's impossible for the male brain to field the amount of information that's being thrown at him in a woman's hyper display of verbal dexterity. His symptoms will include a dumbfounded look, a glazed stare, and withdrawal.

So, ladies, harness that information superhighway. Choose your words carefully and feed him like a slow-burning fire. Applying the verbal brakes will keep your man's attention and spare you the embarrassment of being dubbed a scatterbrain.

A few dates later, Bob picks Jan up from her apartment and they head out to a dinner venue that he won't disclose—it's a surprise. While he navigates Friday night traffic into the city, he tells her about the big contract he landed at work. She shares her thoughts on global warming. As they move on to the benefits of wheatgrass and antibacterial hand soap, out of the corner of her left eye Jan catches the image of a car speeding toward them. Her mouth opens. She screams a futile "Bob!"—but it's too late to stop the impact.

A car ran a stop sign and hit the driver's side of Bob's car. "I never saw it coming," declares Bob.

Men are more likely to be involved in side collisions than women are.

"How could you not see it?" asks Jan. "We were both looking straight ahead, and I'm all the way over here and saw it coming. Are you sure you were paying attention?"

The couple suffer no injuries, so they decide to continue with the evening's plans. But what was meant to be a romantic evening ends up being a meal eaten in relative silence—Jan punishing Bob with the silent treatment and Bob feeling like a failure. His circumstance isn't bettered when he chooses to ogle a passing brunette.

Men's tunnel vision often prompts
them to turn their heads.

GENDER ENLIGHTENMENT: A man's vision and a woman's vision differ in function, thanks to the way that their past jobs affected the evolution of their sight. A woman's vision can extend a whopping 90 degrees from her centerline of vision, in all directions. This lends credence to "the eyes in the back of her head."

Bob's vision boundaries are more tunnel-like, but that doesn't mean that his vision is deficient. In fact, it works particularly well when homing in on objects in the distance. His eyes have a binocular-type effect. What he doesn't have in range of vision, he has in forward acuity.

Early human males needed this tunnel vision to focus on far-off prey and to eliminate distractions from their peripheral lines of vision. Jan's ancestors needed terrific peripheral vision to assist in nest guarding and watching the kids.

In this scene, Bob chose to drive, as most men do, because his long-ranging, forward vision is just one part of the collage that makes men good navigators. However, his lack of peripheral vision helps to explain why many more male drivers and male pedestrians are hit from the side by cars.

What Bob didn't know was that Jan also checked out a hottie at the restaurant. She was able to do it with her wide-ranging field of vision. He had to turn his head to keep the brunette in his view, making his sexual observation abundantly obvious.

Recognizing the individual sight gifts possessed by opposite sexes won't make or break a relationship, but it certainly can help to explain at least a few of the reasons that arguments break out over what seems to be right in front of the other's nose.

A Chauvinistic Vision Test

If you've grown weary of the lettered poster on the optometrist's wall, you may enjoy this exercise, which will demonstrate vision differences between the genders.

Choose a male (your father, brother, boyfriend) and a spot on the floor. Ask him to stand on that spot and look toward a designated area on the wall (it must be straight ahead). Making certain that his eyes remain pointed at the wall in front of him (he might cheat), ask him to identify the objects in his left and right fields of vision that are farthest from the wall. This will determine how far his peripheral vision extends. Now you do the same and compare the results.

Next, choose a bulletin board or a sign and ask your male assistant to start from a great distance and move slowly toward it. He should stop when he can clearly read any words on the sign (but ask him to keep those words to himself). Now start from a distance and halt when you, too, can read all or part of the sign. Compare the words that you can read with those that your male test subject can decipher. This will work best if both participants have 20/20 vision, either naturally or with vision correction.

The results should be largely universal: women have wider peripheral vision and men have better distance vision.

But who can see the forest for the trees? It seems that we might be better at seeing the whole forest, while they're better at seeing the trees.

Bob, Jan, and some friends get together for a game of backyard football. As soon as the first play is completed, it's obvious that the crux of the game will rest with the men, while the women stand, befuddled, wondering which way the ball went. The few passes that the women do have chances to make aren't received; they're too close, too far, or out of bounds.

The play strategies make perfect sense in the men's heads. Each one can work out what will happen if Jim goes left, or if Stan goes long. The girls follow the ball but aren't participating in any kind of strategy for the win. It all seems just a little bit too complicated. Stan suggests that the girls head for the sidelines. The "players" could use "some cheerleaders."

> GENDER ENLIGHTENMENT: This scene might sound like an episode of *Friends*, and that's no accident. Whenever a coed group of athletes are put together on a playing field, the men generally dominate the ball catching, ball throwing, and strategizing.
>
> One of Bob, Jim, and Stan's best brain functions is spatial in nature. This means that they can picture, in their minds' eyes, precisely where an object is in relation to other objects and people, how fast it's moving, the proportions of the object, the virtual three-dimensional rotation of the object, and how to best navigate around the object (even when it's moving and other objects are in the way). A large portion of the male's right frontal lobe is responsible for this spatial ability. This is complemented by four other right hemispherical sites that are solely responsible for performing spatial tasks, plus a few others in the left brain. The spatial portions of a woman's brain are little more than pepperings amid her gray matter, and only 10 percent of women can boast the spatial ability of even the least spatially talented of men.
>
> Dr. Camilla Benbow, a psychology professor now at Vanderbilt University, has studied the brain scans of more than one million boys and girls. She found that boys' spatial talents were evident as early as the age of four, when girls are picturing objects in two dimensions and boys are already starting to see them in three

dimensions. In Benbow's tests, which used three-dimensional rotation questions, boys outperformed girls at an average ratio of 4:1, with most of the best-scoring girls performing more poorly than the worst-scoring boys.

If you're among the minority of women who earn livings as truck drivers or engineers, or if you excel at backyard football, there's a reason you get plenty of attention and second looks while doing so . . . and it's the same reason women like NASCAR and IndyCar driver Danica Patrick gather plentiful fan bases. Women aren't generally talented in spatial tasks, so when one displays these talents, she's considered to be special . . . or spatial.

There's now evidence that suggests that spatial abilities can be learned. A study conducted by David Tzuriel of Israel's Bar Ilan University placed approximately fifty first-grade students in an educational program that focused on seeing and rotating geometric shapes as a whole, rather than in parts. After eight weeks, it seemed that any gender gap in spatial ability had been closed.

For now, no one is teaching girls the spatial capability that comes naturally to boys, so it's simple to view this inborn brain difference through the lens of evolution. It's not hard to imagine why men had to develop spatial skills. They were in the field, strategizing. They had to determine the best and fastest ways to escape from predators and to pounce on prey. Once the javelin came into use, the most successful of males (the most likely to survive) could throw a javelin with the best combination of accuracy and speed to down their family's next meal.

Men aren't doing a lot of javelin throwing or buffalo tackling these days, but what they are doing is golfing, hunting, playing video games, wrestling . . . all to put their spatial talents to use and to burn off the testosterone that fuels those brain functions.

And yes—we must address the players' request for cheerleaders. Sports and sex create the perfect storm for athletes' testosterone levels. Coaches have known this for years: give the team some sideline dishes and their testosterone levels will soar along with the score.

There are some phenomenal female athletes in the world, but

you don't have to be a sportscaster to recognize that men dominate the athletic landscape. That doesn't mean, however, that
coeds can't join in a lively game of tackle . . . uh . . . football.

Jan's thirtieth birthday is coming up, so she's been watching
and listening very carefully for clues to any surprise plans. She,
Bob, and her friends gather at a local coffee shop for breakfast and
talk about the upcoming weekend's plans. Jan listens to Carol
speak about hosting her great-aunt who's coming in from Michi-
gan, watches Laura fold a napkin while she suggests planning a
weekend shopping trip, and sees Bob's fidgeting, his sideways
glances at both girls, and his dramatic insistence on "Jan getting
out more."

The foursome breaks up to head for their separate commitments. In his car, Bob grins to himself, smug in his flawless performance. *Jan won't suspect a thing. The party is going to be a complete
surprise.*

Carol and Laura talk at their cars before leaving, worried that
Bob's ridiculous attempt at lying has tipped Jan off to their party
plans.

Jan pulls out of the parking lot and heads straight for the mall.
She's going to have to buy a new dress for the party.

GENDER ENLIGHTENMENT: The Salem witch hunts are prime
examples of how "women's intuition" has been punished by men
who simply don't understand how women can pull facts from
thin air. And in fairness, the facts that Jan's brain uncovers really do come from virtual nothingness, when you consider that
not one word about the party was uttered. This "intuition" is
the result of Jan's ancestral mothers' jobs. They were home-field
defenders. They needed to quickly determine the intentions of
strangers, and could do so by reading subtleties of intonation,
volume, tempo, inflection, and pitch (aka paralanguage) and by
impulsively recognizing body language that was inconsistent

with spoken words. In modern times, studies have revealed that, in general, women can more effectively hear words in context and decode verbally undisclosed emotions than men can.

Women use this "sixth sense" regularly in modern times. When we interview a babysitter, we might turn her down based solely on a "bad feeling." We might advise our children to stay away from the neighbor only because he gives us "the creeps." We might choose one friend over another because one seems "more genuine." Jan uses the combination of her companions' body language, vocal pitches, and contradictory word inflections to draw the conclusion that she's being lied to. All of these visceral reactions are the cumulative effects of Jan's abilities to read under, through, and over spoken language.

Because Jan has more connectivity between her brain hemispheres than Bob does, her heightened senses are backed up by the ability to make split-second assessments about situations. The corpus callosum, which we covered earlier, helps Jan to integrate visual clues with verbal ones. In Bob's brain, the visual and the verbal remain largely separate, inhibiting his ability to make instantaneous character judgments and truth assessments.

We could go on and on, furthering the biological argument about whether Jan's perception was heightened through evolution, or whether Bob's was suppressed. The answer is probably that both moved in their respective directions, from an average starting point. Ancient woman needed a radar-like "sixth sense" to protect her family from strangers and from accidents. Ancient man needed a "one-track mind," without all the distractions that would come from suspicion and situational analysis, so he could concentrate on his main job: providing food.

Jan will always be able to detect Bob's lies more efficiently than he can detect hers. This brain difference qualifies as one of those modern-day paradoxes that seem unfair, biased, and even sexist. But there's good news: in the future, when Bob makes the decision to admit that he had been golfing when he was supposed to be cleaning the garage, Jan will appreciate his

A woman's keen perception of unspoken language helps her to detect a man's untruths.

honesty . . . the honesty that she'll be able to detect in three seconds flat.

Bob is quiet over dinner. He skirts conversation. He gives only nondescript grunts in response to Jan's questions. Halfway through dinner, he reveals that he lost his job that day, and would really like to go home . . . alone.

Jan breaks into an emotional outpouring. "I can't imagine how hurt you must be. What reason did they give you? Was there any warning? Any chance they'll call you back in?" And then the worst: "Bob, let's talk about it. Talk to me—you'll feel much better if you do."

Bob says nothing. He downs an entire bottle of wine.

Jan suggests that she drive him home. On the ride to his apartment, Bob breaks down, tearfully telling Jan that he feels like a complete and total failure . . . the job had been his lifelong dream.

GENDER ENLIGHTENMENT: Men experience the same emotions that women do. But the expression of those emotions is where the gap is formed.

Jan finds it difficult to disconnect her emotions from her speech. Because she houses emotions and speech throughout both brain hemispheres, because both sides of her brain communicate so well with each other, and because her personal problems don't rest until they're converted to words, Jan imagines that Bob must be bottling up his emotions. She believes that he's been conditioned by his father to keep his problems canned up, "like a man."

Jan's perception couldn't be further from the truth. Bob feels no need to talk about how he's feeling because his brain doesn't prompt him to do so. His emotion is housed neatly in his brain's right hemisphere. His verbal expression is accommodated by his left brain. Considering that Bob's left and right hemispheres don't have the connectivity that Jan's do, he doesn't feel compelled to share his emotions. For him to do so, he would have to consciously think: *How do I feel? Now how do I convert that to words? What words should I use?* After the grand exposition, executed solely for the benefit of Jan, he'll think: *What's the big deal? I don't feel any better. I'm going to go home, pop a beer, play a game of pool, and decide how I'm going to solve this problem as quickly as possible, so this terrible feeling goes away.*

Bob discloses his emotions in the car because alcohol "feminizes" the male brain by knocking down his organized, cataloged brain sections and increasing communication between his two hemispheres.

If you pressure a man into disclosing emotions that he doesn't feel obliged to disclose, you're not providing therapy for him, only satisfaction for yourself. It's true that you feel like a weight has been lifted when you talk about how you feel, but the same is not true for the bearer of a male brain. Where there's little connection (between verbal and emotional centers), there's no need for an outlet. Bob's emotional center is like a self-contained lake. It's perfectly content, existing solely as a product of rain and evaporation. But Jan's brain is more like a pond that is fed by a spring at one end and emptied into a stream at the other. The water that comes in must be emptied, or else her brain's pond will overflow. The release, and the relief, that you feel when you put your emotions into words are foreign to a man. He just doesn't get it (and doesn't give it).

If and when he's ready to talk about his emotions, he'll feel most compelled to do so with someone who didn't badger him. Contradictory? Maybe.

But come on, like we've never confused them . . .

Jan and Bob are headed out to see their first silent movie.
How quaint, thinks Jan. *How am I going to hear the explosions?* wonders Bob.

The theater is crowded. The only two seats that Bob can find are in the left rear, just behind a giant man with a head the size of a basketball. Bob takes the seat just behind the Head and gives Jan the better seat. Bob's view of the screen is partially obstructed, but he can see most of it with his right eye.

As the film's tragic love story progresses, Jan sneak-peeks at Bob's face for signs of enjoyment, empathy, sadness . . . anything. His face is expressionless. As they drive home, she laments the untimely death of the leading lady's lover. Bob has little to contribute. The movie had no emotional impact on him.

Jan assumes that Bob didn't enjoy the movie because no shooting, conspiracy, or full-frontal nudity made an appearance. Of course, he's disappointed that his favorite things weren't included, but there's a neurological reason for his indifference.

GENDER ENLIGHTENMENT: Jan's emotional centers aren't really centers at all. Instead, they're sprinkled throughout her entire brain. But Bob's brain is different. According to researcher Sandra Witleson, his emotion is housed and processed primarily in his right brain. Since all left eyes feed data to the right brain, and all right eyes feed data to the left brain, Bob would have made out better if his one good movie-watching eye had been his left. Because he was watching the movie with his right eye, information was falling on a field that was underreceptive to emotional stimuli. Therefore, little emotion was processed. If Bob had been sitting so that his left eye was the primary viewing device, he would have felt more empathy for the lonely lover.

The takeaway factor here is pretty simple: if you want to elicit more powerful emotions from the average guy, direct the majority of your petition to his left side. Sit at his left side, speak into his left ear, look into his left eye, and stroke his left arm while you make your case. The difference may be subtle, but remember that visceral reactions, including emotions, beat cognitive

thought to the punch when it comes to response speed. Choose your word and interaction placement wisely, and by the time he makes a concerted effort to deconstruct your sentences and decide what they mean, emotion will have already started to bubble up within him.

Appeal to his left side and you'll reach his emotional center.

PMS, a Modern Malady

Premenstrual syndrome, as a chronic and recurrent symptom of hormone fluctuations, is a relatively new problem. Ancient women experienced an average of ten menstrual cycles in their lifetimes (they didn't live long, and the majority of their lives were spent pregnant or nursing). Today's woman experiences 350 to 500 fertility cycles, making her emotional existence the equivalent of a fuel-injected roller coaster with a wobbly wheel and a few loose connections.

During the last week of the menstrual cycle, if your body recognizes that no fertilized egg is in sight, both estrogen and progesterone drop off significantly. This is PMS—the last part of the cycle, and the one with the most infamous reputation. For 1 in 25 women, it can bring severe mood swings, depression, and even psychosis, suicidal thoughts, and crime waves. This is the effect of hormone withdrawal. Like an alcoholic who needs a drink, a PMSing woman's brain needs estrogen for mood heightening and progesterone for its calming effects . . . and fast. But it won't get even half of what it craves until the next menstruation begins, when it gets an estrogen fix and a good mood is restored.

Even if long-term commitment is the furthest thing from your mind, a look into the continuation of Jan and Bob's relationship will give you a valuable glimpse into how men's brains work (which can be indispensable even in the earliest stages of dating):

Bob must choose between two job offers. After the offers come in, Jan notices that Bob is sluggish about returning her calls, is wishy-washy about making weekend plans, and answers her questions with grunts or brusque, one-word responses. It seems that he's too busy conquering the amateur golf circuit to have any time for her. There's golf in the afternoons with prospective bosses, golf all day Saturday with his buddies, golf every Sunday morning by himself . . . he's even changed his voice mail greeting to say, "Hi, it's Bob. I'm probably on the course, so just leave a message and I'll call you back after the eighteenth."

Jan learns to hate golf.

Bob doesn't call. He seems agitated when Jan does. She feels slighted.

Sure, the golf clubs are slimmer, and the balls don't talk back, but is she facing the prospect of being dumped in favor of a sport?

GENDER ENLIGHTENMENT: Bob's brain is made for problem solving. This was his evolutionary role, and the residual effects are still going strong. When Bob has a problem to solve, his spatial brain (also his problem-solving brain) goes into overdrive. This takes so much of his brain's energy that areas that aren't highly specialized, such as those of speech and emotional expression, go into virtual hiding. His right brain is activated. His left brain goes on shutdown.

Often, when faced with a problem to solve, men will do spatially challenging tasks to further activate the portion of the brain in question. Bob's golf playing is a good example of this. Studies show that if a man stimulates his right brain with spatial tasks (golf uses distance, speed, wind estimation, angles, and rotational tasks), his ability to solve problems is bolstered.

The best thing that Jan can do in this situation is to give Bob his space. If she chooses to bleat incessantly, pressing him to talk about his problem or demanding that there's something wrong with *his* behavior, he will see this nagging as yet another problem to solve, and may determine that time with her isn't worth the stress.

Additionally, when women beleaguer men with a generous helping of "things he's doing wrong," the man's rostral cingulate zone (which gauges social acceptance) will alert him that he's making mistakes, and he'll shut the nagger out. In this scenario, Bob would appreciate a simple "I know you need space to figure this out. I'm going to give you that."

Had Rodin's *The Thinker* been a woman, she wouldn't be sitting on a rock alone with her thoughts. She would be sharing cosmos and carbs with a clutch of other females, mouth and eyes wide open. She would feel compelled by the nature of her brain's construction and its estrogen-fueled operations to give her problems an escape with words. She might not solve any problems with spoken words, but she would feel a release of tension, which would provide the calm that's necessary to think rationally (and to sleep at night). Centuries ago, women gathered in groups to support, talk, and build bonds and alliances, using problems as their media. Men, however, could be found (if you could find them at all) perched alone on a high cliff or leaning against a tree next to a crystal lake, emptying their minds so that their problem-solving brains could concentrate power on the dilemma at hand. Then those men might engage in a longer-than-usual hunt or a rock-throwing session to further focus their spatial, compartmentalized, problem-solving minds.

These brain differences are still prevalent today, as are the methods the genders use to deal with dilemmas. Try to change it, and you'll lose.

Men's brains need solitary space in which to solve problems.

The Shopping . . . uh, Hunting . . . Expedition

Historically, men were hunters and women were gatherers. Man left the cave in the morning, testosterone levels at their highest, knowing that his main objective was to find and kill food for his family. His day had a goal, an objective . . . a specific purpose.

Women stayed close to the cave and foraged for berries, fruit, and other gems . . . whatever they might happen upon. If they came back with armfuls of food, that was great. If they didn't, tomorrow would be another day. The men would come back with food that evening, anyway. No worries.

A man generally dislikes casual shopping because there is no goal. His ancestors were failures if they returned without meat; therefore, he feels like a failure if he returns from a shopping expedition empty-handed or without the fulfillment of a specific need. Buying lightbulbs at the home improvement warehouse is simple—there's a goal and a good likelihood of finding what he needs. But a stroll around the outlet mall—that can be utterly maddening for him. The construction of his brain makes this effect almost unavoidable.

If you'd like your guy to join you in a retail romp, you're going to have to provide him with some clear objectives. Imagine that you're chartering an elk hunt instead of a shopping trip. Verbalize goals; even put them in writing. He'll need a spending limit, a list of desired items, favorite designers, and a time limit. Every time he's able to mark something off the list, he'll feel fulfilled. His evolutionary role demands that he come home with a "kill," and if that kill has to be a new five-hundred-dollar bag, so be it.

Jan finds her dream house in an online ad. She calls Bob into the room. He notes that it's conveniently located on Highway 50, and asks her to click on BLUEPRINT so he can see the layout of the house. He studies the drawing for a few seconds and says, "Look at how the living room is open to the kitchen and dining room. That's how a house should be built." He scrolls down. "Wow, Jan. This staircase is huge. Look at how it leads right up to the master bedroom . . . and the bedroom window is facing east. That means sunshine in our room in the morning, when you're at your prettiest." He bends to nuzzle Jan's ear while she stares, puzzled, at the image on the monitor. *Where's the staircase again?*

On the way to meet the Realtor for a showing, Bob decides to drive, since they'll be going through the city. (He worries when Jan comes too close to parked cars and becomes frustrated when she refuses to hold her piece of the road.) He's already circled their destination on a map, which is about twenty-five miles southwest of her apartment. They buckle up and head out to take a peek at their dream home.

"Why not use the GPS?" asks Jan.

"You know I can't stand that woman's voice. That map will get us there faster, and that GPS bimbo won't interrupt Hendrix," Bob retorts as he turns up the radio volume.

After driving for ten minutes, Bob glances at Jan and asks, "Shouldn't we have turned by now?"

Jan doesn't respond. She seems to have been stunned speechless, painstakingly following a path along the map, which she has turned upside down.

"What in the world are you doing?" demands Bob.

Jan slams the radio volume knob to stop a guitar riff and declares, "I have no idea where we're at on this stupid map."

"Why do you have to rotate it? If you're going south, you just make the turn in relation to the direction you're driving. You don't turn the map to match your direction." He swerves around a double-parked cab while looking at the map, swings a U-turn, and drives the rest of the way without assistance.

After arriving at the house, they end up doing little more than looking in the windows and admiring the landscaping. The Realtor never shows. Bob spends half of the drive back to Jan's apartment, which he navigates by memory, yelling obscenities into his cell phone, and the agent's ear. Jan stares out the car window, wondering if the female Realtor had been held up with something like a sick child, heavy traffic, or a faulty, upside-down map.

GENDER ENLIGHTENMENT: This scene could be titled "Testosterone and the Brain." Bob's spatial brain allows him to virtually pull the blueprint off the computer monitor, convert it to three dimensions, see it in an upright manner, rotate it, and determine the house's direction in space by considering its placement on the eastern side of a highway that runs north to south. Bob's brain keeps great track of his place in space, contributing to his gender's overwhelming ability to find north, even in rooms without windows.

Jan prefers the car's GPS because it plays to her brain's lack of spatial ability. Not only does the "bimbo" express direction verbally, which is a female brain's strength, but the GPS rotates the map so that forward motion is always "up," eliminating the need for mental rotation. Jan is quiet (and turns off the music) while attempting to read the map because she's now employing many portions of her brain to attempt to fake the spatial ability that comes so easily for Bob's brain. This is notable because, usually, a woman's brain can perform more than one task simultaneously.

Bob can read a map and talk or listen to the radio at the same time because two separate areas of his brain are at work. He can glance at a map once and navigate the rest of the voyage from memory because his spatial center innately knows how to use speed and distance to estimate where his next turn will be. However, Jan must use segments of both sides of her brain to read a map, causing each activity to impede the success of the other, leaving little brainpower for humming along to Hendrix. Her best bet for navigation is the use of landmarks, which are conspicuously missing from maps.

Jan often confuses right and left because of her hemispherical connectivity. This bilateral association is usually an asset, but in this case the connection blurs the lines. Because Bob's brain is left-brain and right-brain divided, he doesn't usually flub up directions.

When Bob becomes angry, chemical releases in his brain cause that anger to build and build and build . . . until he says or does things he wouldn't do in a rational state. Testosterone, vasopressin, and cortisol flood his brain and he experiences a sort of high from the hormonal surge, making him want to continue to scream at the Realtor. In evolutionary terms, this high would have helped Bob's ancestors win battles by boosting their willingness to go on, their energy, and their fearlessness of injury. In the passenger seat, Jan is silently seething, yet relating to the agent's plight because her brain's emotional centers have a memory that's just as good as her fact-storing centers, causing her to empathize with a busy workingwoman being hollered at by an irate male. Jan's been there and can not only vividly remember how it felt, but is experiencing those emotions all over again. Jan's primal brain calculates how badly Bob's outburst will damage the relationship with the Realtor, while Bob's primal brain is going to great hormonal lengths to prolong the altercation so he can win. Bob's brain's ability to depersonalize (convert the agent into a virtual object to yell at) would have come in handy long ago when men had to injure or kill fellow tribe members for the sake of their own families' safety, but Jan's brain is incapable of separating emotions from actions, people . . . anything.

Brain gender chasms such as spatial ability are best bridged with an understanding of the operation of the opposite sex's brain. Compliment your man's spatial abilities. Stop gasping for breath with

A man's "testosterone high" can cause his anger to escalate and persevere.

every "ingenious" traffic move. His brain is designed to make split-second measurements and decisions with relative degrees of safety. Know that his anger is probably directed at the person's actions, not necessarily at the person . . . then try to introduce him to the concept of empathy, which might serve to break down some of the brick wall that encases the emotional section of his brain.

Bob and Jan, now engaged, must count the wedding reception's party favors and sort them by color, and only fifteen minutes remain before Bob's mom is coming to pick them up. Bob moves chocolate-filled sachets into piles of ten, performs quick multiplication, and looks to Jan for her numerical contribution. But she's got no figure to contribute. She's still counting, "Ninety-six, ninety-seven, ninety-eight . . ." Bob sees her process as painfully slow and unnecessarily cumbersome. Every number grates on Bob's nerves, "One-hundred-two, one-hundred-three . . ."

Jan is likewise annoyed. Bob has sorted the favors into two groups: shades of red and shades of green. "Bob, you're going to have to sort them again. Burgundy is not crimson and sage is not eucalyptus." Jan rolls her eyes. "Now all that time's been completely wasted."

Bob takes on the countenance of a kicked puppy while he struggles to differentiate between what, in his vision, looks like red and red. "I don't know why it even matters," he snaps.

GENDER ENLIGHTENMENT: Jan's ability to speak and listen greatly outweighs her ability to mentally compute. Because of this, Jan can keep better track of her counting if she supports it with the type of verbal reinforcement that her brain specializes in. Conversely, Bob can work quickly if he stays organized. When he catalogs his mental computation, he's mimicking the operation of his own compartmentalized brain. He can "see" groups of two, three, five, or ten without going through the rigors of manually counting them, or hearing the words. He uses the right, visual, side of his brain to count, which is much more efficient than her method of using the left, or verbal, side.

In reverse strength, Jan's perception of color differences is keener than Bob's. On the X chromosome are the genes that supply the cones necessary for seeing three basic colors: red, green, and blue. From those three colors, all 100 million of our perceptible shades are born. A University of Maryland study focused on the role of the gene for red perception in variances between the sexes. Researchers not only found that the red color gene shows significant variation (three times more than other types of genes), but that because women have two X chromosomes, they have twice the color cones that men do. That doesn't mean that women can see twice the number of colors that men do, but if the variations in a woman's genes (when comparing her two X chromosomes) result in red cones that differ slightly from each other, she'll be more astute at picking out differences in colors that contain red. (It's estimated that 40 percent of the female population has this talent.) This chance at superior color perception would have benefited women throughout evolution because their jobs were more color-sensitive (picking fruit and berries) than their counterparts'.

To widen this color chasm, men experience color blindness (or color perception deficiency) when a variation in genes fails to highlight differences between red and green. This genetic woe is felt in as much as 8 percent of today's masculine population. Women can suffer from this malady, but because they have an extra cone to pick up the slack, it's rare. Women who carry a deficient color gene can, however, pass it on to their sons (making them color-blind), and can replicate it to their daughters, who will experience color perception problems if they receive a "dud gene" from each parent.

Jan reacts like most other women when she uses the words *all* and *completely*. Women take much broader freedoms with vocabulary than men do because women have learned that one word can mean a multitude of things, when accompanied by inflection, intonation, and body language. Because men aren't privy to this ability, they speak and hear words literally. This is often why men will display a wider vocabulary than women— they want to search for the perfect words because their communication abilities don't allow them to apply artistic license to language. When Jan asserts that "all" their time has been "completely" wasted, she thinks she's making a valid point. Bob simply thinks she's overreacting.

Bob feels downtrodden about his mistake because, for evolutionary reasons, men don't like to admit that they're wrong. This goes way beyond pigheadedness, ladies. There's actually a very noble reason that men avoid admitting fault. In the wilds of the savannahs, a man's job *was* simple: get food. What's more, it *wasn't* simple to get food. When he set out in the morning, testosterone high and ready for conflict, he envisioned himself coming home with a kill, on which his family's survival rested. If he came home empty-handed, testosterone levels scraping the bottom of the masculine barrel, he was deemed a failure by himself and by those relying on him. He had one job. There was no room for mistakes—too many lives depended on his performance.

The best prescription for getting through this? Patience. Most men and women haven't counted and colored together since kindergarten. The chances of doing so as adults, on a daily basis, are slim, at best.

Let's Stop Here to Ask . . .

Men refuse to stop and ask for directions. It's one of the oldest jokes in the gender-bashing book. But the reason is even older.

Men don't like to admit failure because, in the past, failure meant that someone might die. By refusing to ask for directions, a man is creating a fallacy—that he's in control, and that his male brain can be relied upon for your "survival." When you browbeat him into stopping to ask for directions, he hears "You're failing me. Let's find someone else who can take better care of me than you can."

Want proof? Ask any gas station attendant. Men are much more likely to stop and ask for directions if they're alone in their vehicles.

Bob's been working lots of overtime, but his sex drive refuses to suffer. To the contrary, Jan's sex drive has plummeted in response to the upcoming opening of her new boutique. At the end of every taxing day, Bob makes an attempt to seduce Jan. But Jan is in no state of mind to entertain his advances—there's a rolling boutique to-do list siphoning through her brain, she's too tired for sex, and she feels disconnected from Bob . . . she hasn't had a chance to bond with him for weeks. Bob says that sex will help them to reconnect.

Jan needs to feel emotional closeness to Bob in order for her libido to be kicked into action. Bob can't feel close to Jan without sex for an appetizer. There's a stumbling block in their bed, and it runs right through the middle.

GENDER ENLIGHTENMENT: The areas of the male brain that are reserved for sexual drive and function are twice the size of the corresponding parts of the female brain. The hypothalamus is the brain's sexual control panel, and few women are surprised to learn that Bob's is significantly larger than Jan's. Not only is Bob's larger, but this organ is stimulated by testosterone. Since Bob has a load more of the big T running through his system than Jan does, his hypothalamus experiences a steady stream of fuel.

It's no surprise to any evolutionist that a man's sex drive should be stronger than a woman's (on average), because men have historically had the job of making sure that humans stayed off the endangered species list.

Bob feels stressed, and he needs sex to calm himself. Viewed through an evolutionary lens, his desire makes perfect sense. Long ago, when stresses like lack of food, dangerous weather, and predatory attack were high, every new life meant another chance to further the species. As a result, when men felt that their own lives were in danger, their desires to procreate were boosted so that the next generation could take over in the case of their demise. If a saber-toothed tiger was licking its lips outside the mouth of the cave, a man might want to take a quick shot, knowing that it might be his last chance to plant his seed. On the other hand, the woman may have refused the man's advances because she knew that if she conceived, and the man was eaten for lunch, she would be left to raise the child on her own.

Another clue to this evolutionary conditioning is a man's state of mind during sex. When Bob's getting busy, he's thinking of nothing else but getting busy. Bob's ancestors needed this type of concentration in order to "get it up" in dangerous situations. On the other hand, Jan can make the grocery list in her head, keep up with a movie's storyline on the TV, and check the condition of her manicure while Bob is satisfying his, and her, needs. Why? Because her female ancestors were conditioned to watch for danger while copulating . . . because the men were too focused on making new humans to do so. Her brain is designed to defend the nest with her heightened sensory abilities.

In order to close the sex gap in a stressed relationship, both genders need to bite the bullet, suck the earlobe, or chew the fat. Sometimes, ladies, you'll need to "suck it up" and give him the sex that will speak to his primal need for tactile activity, which will, in turn, stimulate his communicatory abilities. Remember that speech is not emotive for him, but sex is.

On the other hand, sometimes men simply need to sit and chew the fat with their best ladies. Remind your lover that your brain's verbal centers are intertwined with your emotional ones, and touching your emotional hub will leave you wanting to touch his sexual hub.

Know your mate's hypothalamus. Learn that a man's brain demands sex before love. Tell him that your brain demands the exact opposite. This will result in a zigzag pattern that touches on both sides of the bed.

Jan and Bob have their own bedside lamps. When Bob rolls over and begins to kiss Jan's neck, she places her novel on the nightstand and turns off her lamp. Bob reaches over and turns it back on.

Jan enjoys the rest of their coupling with her eyes closed.

GENDER ENLIGHTENMENT: Men can easily be led to believe that women are disgusted by the male form. Present a man with a naked woman, and he'll be rendered speechless. Present a woman with a naked man and she'll likely burst into laughter. This has nothing to do with one gender being more attractive than the other, and everything to do with how each gender experiences erotic feelings.

A man's brain is primarily stimulated by vision. This is why men prefer sex in brightly lit rooms and centerfolds wearing come-hither facial expressions. They'll go to great lengths just to "sneak a peek," and can fuel a generous number of sexual fantasies from just one visual experience. When a man's visual cortex processes a feminine sight that speaks to his evolutionary drive to procreate (narrow waist, ample breasts, full lips, etc.), it's not long before his hypothalamus (sexual hub) is energized, followed closely by his reward centers. This process helps to explain why men are more likely than women to fall in "love at first sight."

To the contrary, women's brains are programmed to enjoy romance novels, verbal exchanges during lovemaking, and the imagining of passionate pre-sex encounters. Sex with the lights off takes a woman's visual skills out of the sensory equation, inevitably sharpening her senses of hearing and smell, as well as her already acute verbal abilities.

Breaching the sex lighting chasm in a relationship is as simple as compromising. Find a level of lighting that satisfies both brains' ideas of great sexual atmosphere. Allow his visual brain to take in the full view of you. And then explain that you need to take in the scent, the feel, and the sound of him.

"Whadya Say?"

It really depends on who's talking, or crying, or babbling, or whining, when determining exactly how much, and how well, a man can hear.

The human male's ear and the human female's ear differ little in an anatomical sense. Any hearing differences that are noted (such as higher frequency recognition by women) originate in the brain and not within the hearing mechanisms themselves.

Sound processing seems to occur only in the left brain for men, and in both the left brain and the right brain for women. Because of this, men primarily hear words and often have a harder time picking up on the manner in which those words are spoken. Men's hearing tends to block out repetitive noise, thanks to testosterone marination in the womb (finally, an explanation for girlfriend and wife block-out), and they also tend to hear lower-volume sounds (2.3 times lower than that of women). This might help to explain why men can hear a snail creeping along the forest floor but can't hear the neighbor's baby wailing at 2 a.m.

Jan wears sweatpants and a T-shirt to bed. This didn't bother Bob at first, but now he finds sex a bit boring, and often resorts to the easiest and quickest way to gain his own satisfaction. As a result, Jan feels overlooked.

For their first wedding anniversary, Bob gives Jan a piece of sexy lingerie and asks her to put it on right away. Jan is peeved at his selfishness for only a few moments, until Bob gets to work, proving that the lingerie truly is a gift for her, worthy of a standing O.

GENDER ENLIGHTENMENT: The human male's brain is wired to be excited by new and unfamiliar bodies. Pornography is not responsible for this tendency toward promiscuity, nor are ideas interjected by fathers or friends. As discussed earlier, the size and activity of the hypothalamus make a male brain naturally hungry for sex. You may have heard men joking about "getting some strange." This speaks directly to their hypothalamuses.

Consider a bull, or a ram, or a rooster. For polygamous males of other species, five episodes of copulation with the same female represents their limit for sexual familiarity. If a bull will no longer perform for a cow, a farmer will present a new cow. This causes all parts of the bull to wake up. Similarly, a rooster will usually only breed a single chicken about five times, until he loses interest and moves on to another hen. Put a bag over the head of a ewe that a ram has bred numerous times, and he'll still walk away. He can't even be fooled into erection.

Bob adheres to this principle in one way but departs from it in another.

He craves variety. Historically, man had to sow his oats in numerous fields to increase the chances of his genes' propagation. By the time he'd copulated with one woman a few times during her fertile period, he had likely done everything he could to plant his seed there. She would then be nursing his child for five years before going into another fertile phase. It made procreative sense to move on to another plot.

That's what the polygamous male brain has in common with

males of many other species. But what Bob doesn't have in common with the ram is that he can be fooled. Put a red teddy on Jan tonight and a black one on her Friday night, and he'll be happy as a caveman with his very own basket of cavewomen berries. Social conditioning has asked today's man to curb his polygamous tendencies. Thankfully, entrepreneurs like Frederick and Victoria have recognized that outfitting women with variety is a good way to accomplish this. The ram may not have been convinced, but men are a bit easier to fleece.

The prescription for bridging this brain gap is simple: save the sweats for the gym and put a variety of lace numbers through some exercises of their own.

After Jan and Bob retire, they seem to trade roles. Bob's sex drive droops. He looks back on his professional conquests and wonders why he hadn't spent more time with his family. Jan is more self-assured, is more likely to make off-color comments, and values time for herself over dusting and vacuuming. Bob takes a cooking class and decides to plant a vegetable garden.

GENDER ENLIGHTENMENT: As we all age, hormone levels reduce. Jan's plummeting estrogen levels take her nurturing tendencies with them and Bob's loss of testosterone takes with it his conquistador attitude and his sexual energy. This shift accounts for the belief that people morph into one another after decades of living together. They're actually just coming back to home base, without their hormones in tow, the way they were as children.

Most of these brain gender differences will become obvious in your present and/or future relationships, as they have for many, many generations before you. But one noted difference in the experience is that you are among only a few age bands that have been privy to the data supporting these differences. Only since the

1960s have female brains been studied in the same depth as male brains had (before that, most brain studies were conducted on war victims . . . who were men).

In the recent past, men have been dubbed as "pigheaded" and women as "nags," and it was widely believed that upbringing and social norms had induced the preservation of these perceptions. We now know that these differences are innate, they're biological, and in the large, cannot be changed without collective human nature eliciting an evolutionary shift that affects the structure of the brain.

Some say this shift is on the horizon (if you can call hundreds of thousands of years the horizon). As more women enter the workforce and vie for the jobs that have not traditionally been suited to their thinking patterns, and as more men find themselves in white-collar jobs and raising children, the need for the gender divisions between brains may fade.

Until then, use the differences to enhance your relationships. By giving your man the room that he needs to solve problems, or by lending him the power to defend your honor with his directional skills, or by being the eye candy that his brain craves, you'll be giving him not only what he wants, but what his brain is telling him that he needs. Likewise, teaching him how to appreciate your unique talents, without burying him beneath profuse language and emotional exaggerations, will teach him to give you what you need. When brains are understood, relationships are mutually satisfying.

A Prescription for Existing Peacefully with the Male Brain

Because the male and the female brain seem to be contradictory, any number of hurdles can surface in a single day. Your newfound understanding of your man's gray matter is bound to ease some of the strain, but I've always found that keeping some practical advice "in mind" can be helpful in navigating the chasms:

1. Don't swear off parallel parking and pigskin pass receiving altogether. Instead ask your boyfriend to teach you. Remember, your brain might not be gifted with spatial ability, but you can learn with practice. You can also feed his brain's need for social acceptance, problem solving, leadership, and protection at the same time.

2. Don't turn paying for dinner into World War III. When a man pays for (or prepares) dinner, he's "catering" to his primordial brain's need to provide for you. This simple act helps to supply a positive testosterone swell, which will satisfy him.

3. If you want his cognitive brain to trump his reptilian one, tell him so. If you want him to listen to you without simultanesouly surfing the Web or if you want him to understand how you feel without offering a solution, give him a heads-up (and don't forget to stay to his left side).

4. When speaking, stick to one subject. Shut up while he reads the menu or the cable listings. Avoid using words like *everyone* and *worst* unless you really mean them. Otherwise you'll lose his attention and your credibility.

5. If he wants to drive, let him. This allows him to demonstrate the maneuvering talents that his ancestors scored for him and it feeds that testosterone wave his brain craves. Remember, he doesn't like to make mistakes, so show some faith in his navigational abilities and get your foot off the passenger-side brake pedal.

6. Don't rely on him to detect nuances in your voice, expressions on your face, or subtle body language cues. He's just not

good at it. Sure, if you're slamming cupboards and calling him a slimeball, he's going to pick up what you're laying down, but in most situations you'll need to use the words that accurately describe your feelings instead of leaving breadcrumb trails.

7. If he wants to come home from work and stare at the television, allow him the space to do so. Just as ancient men hunted all day and then came home to stare blankly into fires, your significant other's brain needs that same "shutdown" time.

8. If you ask him to do something while he's engrossed in a televised ball game or the newspaper, and he ignores you, understand that his brain is deeply compartmentalized and focused, and his "selective hearing" is probably not voluntary. Get his attention first and then ask for what you need.

9. Don't press him to talk about his feelings. This might frustrate him and cause resentment toward you (for imposing your brain's needs on his). However, if he's had a bit too much to drink and wants to talk, listen to him. The alcohol breaks down barriers in his brain, feminizes it, and makes speech a satisfying emotional release.

10. Don't dwell on his mistakes. His brain is hardwired to perceive mistakes as life-threatening (because they often were for his ancestors). True, you will always be able to call up the emotional pain you felt when he made his mistakes, but for him, your remembrances are just stabs at his manhood. Instead, only bring up current problems and soften each piece of bad news with five complimentary statements.

11. If he's pondering a conundrum, give him space. When he's golfed, shot, thrown, and calculated his way to a solution, be there to congratulate him.

12. Though excessive anger and aggression from him should never be things you have to live with, understanding that his occasional outbursts are products of his chemically marinated brain, and not of animosity toward you, can help you to comprehend the differences in your brains. Often, while he's ranting about your mother's cabbage appetizers or the sluggish Sunday drivers on the road, he's simply riding a testosterone high.

13. Recognize that a man's sex drive doesn't spring from his loins or from a selfish desire for satisfaction; it comes from his brain. A fitting movie line might be "Is that your hypothalamus, or are you just glad to see me?"

14. Once your relationship has escalated to a physically intimate level, take it all off. Remember that he's stimulated by vision. If you refuse to bare it for him (at least once in a while), he'll feel as slighted as you would if he refused to talk to you or touch you after sex.

15. Don't forget to keep some sexies in your dresser drawer. When you dress up differently, fix your hair differently, or temporarily pretend to be someone else, it will excite his libido with that "first time" feeling.

16. As he ages, understand that a drop in testosterone will effectively feminize his brain. He might take up hobbies that don't involve shooting or hitting things, his outbursts will soften, he'll be more likely to feel lonely . . . but don't panic. There's nothing wrong with his brain—this is him "off" testosterone.

17. Finally, when he doesn't understand the way that you operate, explain it to him. Your brain is a mystery to him, too.

What every man wants is an expression of appreciation for his efforts. He's a provider by nature. He hates failure. He wants to protect you. And he wants to know that you see and value his endeavors.

When he feels that he has fulfilled his evolutionary role, he feels valuable. And when he feels valuable, real, lasting love can take hold.

CHAPTER SEVEN

"Hmmm . . . You Look Familiar"

THE ROLE THAT YOUR MIRROR PLAYS IN MATE CHOICE

For centuries, that little lady named *Mona Lisa* has been agitating spectators and speculators around the world.

Who is she? Is there a greater significance to her countenance than meets the eye?

Some claim that she might be the wife of a wealthy merchant; others say that her lovely face was borrowed from that of Isabella, Duchess of Aragon; analytical readers believe she may be Leonardo's mother; and, most interestingly, another theory states that Mona Lisa's visage is actually that of the artist—a self-portrait.

Of course, Leonardo da Vinci was a genius . . . an inventor, an artist, a mischievous brain teaser . . . so it's likely that there's at least one secret hidden in Mona's smile. But there's also another, more innocuous, possible plot that might surface. What if Leonardo had begun his masterpiece with the intention of pleasing the admirers of the duchess but had unwittingly tweaked Mona Lisa's features to resemble what was familiar, what was safe, and what was most highly attractive to him? What if Mona, above all else, resembles Leonardo?

Ask any artist, writer, or musician what their work means to them, and you'll get a variety of answers, but none that depart from the general meaning of "love." They'll all speak of an attraction that pulls them toward their work.

Studies, a few of which we'll cover here, have concluded that human beings are largely attracted to those who look similar to themselves. If Leonardo did feel attachment to his work, even love for his work, and he held a brush with which he could create the face of his choosing, is it impossible that he would have designed a mug that resembled the one he knew best?

You decide. Maybe Mona Lisa never existed. Maybe she was simply a fantasy of one ingenious, but still very human, artist.

Is Mona just a Leonardo look-alike?

"Mirror, mirror in the pub, who most resembles my mug?" When singles are looking for love, this might be the very thing their subconscious minds are chanting.

Sure, opposites attract, but people aren't atoms. They're programmed, by Mother Nature, to find the mates who will best carry on the features that have gotten them to adulthood, and promise, tongue in cheek, to take them to a timely death.

In order to demonstrate this idea to yourself, think of your own facial and bodily features. What have they done for you lately? Of course, there are the superficial: the job promotion, the hot one-night stand last year, the gig as a catalog model . . . but there's one chief thing that your features have afforded you up to this very minute—life.

At the risk of sounding redundant, evolution has given you your features, both on a generally human level and on your individual family level. You look the way that you do because you are the result of successful breeding. In other words, your whole physical being is a representation of the features that helped your genetic ancestors to survive. Whoever gave you that big schnoz used it to survive a dry climate. Those long legs are the result of someone being able to outrun a rabid, angry boar or a rabid, angry stalker. Your big, blue eyes helped someone in your past to score the sperm that caused the family tree to sprout a new bud.

So, logic would tell you that if your features have worked well enough to bring you to this point, they're worth perpetuating, right? This is the thinking that helps to explain the tendency that humans have to choose mates who bear a reasonable resemblance to themselves.

Take a look at the engagement section of the newspaper and you might get a better grasp on this concept. People often choose those who share common features, including eye spacing, nose and lip shapes, hair color, height, weight, earlobe length, and general attractiveness (as defined by averageness and symmetry). It's been said that as couples age, they begin to look like each other. This can be supported by lifestyle, habits, and diet, but it can also be supported by the idea that they probably started out not too far from center.

These two resemble each other, and that factor probably contributed to their initial attraction.

The concept of being attracted to your own self-portrait with a masculine twist is supported by the evolutionary concept known as assortative mating. Positive assortative mating operates on the premise that *like* attracts *like,* as long as the similarities don't flirt with the possibility of genetic repercussions.

To break it down, if two people are too genetically similar, their offspring can suffer from the compounding of already injurious genes. We've all heard the joke that if brothers and sisters procreate, the babies will have three heads. This is a bit of an exaggeration, but evolutionarily speaking, being too genetically similar to a mate could result in less-than-sturdy children, especially when both parents share a serious genetic shortcoming.

On the other end of the spectrum, if the genomes of mates are too dissimilar, the results could be that the features that have worked so well to foster the survival of the parents run the risk of drowning in a new, unfamiliar gene pool. This is why the majority of the United States' population still subconsciously (or consciously) insists on marrying into their own ethnic groups, according to a Pew Research Center study released in 2010.

The idea of assortative pairing means that the best dating, mating, and marriage candidates are those who are good genetic averages, somewhere between blood relatives and polar opposites. This means that the majority of humans will choose those who bear similarities to themselves, but who are not closely related.

Cousin Quail, Not Once Removed

English biologist and professor of ethology Sir Patrick Bateson tested the assortative mating theory with Japanese quail. Quail chicks were raised with their biological siblings for only one month, and were then isolated until they reached reproductive maturity. At that time they were reintroduced to their siblings. But those siblings weren't alone. They shared the playing field with first cousins of the prowling quail, as well as complete strangers. The quail, both male and female, spent the largest amounts of time interacting with their first cousins. The siblings and the strangers got little or no attention. When the quail were finally permitted to mate with their first cousins, eggs were produced days earlier than the eggs laid by non-first-cousin pairings. The other pairs did produce offspring, but the initial "chemistry" wasn't nearly as explosive.

The parallel between the quail study and the tendency of humans to choose similar-looking mates cannot be denied. Like humans, the quail went for the mates that were familiar enough to feel safe (to eliminate the chances of losing good genetics), but different enough to prevent problems that can arise from inbreeding. This represents the reproductive balance that *is* assortative pairing, and explains why you're attracted to the faces that most resemble yours (as long as those faces don't show up at your family reunion).

This leads to the question of incest. If similarity is good for the propagation of features, and important to attraction, why do brothers and sisters cringe at the mere mention of incest? For that answer, we'll turn to imprinting, sexual inhibition, incest, and two men with opposing yet strangely harmonious theories.

In 1891, Edward Westermarck, a Finnish philosopher and sociologist, hypothesized that adults rarely desire to have sexual relations with those whom they grew up with. His theory had little to do with genetic relations, only familiarity. One example of nongenetic sexual imprinting was the Chinese custom of a young girl moving in with her future husband's family and living with them until the marriage took place. These marriages often resulted in low birthrates. The couples simply weren't significantly attracted to one another. Another example is the Israeli kibbutzim, in which children are raised communally, with no concentration placed on sibling relationships. As adults, these children were highly unlikely to pursue a sexual relationship with any person who had been raised alongside them. This explains why, when estranged since infancy, a biological brother and sister have a good chance of pairing up. They look a lot like each other, but haven't been raised together. (Wouldn't you like to be a mouse at that premarital blood test?)

Westermarck attributed this sexual aversion to family members and close playmates to a critical imprinting period between the approximate ages of eight and fourteen, in which adolescents develop a sexual distaste for those with whom they live or spend a large portion of time. He maintained that this imprinting could only take place during a portion of time, not an entire life span. If it was to remain alive and well throughout life, husbands and wives would grow sexually sour toward one another after only a few months of living together. This is Westermarck's explanation for the overwhelming repugnance for incest, but Sigmund Freud had a different idea.

Freud maintained that incest was a natural human behavior. He cited the need for taboos against it. His thinking went something like this: *If incest is naturally repulsive, why are taboos even necessary?*

Tied into this manner of thinking is the Oedipus complex, in which Freud theorizes that children, between the ages of three and five, experience a desire to kill their same-sex parent so that they can enjoy an exclusive relationship with their opposite-sex parent (bring that one up at Thanksgiving and watch the stuffing come up).

Freud believed that at the age of five, when children begin to identify themselves as either male or female, they grow to distinguish themselves as having more in common with the same-sex parent than the opposite-sex parent (accompanied by a dissolving of the desire to kill the former). This theory shares a vein with assortative mating when the children finally reach adulthood. They will then most often be attracted to those people who resemble their opposite-sex parents. Can anyone say "fickle"?

The reference has been made for decades: people tend to choose mates who resemble their parents. This makes perfect sense. We all resemble our natural parents in some way, so when we choose mates who resemble a parent, those mates also resemble us.

In the case of similar-looking mate choices, familiarity does not breed contempt; in fact, it often breeds affection. When you hit the club, or the church social, or the singles cruise, take note of your opposite-sex facial preferences. If you tend to choose those faces that could belong to your brother, you probably either have a solid relationship with your father or hold your own features in high esteem. If you find that you're attracted to those of other races, or those whose characteristics differ greatly from your own, you're in the minority . . . but that doesn't mean you don't have good reason. You could subconsciously be looking to enrich your own genome with some fresh DNA to soften an undesirable family characteristic. Or you could be looking to steer clear of anyone who reminds you of your father.

Most of us will look for mates who resemble ourselves. Our features have worked to bring us to this point, so they must be worth keeping. Likewise, others will see our faces as either familiar or foreign, and respond in the same manner.

If Leonardo da Vinci held affection for Mona Lisa, in the same manner that most every artist holds fondness for their work, he may have naturally infused some of his own features into the painting (or he could have done so for a good chuckle from the grave). This conjecture is so robust that it has prompted Italy's National Committee for Cultural Heritage's art historians and scientists to suggest exhuming the body of Leonardo, who died in 1519. They want to rebuild his face and determine if he does indeed resemble his most famous work of art.

The bigger question for us is "Was Leonardo in love with the image of Mona Lisa?" If her face is determined to be the feminine version of his, the answer could be yes.

Scrutinizing the faces that approach you can offer some insight into suitors' intentions. If the guy who's hitting on you looks like he could be your cousin, his genes just might be worth considering.

Sure, it's the oldest pickup line in the book, but maybe "Haven't I seen you somewhere before?" should be revisited as a viable opener for coupling up. Maybe instead of answering, "Security!" you should consider a simpler response: "Yes, in your bathroom mirror."

CHAPTER EIGHT

The Faces of Reproduction

OUR PART-TIME LOVE AFFAIRS WITH DOMINANT FACES

Two men walk into a bar.

The first man's face is robust, with a heavy brow, protruding cheekbones, square jaw, and thin, straight lips.

The second man's face is softer; his eyes are large, his lips plump, his chin small, and his face animated.

Which of the men are you most attracted to? Before you answer, remember that our preferences change depending on where we are in our menstrual cycle, so figure out the date of your last period. And while you're doing that, thank your lucky stars that I didn't add the traditional priest and rabbi to this enduring joke.

Generally speaking, women are attracted to rugged or delicate male features for notably different purposes. The face of man number one in the above scenario has been shaped by generous genetic doses of testosterone. Because his resulting features are indicators of high testosterone levels, it can also be assumed that testosterone's other achievements are being realized in his mind and body. For instance, studies show that he is probably more aggressive, has a stronger immune system, is more fertile, has a higher social status, and is more dominant among his male peers. He is probably also less likely to be a doting father and a faithful husband (or at least one completely satiated by monogamy).

As is also shown by studies, the second man, with the less masculine face, is probably not as confrontational and is shier, more susceptible to disease, less fertile, weaker, and less likely to win any type of battle, unless it's a battle of wits. However, he holds a high propensity for being a nurturing father and a faithful spouse.

The man with the more masculine face is a good candidate for a tempestuous tryst; the feminized face is better for long-term commitment. As discussed in chapter 5, each one holds noted advantages, depending on your own long-term or short-term relationship intentions. But that doesn't mean that your own chemical concoctions won't try to sabotage your objectives.

Testosterone plays a critical role in attraction. That's what Dr. Ben Jones, a psychology lecturer at Aberdeen University, discovered when he collected and recorded the facial preferences of both male and female subjects. During a one-month period, each subject donated a saliva sample from which testosterone levels were tested. Then each participant was asked to rate the attractiveness of a pair of faces, one male and one female.

Before reporting the results of the test, I need to point out that, though men's testosterone levels do fluctuate seasonally, with success and with sexual activity, women's fluctuations are more regular, more dramatic, and orchestrated by their fertility cycles. A woman's highest levels of the big T are felt during the days just before ovulation, when her sex drive is at its highest. From the results of Dr. Jones's study it is evident that testosterone not only contributes to a man's reproductive fitness, but also heightens the viewer's sensitivity to that fitness.

Jones found that men with the highest levels of testosterone favored women whose faces were the most feminine. Women with the highest levels of testosterone (preparing for ovulation) chose the most masculine male faces.

Also interesting was the fact that men's ratings of other men's faces didn't change with testosterone fluctuations. However, women whose testosterone levels were high often rated masculinized women's faces as the most attractive. This is probably due to the fact that when ovulating, women see feminine faces as threatening to their reproductive success. The ovulating women's preferences for masculinized female faces weren't preferences at all, but rather choices that would make their own faces appear more female, and more attractive to the opposite sex.

These findings support the reasoning behind my asking, in the beginning of the chapter, about the date of your last period. Fourteen days from the beginning of your most recent period, you will ovulate. Just before that ovulation, your system will experience a spike in testosterone and estrogen. This radical increase speaks to your most primitive brain and drives it to find the best, most efficient, and most effective way to fertilize your egg. A man with high testosterone (one whose face is rugged and manly) seemingly offers the best route to accomplishing that fertilization.

Researchers have found that women who are in committed relationships (probably with baby-faced men) are most likely to step out to affair-land during the times when their testosterone levels peak. After the testosterone and estrogen levels fall (just after ovulation), progesterone takes over and brings on a nurturing, calm attitude without all of the sexual drama. This is the point when women are most likely to once again appreciate their long-term commitments.

Luckily, the average human courting ritual lasts for more than four days. Otherwise, there would be more than a few couples for whom the honeymoon wore off before it was over.

The logic behind attraction to masculine faces during ovulation is, of course, rooted in human evolution. In the brutal environments that humans once inhabited, having a father around to protect and defend the family was an advantage, particularly if his offspring were ill or weak. For this reason, early women probably chose as long-term mates those men with lower levels of testosterone during the largest portions of the women's reproductive cycles. They knew those men were less likely to stray.

But there was another course of action that could be taken with reasonable success. The higher-value reproducers, the men with masculine faces and high testosterone levels, had higher-quality genes to pass on to their offspring. If an ovulating woman was drawn to one of these brawny men, there would be forgiveness for her rash decision. The resulting child would likely be hardy, robust, and able to gain independence earlier than a child who inherited the weak genes of a baby-faced, faithful man. Even though the children with the good genes had no fathers present, they were healthy enough to demand little attention from their mothers.

When you stop to consider the ways that our hormonal fluctuations change our attitudes toward mates, you can understand how it might make good reproductive sense to produce children with sexually dominant men, but maintain long-term relationships with quality nurturers. The children would be vigorous, with healthy immune systems, and they would also benefit from the protection offered by devoted surrogate fathers. This thinking is why so many women (one in five) stray from loving relationships for flings. This is also why these flings happen more often during the hormonal fluctuation that occurs just before ovulation.

Early women may have had to choose: one-night cave stands with adulterous hairy hunks (for healthy children) or long-term bedrocks with faithful, baby-faced men (for children that might be of average health). Chances are the women didn't choose at all. Their hormone-laden brains did so for them. Much in the same way that ours do today.

Since our prefrontal cortexes have taken over much of our thinking, we can reason more efficiently than our early ancestors did. We have social norms and moral standards that we use to govern our actions. That's why the majority of today's women look for a good average—a man whose face falls somewhere between dominant and submissive. A man with good reproductive ability and the desire to stick around for more than breakfast. Who says you can't have it all?

Faithful mates aren't without their evolutionary tricks. During a woman's ovulation, competition for her sexual attentions runs high. Men with high testosterone might spar (literally or figuratively) for a reproductive chance at what they determine to be a sure thing. This behavior doesn't depart from that of other species who wrangle for the first shot at a female in estrus.

You might notice this phenomenon in your own dating efforts. Some nights maybe no one will ask you to dance; other nights you'll choose from a host of salivating suitors. Look at the calendar before you hit the dance floor, and it all might start to come together. If you're ovulating, you're likely to get more attention from the opposite sex.

But what about the low-T men who would make good fathers? How can they thwart this power struggle in order to get, or maintain, the attention of their ovulating sweetie?

Women often note that their mates are more doting, more attentive, and more loving during ovulation. Likewise, on a night

out, an ovulating woman's date might feel inclined to attach himself to her side to defend his rights to her. This is a counteraction
strategy from those men who aren't endowed with the testosterone levels that push them to be competitive in a visceral sort of
way. Instead they use affection and attention, their best weapons
in the sexual war, to win over, and/or keep, their ladies.

**Men with high testosterone levels have their own repro-
ductive standards,** and those standards have everything to do
with high estrogen in potential mates.

Historically, men have not preferred dominant mates. If a man
boasts his own high testosterone levels, he will see a woman with
a masculinized face as someone who might struggle with him for
power. Instead he prefers the softer, more estrogen-influenced
face because it offers indications of fertility and the appearance of
submissiveness.

The faces that reproductively dominant men are attracted to
are generally those with large eyes, full cheeks, small chins, diminutive jaws, and full lips. If your smile is active and large, this
is also an indicator of high estrogen, and will attract a high-T
male.

A woman's face that has a straight, thin-lipped mouth that
rarely smiles, along with small eyes, and heavy, bony facial features, speaks of a woman's relatively high testosterone levels and
her propensity for dominance (both of which are unattractive to
a man . . . unless he's looking for a defense lawyer).

Just as there are seemingly cruel standards for men, there are
equally cruel ones for us ladies. It seems that dominance and reproductive success do not go well together, at least for those of the
feminine persuasion. The two characteristics are complementary,
even catalytic relative to each other, for men. But for us it seems
that our features usually speak of either power or reproduction—
not both. Of course, there will always be those dominant-looking
women who bear children fruitfully and who take on submissive
roles at home, but the law of averages is, once again, at work here.

Body Watch: Is your face more like Jessica Alba's or Hilary Swank's? Both are certainly beautiful, but there's no denying that Jessica's face is more rounded and feminine, while Hilary's is more angular and masculine.

If you can't judge a book by its cover, you can at least judge a reproductive prospect by his face. Though there are plentiful exceptions to every rule, the standards of testosterone, brawny features, reproductive fitness, and levels of attraction as determined by hormone fluctuations will remain largely constant.

If you revisit the beginning of this chapter, you'll be reminded of the two men who walked into the bar—one with rugged features and one with softer features. Each face holds different clues to the strengths housed within its corresponding brain.

You can revisit this chapter a number of times, and chances are that your facial preference will vary, at least once. This is the nature of your reproductive system. For the success of our species, your libido has struck a balance between gene proliferation and family protection. Children need both. They can't always get both from one father. This is the paradox of monogamy, and it seems that until it goes viral, these facial differences will prevail.

CHAPTER NINE

Men with All the Trimmings

THE COURTSHIP ADORNMENTS OF THE HUMAN MALE

When you think of colorful or extravagant males, what comes to mind? A rooster strutting through the barnyard, spurs sparkling and scarlet comb waggling? A peacock fanning his trunk ornaments for all the horny peahens to see? Or does the large size of successful males pervade your thoughts? Bull elephants? Mammoth elephant seals? Gorillas with flaring nostrils, large chests, and brute strength?

Courtship is prominent in the animal kingdom . . . so prominent that television surfing at nearly any time of the day will produce some nature program that touches on the adornments of males and how those adornments aid them in scoring the most genetically valuable females. But what many of us fail to realize is that for every gettin'-busy-in-the-forest animal show, there are at least one hundred others that show equally flamboyant displays of human male courtship ornamentations. These shows are soap operas, medical dramas, sitcoms, and talk shows.

Because nature has assigned the spreading of genes as one of man's "jobs," he must sell those genes. There are lots of other pushers out there, most with the same goal. In order to elevate himself to the front of the pack and land himself in the ultimate sack, he must flaunt the results of his quality genes. His body must say, "If you like what you see, and you want some of this for your own children, I have the secret ingredient right here."

Sexual selection is Charles Darwin's sequel to natural selection. It was sparked by the existence of ornamentations like peacocks' tail feathers. He wondered why the most successful breeders were those with the implements that slowed them down, used up metabolic resources, and made it easy to be targeted by predators.

The only answer seemed to be that females preferred the larger, more colorful plumage. But why? After years of deliberation, the biological jury seems to have come to a viable conclusion: if a male's system is strong enough to support these embellishments, then he must be one hell of a specimen. Plus, females want to pass those genes along to their offspring, for the future propagation of their own genes (in other words, the next generation's peahens would go gaga over their sons).

Think a human male can't possibly stack up to a peacock's plumage? Think again. He may not be wearing a sandwich board, but a careful eye will reveal the many parts of the human male's body that advertise what he's selling.

Beards have gone out of vogue in the last few decades, mostly for grooming or sanitation reasons. But before the baby face was all the rage, beards could be compared to the lion's mane—symbols of power and regality.

Earlier, we spoke about the evolutionary purpose of the beard. Sure, it hides the jugular and insulates from both cold and sun. But there is another, sexier, theory as to why males sport beards.

A full, fast-growing beard is a good indicator of generous levels of testosterone. It adds to the heaviness of a man's jaw. Along with goatees, mustaches, sideburns, and five o'clock shadows, it stresses the sexual maturity of any given male. Long ago, a male who couldn't grow a beard could have been cursed with the eternal look of youth (it doesn't sound like a curse until you consider that it spelled i-m-m-a-t-u-r-i-t-y to females). A beardless man would have been the equivalent of a rooster with a tiny comb, or a deer that couldn't muster more than a few antler points. In other words, he wouldn't get many opportunities to reproduce.

Even today, the fullness of a man's beard is a clear signal of his sexual maturity. I can't imagine that any woman would find that the wispy peach fuzz of a teen's face or the translucent tendrils of a senior's chin sexy. We equate skimpy beards with skimpy reproductive abilities, and rightly so. Dense, fast-growing facial hedges advertise a man as a reproductive superstar. When older men experience decreased testosterone levels, they undergo symptoms such as reduced energy, diminished sex drive, reduction in number of erections experienced . . . and yes, reduced beard growth.

Not quite a beard, but a reliable harbinger of one, the five o'clock shadow takes the prize for facial landscaping, according to women who participated in a study at Northumbria University in Britain. When presented with photos of fifteen men, each Photoshopped with different lengths of facial hair growth (from baby's butt to Santa Claus), "light stubble" reigned supreme. It seems that women want reliable reproductive indicators but don't want to suffer through spittle, food particles, bacteria, and all the other turnoffs that come with lumberjack beards. They also don't care for the ambiguity that accompanies the clean-shaven face. (Is he a boy or a man?) But the five o'clock shadow—now there's a look that will take any girl through to midnight. It's rugged, it's sexy, it's clean, and it says that he's got so much testosterone coursing through his veins that he can't even make it past dinnertime without oozing manliness.

If women were still looking for men who could tackle and kill wild game, the beard might still be a highly successful courting adornment. But for now, until wild game takes over Wall Street and beards can shake their grubby reps, the daily shave will hold its place in men's morning routines.

Tall men are products of both natural and sexual selection. Nature chose to spare them; women chose them because they expected nature to be kind to them.

The ancestors of men and women showed little difference in sizes between genders. Much like cats and dogs, one may have had to seek out primary gender cues (genitalia) to differentiate between males and females. Tall men were selected more often than short men. Therefore, men grew to be (on average) taller than women.

It seems that women prefer taller men just as female gorillas and female elephant seals prefer bigger-than-average males. Taller or bigger males are more likely to win a mating battle, but females of some species, like humans, will bypass that whole show and go straight for the favored winner.

A Tall Order, Fulfilled

It is believed that throughout human evolutionary history, taller men have been chosen as leaders because they looked more formidable than their vertically challenged competitors. Nicolas Sarkozy, the French president who literally and begrudgingly looks up to other leaders of state, inches into power at just around 5'6". Shorter than Napoleon, Sarkozy goes to great lengths to increase his height, including the use of heeled shoes, platforms behind lecterns, and employees who are shorter than him to surround him for public shots. His wife, a tall model, never wears heels. Next to her, Sarkozy walks on the balls of his feet, with a noted bounce, probably in an effort to suspend himself a few centimeters higher in space.

Time has passed since height made any significant difference in survival, but little about our preferences has changed. Today placement in space is a significant consideration in power: that's why speakers are placed on podiums and pharmacists have to climb to their stations. If someone is relatively high, an aura of trustworthy leadership is created. When a man is born to naturally tower over people, even look down his nose at them, that podium impression is affected. We've all been told to stand tall to show confidence, and it seems that when you're already tall, a baseline of high confidence (at least in the eyes of others) is accomplished.

A study by Timothy Judge and Daniel Cable proved this theory when it found that men who exceeded the mean height of 5'9" earned up to $789 more per year. Clients wanted to spend more money with them, and they were given more initial career opportunities with which to prove their aptitude.

Similarly, an Australian study measured the perception of height in relation to professional status. An actor was introduced to five different classrooms of students, first as a fellow student, then as a demonstrator, a lecturer, a senior lecturer, and finally a professor. When asked to estimate his height, participants' average guesses increased one-half inch for every step up in manufactured authority. It seems that height is so deeply married to the ideas of trustworthiness and status that perceptions travel in both directions.

If you enjoy trolling the big-and-tall section in search of Dagwood Man Sandwiches, you're not alone. Whether a client is spending money, a listener is investing trust, or a woman is looking for love, it seems that the higher it's stacked, the thicker the wallet, the loftier the trust factor, the higher the power perception, and the healthier the sex appeal.

When you consider all the career, monetary, and sexual benefits that tall men enjoy, it's easy to understand why Napoleon started his own complex.

Men's shoes often have thick soles and men have been known to wear lifts in their shoes in order to gain attention from the ladies. This is a form of courtship ornamentation. Though the average barefoot male measures around 5'9", females' preferences hover right around 6'. This differential is a good indicator that men's heights will continue to increase as generations pass.

Penises have largely been shaped by women, and I don't use the term *largely* frivolously. As we've discussed before, the human penis is the largest, in relation to body mass, of any mammal. Because the vagina is collapsible, and can adapt to most any size penis, a small one will most often do an ample insemination job.

So, why the extra baggage for the guys? The glaringly obvious answer seems to be that women chose penises that were both longer and thicker than average simply because they preferred the sexual experience that they offered. A penis with more girth was more likely to rub against the clitoris during intercourse. A longer penis was more likely to reach the point of stimulation near the cervix and the bladder. In short, bigger was deemed better by the maidens, and the best-endowed, best-"peacocking" cavemen got the most, and best, chances at procreation.

Across the animal kingdom grid, the species with the most elaborate penises are those in which the females can choose from a significant number of suitors. If a penis looks intriguing, it's going to warrant a romp, which may be all it takes to distribute those funky penis genes. One Argentine lake duck specimen takes the prize for longest bird penis, at 42.5 centimeters. Dr. Kevin McCracken of the University of Alaska, Fairbanks, maintains that this well-endowed quacker blows previous records (20 cm) out of the water, citing extreme sexual selection as a possible cause. (While male ducks orchestrate elaborate courtship routines, Lady McDuck and her feathered lady clique get all foamed up over oversize organs, giving the big-duck-dick gene plenty of opportunities to spread its wings.)

The male damselfly's penis displays elegant lines and offers

The damselfly's penis
is elaborate.

Normally coiled within the
abdomen of the flea, this
penis looks like a special order
from the Phallic Factory.

interest for every season. Its specially designed hooks work to scoop sperm of other males from the female damselfly's sperm storage facility (see photo).

The bird flea's mating lasts for one to nine hours, and it's no wonder. It probably takes both flea parties that long to figure what to do with this thing (see photo).

The human male's penis might not be as intricate as some, but the human female's vagina doesn't require all the bells and whistles that the female bird flea's vagina does. Our ancient grunt-and-whistle sisterhood chose the penises that worked best for their purposes, and we're left with results that fit like gloves.

You're probably puzzled, wondering how a penis can be a courtship adornment, particularly if it's not unveiled until courting has been successful. Remember that for most of human history, the penis was as commonplace as the nose. Clothing is a relatively new invention. We're just reaping the hidden benefits of our ancestors' blatant choices.

Body Watch: When a man hooks his thumbs into his belt loops, or places his fingers into his pockets but keeps his thumbs out, he's using his thumbs (his most powerful digits) to point to his pride and joy. One could presume that only a significant appendage would be worth pointing to.

Brains are survival tools today, but they were particularly valuable when our ancestors descended from trees and had to devise methods for staying alive. As man's brain grew, his ability to solve problems also expanded. There's no doubt that females saw value in a man who could create a plan for keeping her and his offspring fed, warm, and safe.

Today, when men flaunt their IQs by questioning Alex Trebek's answers, posting their SAT scores on their Facebook pages, or offering directions to a beautiful woman who seems to be lost, they are using the size of their most valuable organs, their brains, to woo potential mates.

Not All Male Trimmings Are Genetic

Some trimmings are manufactured. Examples include brightly colored clothing (yellow, orange, and red); suit coats that expand the broadness of the shoulders, taper the waist, and make the arms appear larger; graphic tees; off-center parts in the hair; and asymmetrical chest adorn-ments like crests and bouton-nieres. Many men will choose accessories that attract attention. A roadkill fur hat, an over-size pendant or watch, shiny or extravagantly adorned shoes, bejeweled jeans, or a belt buckle large enough to draw attention to his most prized possessions bids others not only to look, but to use the topic of that adornment to start a verbal exchange. Embellishments that have traditionally been reserved for the female sector might also be used to attract attention. Fingernail polish, ponytails, and earrings all provide a desired effect. If a man employs any of these "helps," he's attempting to call attention to himself, in hopes of gaining the opportunity to embark upon a mating dance. Additionally, T-shirts that advertise popular soda and bread brands probably have nothing to do with dietary preferences and everything to do with starting conversations. "Wonder Bread . . . I haven't eaten that since third grade" might be the greatest conversation starter since sliced bread.

Wealth and success have proven to be almost as valuable as a handsome face in attracting females. In chapter 2, we discussed how women generally go for looks first . . . but what if men suspect (or know) that their looks aren't making the grade? What if they need a Plan B? It's simple: they'll use the same approach that unsightly men of yester-century used to bag women. They'll peacock their wealth and status.

Long ago, a wealth and status symbol was a man's potbelly or his winter store of food. Later, a massive and colorful headdress would do the job for a chief in an American Indian tribe. For today's A-lister making a public appearance, it might be a Mercedes-Benz, a Versace suit, and a watch that blinds his friends when the spotlight sweeps the club.

The Benz, the suit, and the watch are all equivalents of bright, gaudy plumage, intended to lure the highest-quality females. Sure, these implements aren't hereditary (unless he's an heir), but they prove that a man's frontal lobe can go to work to make up for any genetic deficiencies he may have.

The Jack Nicholson/ George Clooney Conundrum

Hunk? Maybe not at first glance.

The richness of Jack Nicholson's love life offers proof that women value status in a masculine prospect. Despite the fact that the good looks of his youth may have faded, the star of such films as *Terms of Endearment, As Good as It Gets,* and *Something's Gotta Give* is still a silver screen lady's man. He exercised his power in *The Witches of Eastwick* when he put his three female costars into lust-crazed dazes, and he does the same thing off-screen. It seems that he's like some kind of old-dude drug that puts women from eighteen (his preference) to seventy in some kind of cross-eyed stupor. There's no question that his intense personality, mysterious aura, and deep voice contribute to his woman-luring skills. There's also something to be said for all the "practice" he got during the days when he was a hot tamale, but the factors that contribute most to his recent success have to be his status and the monetary benefits that come with it.

Women seem to think they want wealth and status (at least on paper), but when given the opportunity to choose, they jump on the best-looking male specimens. However, that's only one side of the looks-versus-status argument. Here's the other: Psychologist David Buss spent five years following the mating preferences of more than ten thousand people in thirty-seven cultures around the world. What he found might be shocking to some—but not Jack Nicholson fans. Regardless of a woman's status, she was most always more likely to choose a man with higher levels of material goods and high-status connections, while paying little or no mind to his physical appearance. In fact, physical appearance seemed to wither into the background once a man's social and financial rankings were revealed. The findings of these studies, though contradictory at first glance, work to prove one common concept: Money and status are plumage, displayed through attained possessions and a prominent air. However, this "plumage" isn't foolproof. It's simply a tactic that is sometimes overridden by genetics and what those genetics can do for a woman's offspring.

Enter George Clooney, the whole ball of wax, who not only has the good looks that point toward his quality genes, but also exhibits all the signs of wealth and status. He possesses extraordinary appeal for women of all ages, which comes as a surprise for some. Many would consider him too old to be cougar food. But as it turns out . . .

Researchers at the University of Abertay Dundee in Scotland were surprised to find that successful women "of a certain age" don't always turn toward fresh, young hunks, but instead choose to gravitate to older, attractive,

George Clooney's age and status work in conjunction with his good looks.

successful men. At first blush, a casual observer of humanity might guess that older, single, affluent women would take the same route that Jack Nicholson does and gather clutches of younger, attractive members of the opposite sex. This theory holds true only in part. Cougars like Demi Moore, Kim Cattrall, Mariah Carey, Susan Sarandon, and Fran Drescher seem to be the exception to the rule.

Psychologists now know that as women age and move up in the world, they will generally demand more attractiveness from a partner while their desire for prosperity and maturity in a man remains constant. That's probably why they're swooning over George and not Jack. Jack gets the young ones, who haven't yet begun to demand it all, while George continues to be flooded with attention from all generations.

Translated, these studies show that men who've got the cash can score with women of any age, but in order to land the mature women, they've gotta look like Clooney.

Many species risk life and limb just to procreate. Salmon swim upriver to spawn, risking violent death and starvation. Antlered animals will often become locked together during a fight and die of hunger. Likewise, human males will go to great lengths to prove that their genes are just right for molding your offspring.

In many ways, man's adornments are products of sexual selection. Long ago, naturally competitive males who boasted significant size (in posture and package) and who displayed the benefits of wealth and rank won more battles (bloody and brainy). They seized more chances to produce young. Thankfully, men are no longer stepping into blood-spattered arenas to fight for fornication rights—they're simply showing us, with outward signs and symbols, that if trends were to revert, they could assume the duty.

Today, evidence of this mind-set, this tendency, and the features that have come along for the ride are obvious in supermarkets, clubs, church socials . . . anywhere that holds the potential for mate acquisition.

He may not have an engorged comb, two hundred feathers

sprouting from his rear, or a wild tan-
gle of mane springing from his head.
He may not have the plumage or the
beard of a spring gobbler who's strutting for the hillside hens, but he is, for
all intents and purposes, a bird with all
the trimmings.

CHAPTER TEN

Your Hot-to-Trot Tip-offs

THE BODY LANGUAGE THAT DIVULGES
YOUR INNER DESIRES

Charles Darwin first alluded to universal expressions and gestures in his book *The Expression of the Emotions in Man and Animals,* published in 1872. In the 1930s, biologist Alfred Kinsey acted as a catalyst for the sexual revolution that would come three decades later, by challenging socially accepted human sexual behavior through scientific studies. Later, in the 1960s, Austrian ethologist Irenäus Eibl-Eibesfeldt isolated a feminine flirting sequence that spanned geographical and cultural terrain. Similarly, but more currently, Paul Ekman and his team of researchers managed to isolate seven universal facial expressions—ones that show no difference across ethnic, cultural, and social realms.

What do all of these findings have in common (besides a brilliant and driven researcher)? They speak of the universality of human expression. Much of what we know is learned, but there are certain behaviors that we just can't shake. They're wired into us, programmed like an operating system into a computer . . . and the way that we flirt is no exception.

David Givens and Timothy Perper also deserve places on that list of illustrious discoverers of universal characteristics. In the 1980s, Givens and Perper spent more time watching singles interact and take each other home from U.S. bars than a bartender working double shifts would. Not only did these researchers see the same courting choreography performed again and again, but their separate notes lined up to a degree that makes the existence of a universal human mating dance irrefutable.

Women have long been cajoling men into making "first moves." I can't speak for cave chicks, but I do know that women of today send nonverbal messages to the men of their desire in order to elicit approaches in about two-thirds of dating encounters. More than a century ago, a man was advised to only call on a lady if she had already expressed interest in him. Address today's single man and he'll probably either complain or crow that men make all the moves, but what he may not realize is that often he's simply responding to the body language of interested females. As we discussed in chapter 6, men do not like to make mistakes. For evolutionary reasons, they dislike showing weakness and crave the feeling of being in control. This mind-set pushes them to throw passes only to female players who they clearly believe are receptive, and lends authority to findings that show that only 50 percent of men will attempt to approach a woman who is showing no signs of interest.

As also covered in chapter 6, men aren't nearly as astute at reading nonverbal signals as women are. This means that your friendly body language could easily be misconstrued as flirtation, unless that body language is so unmistakable that even the most challenged of men could not mistake it. Messages must be clear if you don't want to find yourself ducking and dodging space invasions from every Bomb, Dick, and Scary.

If you're at all concerned about men taking credit for something that women initiate most of the time, don't be. This state of affairs really is advantageous for us.

What's the harm in allowing him to believe that his first words to you are fished strictly from his own courage? There is none, really. You get what you want and he gets his, too. Sure, you could walk up to any man and ask, "Buy me a drink?" but behavior such as this poses significant risk. For one thing, he could openly reject you, potentially smashing your confidence. Instead, you can use body language that will mark you as gorgeous, allowing you to compete with those women who do little, or nothing, to elicit attention. In short, there's not a single reference in the evolutionary or body language handbook that says you have to be a perfect ten; in fact, fluent daters rarely are.

Our beloved couple from chapter 6 is back, but this time, they haven't met yet.

Let's look on as Jan, a woman who is well versed in the nuances of flirtatious body language, uses her own outward signs of attraction to quell Bob's rejection-sensitive brain and prompt him to respond wholeheartedly to her sexy, yet stealthy, moves. Keep in mind that, for teaching purposes, Jan's actions are a bit exaggerated. This is necessary for proper visualization.

Now please allow me to introduce a mating dance that's as old as humanity itself, and just as effective.

SCENE ONE

Jan rings the bell, greets her hostess, and hands over a bottle of champagne she found buried in the back of her cabinet from last New Year's Eve. She enters cautiously, reliving the nervousness she tried to talk away in the car. She's sure she won't know anyone, and is fully prepared to leave after one drink.

A bar has been set up, fondue fountains are overflowing with cheese and chocolate, furniture has been arranged in small clusters, and lighting has been lowered so that glitter, sequins, and eyes sparkle. Singles abound: small groups of men and pairs of women are sprinkled around the room. Roving eyes and hushed conversations lend a whispery quality to the air.

Not only are there plenty of male prospects, but there's also a plethora of female contenders—all gorgeous and dressed from Fifth Avenue.

Jan appraises her choices: she can saunter in and claim the room as her own without hesitation, or she can order a white chocolate raspberry martini, slump into a corner, and call it a caloric forfeit. While contemplating the evening's possible agendas, she approaches the bar. Her eyes meet those of a gorgeous, manly specimen . . . strong jaw, prominent cheekbones, deep-set eyes, wide shoulders, a confident pose to go with it all . . . comically perched on a bright pink ottoman. Her eyebrows shoot upward with interest. Her lips part slightly. She smiles with relaxed lips, revealing only her upper teeth, being careful not to bare or clench them with nervousness.

As she nears the bar, her confidence and her heart rate spike. She contemplates pulling a Kanye—wrestling the mic from the MC and announcing that she's hot under the Spanx for Mr. Magnificent. But instead she opts for a classier and more effective approach.

Jan thrusts her chest forward, allows her arms to fall to her sides, and orders a vodka martini. While she waits, pondering Mr. Magnificent's odd seating choice, she claims a bar stool and crosses her legs.

Erect and Ready: The theme seems to be universal. A straight and long core, shoulders pushed down and back, neck elongated, and chest thrust forward equate to being ready for his approach. Slouching is synonymous with boring contentment and sends the message that you are uninterested.

Open for Business: Just as a storefront seems more inviting when the front doors are wide open, a woman's body seems more inviting when its frontal view is unobstructed. Crossed arms block advances and hinder information absorption.

This woman's upright posture invites an approac'

The Eye Lift: At the risk of sounding like an eye cream commercial, I assure you that a woman can look pleasantly surprised, interested, and intrigued without a scalpel, stitches, or screaming with horror into a handheld mirror. I'm talking about the eyebrow flash, or a quick rising of the brows and widening of the eyes. It often happens involuntarily when people see someone who piques their interest or when they see someone whom they recognize. Its duration, though fleeting at one-fifth of a second, is enough to send a subliminal "omg" message to a man. Anyone can intensify this unspoken, universal hello's effect by allowing it to linger. Eyes will catch a glimmer and say, "You are so fascinating; I can't believe my eyes."

Jaw-Dropping Joy: When humans are flabbergasted, they often experience both the literal and the proverbial jaw drop. By slightly parting the lips, one mimics the effect of a subtle jaw drop, letting a man know that a woman has been taken aback by the sight of him.

Her parted lips suggest a slight jaw drop, a signal of interest.

The Genuine Grin: The human psyche can differentiate real smiles from contrived ones. Though it may be difficult to define a genuine grin with words, our primal instincts are perfectly capable of doing so. A genuine smile not only gives away the good feelings of the smiler, but also elicits good feelings in all who see it.

Facial muscles should be relaxed, the cheeks should rise, and laugh lines should form around the eyes. The mouth should stretch broadly and the grin should fade away slowly. Smiles that don't alter the upper face, that are stiff-lipped, and that disappear quickly look manufactured, and can even indicate deception.

A genuine smile will come naturally and cause a man's frontal cortex to light up like a red-hot neon sign. Anyone will be hard-pressed not to return this form of genuine goodwill.

SCENE TWO

Jan, under the gaze of the handsome man, intertwines her legs and presses her thighs and calves together to accentuate their muscle tone. As if equipped with a laser pointer, her top knee points directly toward the object of her desire. While Jan waits for her drink, she slowly uncrosses and recrosses her legs, satisfying her inner thighs' hunger for touch and sending a clear "touch me" message to the man on pink. She strokes her legs to soothe her nerves' heightened awareness while dangling her pump from her toes and thrusting her foot in and out of the shoe. Every time she crosses and uncrosses her legs, she offers a pinch of bonus skin for his eyes to devour, while releasing sexually arousing pheromones into the air.

The Crossing at "Leg Junction": If legs were roads, a man would want to drive sports cars along their curves, while focusing attention on the point at which the two converge: a pit stop, a junction at which to test the responsiveness of his vehicle. Using legs to show interest works because they're, well . . . already interesting to him.

The Stripper's Shoe: When a woman allows her pump to dangle from the toes of her top (crossed) leg, with her leg and partially stripped foot pointing in a man's direction, she's sending the message that she's waiting for the proverbial shoe to drop—that she'd like to undress more than her feet for him. By adding a slight forward-and-back swing to her leg, she subtly reminds him of another cherished thrusting motion.

Prop note: Only attempt this move with a pump, thong, or sexy slip-on shoe. If you have to untie your gym shoe or pull off your penny loafer before you perch it precariously over your tube sock or torn hose, you'd best leave the shoe in place.

Body Watch: Clothing that is relentlessly risqué leaves nothing to the imagination, so there's little to discover. However, if your blouse "accidentally" reveals a bit of flesh when you bend to get your purse, or your skirt "coincidentally" reveals a touch of thigh when you dismount from a stool, you will incite a quiet riot.

SCENE THREE

Jan tilts her head to the left, away from Mr. Magnificent, to reveal the soft, fleshy lifelines held within her neck. She brings her left hand up to her face, pointing the exposed underside of her wrist in his direction.

A Jugular Invitation: The fearless display of the jugular invites attention from a man because it says, "I know you won't harm me. I trust your approach."

This woman is displaying her jugular, a clear signal that she doesn't fear approach.

Body Watch: Tilting of the head doesn't just display the jugular; it also shows attentive listening and receptivity. If you want to use this body language cue while interacting with a man who's directly in front of you, and whom you find sexually appealing, tilt your head to the left. If you're interacting head-on with a man who holds the power to hire or fire you, tilt your head to the right. Just eight degrees will do, according to the *Journal of Nonverbal Behavior.*

Twist of the Wrist: Just as vulnerable and alluring as the neck are the wrists. When a woman displays the underside of her wrist, she welcomes approach by her target. When an upturned palm is added, the message is enhanced to include "Welcome. I'm unarmed."

This wrist display shows willing vulnerability, approachability, and harmlessness.

SCENE FOUR

Jan's mouth is watering for her drink, but the bartender is still flipping through his pocket guide, looking for a list of ingredients for a vodka martini. If she weren't under the scrutiny of a gorgeous piece of manflesh, she might be annoyed. But this turn of idiotic events is perfect. It gives her a chance to show the rugged man on pink that she's perfectly willing to submit to what she believes is his dominant nature.

Jan speeds up her normal blink rate by adding about ten extra blinks per minute. She nonchalantly twists a lock of hair around the index finger of her right hand. By adding these submissive acts to her displays of vulnerability (neck and wrist), she feels certain that she's churning the brute on pink into a steamy froth.

Twisted Tresses: Some men, particularly the more dominant type, get all whipped up over the sight of a woman twisting her hair around her finger. This is not only a form of self-touch; it's also incredibly childlike, sparking a paternal, or protective, instinct in some men.

Beautiful Batting: Daisy Duck does it. Olive Oyl does it, too. It's eyelash batting, and it will be effective on characters like both Bluto and Donald. All types of men will respond nicely to this look of juvenile vulnerability.

SCENE FIVE

Jan knows that in order to show Mr. Magnificent that she's interested, she must look in his direction and make eye contact that is generous and deliberate. *Here goes nothing,* she thinks as she looks to her right and locks eyes with him. *Ah, he's even more gorgeous than I'd first thought.* She holds his gaze with hers for several seconds, slightly lowering her chin toward her neck and allowing her eyes to scan his face with fluidity, as if they're floating in liquid. She smiles with her eyes, widening them to allow light to reflect from them.

In order to convince him that she's absolutely certain of the seduction that she's instituting, she slows her blink rate to half its normal speed. She looks down, toward her right shoulder, for a moment and then back up to him with a smile. She turns her head back toward the bar while holding his eyes with hers, in a coy sideways glance, for a few more seconds.

After checking her drink's slow progress, she notices that Mr. Magnificent is standing up. He's run into a friend . . . is shaking his hand. But his eyes continue to drift toward her. *Now's my chance.* Jan openly and unabashedly sweeps his body with her eyes, putting on the brakes as they brush over his chest, his torso, the seat of his manhood. Obviously shaken, he runs his hand through his hair, over his eyebrow, and down the side of his face. In imitation, Jan touches her own brow and allows her finger to trail down her cheek. She brings a finger to the corner of her mouth. While still engaged in friendly conversation, he does the same.

Peek-a-boo Peepers: Eye contact is essential to sending messages of interest, but unfortunately, standard messaging rates do not apply to men. Men need as many as four to five seconds of uninterrupted eye locking to get the point . . . and then, it must be solidly reinforced with a pattern of intent.

A sideways or over-the-shoulder glance is a coy way for any woman to gaze seductively without glaring. A woman should never use a stalker stare in place of seductive eye contact. Lowered brows and an intense, piercing glare are just plain scary—even when emitting from an otherwise demure-looking woman.

Her eye contact and innocent smile say, "Approach me."

Vanessa Hudgens's over-the-shoulder eye contact and harmless smile during the premiere of *Beastly* are anything but beastlike.

The Full-Body Scan: Men do it all the time: they check women out from head to toe without a stitch of awkwardness. As discussed in chapter 6, men are not only visual beings, but their lines of vision require that they move their heads to fully grasp the impact of the feminine form. Since women's vision is more encompassing, reaching farther both peripherally and north to south, we rarely need to make a full scan to take in the landscape.

However, since men can relate to the importance of the full-body scan, seeing a woman perform one sends an interest message that's unquestionable.

Motivation via Imitation: A brain scan would show neurons firing when a person performs any type of activity, but—and here's the kicker—it would also show them lighting up in another person, watching the activity being performed. This explains why yawns and smiles are contagious. Our brains crave imitation.

SCENE SIX

Jan knows she's grabbed Mr. Magnificent's attention, but now she's got to coax his courage. While he looks on, she buries her hands in her shoulder-length hair, fluffs it up, pulls it back, and lets it fall over her shoulders.

Her ears tingle. A touch from her own fingers helps to satisfy the nerve endings that are screaming out for Mr. Magnificent. Her hand trails down her neck, unhurriedly. Both hands fall to her thighs and travel lazily around her knees and back toward her torso.

Her martini arrives. She plucks one of the two olives from the pick, sucks deliberately on its saltiness, and inserts her fingers into her lips to deliver it to her tongue. Ensuring that none of the deliciousness is wasted, she sucks on her thumb, then her forefinger, with slow seductiveness. A lick of the lips is completed just before she raises the glass to her mouth.

The first sip is followed by another lick of the lips, accompanied by the stroking of the stem of the glass with her left hand and the tracing of the rim with her right—all part of a sight that Mr. Magnificent can't seem to ignore.

Hair in Motion: A well-timed hair preening, in the form of a fluff, pullback, or finger comb-through, will create a flash of movement to attract a man's attention, will distribute the woman's personal scent into the immediate area, and will speak of her inner desire to have his hands locked up in her locks. It also pulls her hair away from her face so that he can take in her profile and the vulnerability of her neck.

Touch Yourself: If you haven't listened to the Divinyls' song "I Touch Myself," I would suggest doing so. A swooning female voice sings, "When I think about you, I touch myself." This is the principle that drives the Touch Yourself tactic. When the object of a woman's desire looks in her direction, the stroking of her neck, ears, lips, face, or thighs will not only be enticing for him to watch, but will send a clear message that she's fantasizing about his fingers taking the place of hers.

By stroking her neck, she's stimulating herself and inviting him to do the same.

Touch On Oral Inspiration: Oral, or "of the mouth," elicits all types of visions for a man, and it's easy for a woman to intensify these imaginings by holding her eyeglasses in her teeth, by licking chocolate from her fingers, or by eating slowly and deliberately. Don't forget that facial lips, in a man's eye, closely mimic the texture, color, and feel of another tropical set. A woman can create an entire collection of naughty images in his mind by applying lip gloss with her finger while he looks on.

Lick His Hesitation: If she wants to incite a man to strike up conversation, a woman will often allow a man to witness her licking her lips. When done purposefully and with sensuality, rather than with quick, nervous flicks of the tongue, the lips' resemblance to other girly bits becomes excitingly obvious to male onlookers. A man's dillydallying from the other side of the room might quickly be upgraded to a swagger with purpose . . . in her direction.

Phallic Glassware: No, it's not a new fashion trend for guys. But it is an effective trend for attracting the attention of the man whom a woman's gone glassy over. If drinking from a bottle, a woman can stroke its neck seductively and fondle the mouth of it. If wine is her drink of choice, running her finger around the top of the glass and polishing the stem with her fingers will create a seductive scene, right there in front of him. He'll hardly be able to ignore her dexterity.

By fondling the stem of her glass, she's demonstrating an interest in doing the same to him.

SCENE SEVEN

Jan heads for the restroom, but doesn't take the direct route. Instead she meanders by a tropical plant and coils left around the punch bowl, all to put her form and her intentions in full view of Mr. Magnificent.

After checking her face in the bathroom mirror, she reenters the party and moves toward a painting she intends to admire—one that happens to be mounted on the wall to Mr. Magnificent's left.

The Detour: Whether headed to the chip bowl, the punch bowl, or the toilet bowl, a woman who takes a detour and walks past the object of her interest is literally going out of her way to place herself in proximity to the one she can't resist.

On the Fringe: As a nonverbal invitation proceeds, a woman may find herself transported, seemingly apart from her own power, toward Mr. Magnificent. As the gap closes between the two of them, she should orient herself at his side, rather than head-on. To a man's brain, frontal approach spells c-o-n-f-l-i-c-t, which is not the intention of most hot-to-trot women.

SCENE EIGHT

As Jan admires a contemporary painting that could either be a wolf devouring a child or a tacky necktie, she rests the majority of her weight on her left foot, causing her to lean in the direction of Mr. Magnificent. He breaks from his conversation to whisper, "Can you tell what it is?"

Jan turns wide, toward him, bumps into his shoulder, begs his pardon, and replies, "Is it mounted upside down?"

"I don't know, but my eight-year-old niece could give that artist a run for his money."

Jan places her hand over her heart and exhales abruptly. "Oh, how sweet. Your niece paints?" She turns her body so that her feet are pointing toward him.

"She does. In fact, I'm her art teacher."

Jan nods her head slowly and responds, "No kidding."

The two introduce themselves. They shake hands. They face each other and engage in eye contact. Jan scans his face, occasionally stopping to look at his mouth, while he lists his favorite French Impressionists.

The Lean-to: At any distance, a woman can lean toward the object of her desire and silently speak a wealth about her intentions. As women and humans, we naturally lean toward where we want to be and away from that which we'd like to escape. When a woman leans in the direction of her target, she runs a good chance of becoming his bull's-eye.

The Deliberate Accident: "Unintentionally" brushing against a man on the dance floor, "accidentally" dipping into the same fondue stream, or "mistakenly" picking up a man's cell phone instead of her own can turn a woman's "I'm sorry" into his "Would you like to dance?" Additionally, if a woman brushes against a man's hand while passing a napkin or plucking a snack from the pretzel bowl, she can conduct electricity that is difficult for him to ignore.

Purposeful Pigs: There's a reason that the children's rhyme says, "This little piggie went to market," and not, "This big callused heel went to the pedicurist." Our toes lead our bodies in our bipedal navigation. Our minds know this, and other minds know this about us. That's why a woman should always point her toes in the direction of the man who's captured her interest. This tells him not only that she's actively thinking of him, but also that she's poised to move closer to him at a moment's notice.

Body Watch: Neurons related to the feet take up so much room on the brain's circuit board that it's easy to see why they're so expressive of inner intentions. The feet contain more neural connections than the arms, shoulders, legs, or back, and those connections rest adjacent to the neural field for genitalia stimulation. This helps to explain the powerfully sexual foot fetish held by some individuals. British zoologist Desmond Morris calls the feet "the most honest parts of the whole human body," citing their uncanny abilities to leak inner moods and intentions to onlookers.

Space Invasion: Anytime a woman interjects herself or one of her possessions into a man's personal space she communicates a desire to take more of that space. She can move her foot, a cell phone, an elbow, or a glass into his eighteen inches of personal space and thereby say, "I want to be close," without uttering a word.

Nod Your Approval: Women perceive nods as signals of understanding, but men perceive them as agreement. Men, thanks to their evolutionary roles, value approval because it indicates that they're doing a commendable job. If a woman wants to commend a man's "piece of work," she'll do well to nod in his direction, even if she's being held by another conversation.

Heart Touching: When we're moved by a poignant story, or when we're expressing our love for someone or something, we often find ourselves bringing our hands up to our chests, over our hearts. When a woman accompanies this gesture with a small gasp or a gulp of air, she's showing a man that her heart has been touched—to make it any clearer she'd have to rip it from her chest and show him how it bleeds.

Watch His Mouth: A woman can't control what a man says, but she can control how he feels while he's saying it. As he's speaking, her eyes should travel around his face, coming to rest frequently on his mouth. This is a universal precursor to kissing and will inevitably cause him to flush with heated desire.

Blushing Brides vs. Romping Rides

Women blush as many as five to six times more often than men do. At the risk of sounding redundant, this feature has evolved for reproductive purposes and should not be dismissed or hidden.

Blushing was a clear indicator to the men of yesteryear that a woman was shy about performing sexual acts, and this behavior pegged her as inexperienced in the bedrock. And, if he was lucky, she was also a virgin. This method for choosing inexperienced, unsoiled, never-pregnant women had worked for millennia, until Madonna crashed onto the pop scene with her hit "Like a Virgin."

Authentic blushing by a sexually timid woman begins as a reddened point in the center of the cheek and spreads out to all points of the cheeks and even down the neck.

Often body language signals are sent on a subconscious level. But social taboos, nervousness, or a lack of self-confidence can interfere with their displays. For this reason, a good body language vocabulary is essential in the realm of dating, in case outside influences threaten to interfere with your natural performance. In the case of flirting, practice really does make perfect. You could say that the natural choreography is there, but without a few performances under your belt, every night is like opening night.

Men need to see and comprehend at least twelve sexual signs of interest to get your point. Sure, you could make a list of all the signals, but you'd spend more time reading the smudged notes on the palm of your hand than in actual presentation. To make their implementation simpler and more natural for you, I'll group signals into clusters.

Rehearse these clusters before heading out so you'll be armed and ready to induce that "first move":

Slight head tilt, sideways gaze, smile, hair preen, wrist display, pheromone release from underarms.

Hunched shoulders, jugular display, hands pointing to genitals, thumb display and point, sideways gaze, playful smile.

Thumb display, self-touch, spread legs (useful if target is behind you).

Glass fondle, eye contact, jugular display, open posture, smile revealing upper teeth.

Wrist display, smile, hand in hair, upper body point.

Space invasion with foot, top leg point toward him, leg touch, head tilt, upright posture, smile.

Lean-in, jugular display, head tilt, touch, elevated foot, lower foot point.

Hand in hair, pheromones from underarm, top leg point in direction of gaze, head tilt, jugular display, wrist display.

Jugular display, leg cross in his direction, smile, head tilt.

Self-touch, wrist display, lip part, jugular display, head tilt, upward gaze.

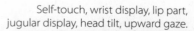

Wrist display, smile from mouth and eyes, self-touch, finger in mouth.

Coy gaze, eyebrow raise, seductive eating.

Forward lean, straw fondle, mouthing of
straw, sideways gaze, lip part, head tilt.

Which girl is displaying the largest number of interest signals? The least? *Take a good look at the photo before continuing.* The girl at the far end is sending out the most signals of interest. She has her upper torso angled toward him; she is smiling with her head tilted and running her hands through her hair to demonstrate her desire to look good for him. Her hand position is offering a wrist display and drawing attention to herself. The woman in the foreground appears to be smiling, but notice how she is using her arm as a barrier between herself and the man. She clearly feels that he is too close for comfort and is blocking any potential approach. In addition, notice how she keeps her body straight and rigid and allows only her head to turn toward him, keeping her body angled away.

Body Watch: Flirting doesn't always have to happen in a full frontal manner. Sometimes full rear is good, too. If a hottie is behind you, place four fingers into a back pocket with your wrist turned out. This will tighten your britches to show more of your shape, persuade him to want to touch your rear end, and make a blatant, but vulnerable, wrist display. The protruding thumb is also a solid sign for being in control.

In the Mating Dance, American Women Have Two Left Feet

A recent Internet poll has pegged U.S. women as one of the least likely groups to initiate sexual encounters through flirting. Apparently, women in Spain and Poland enjoy an intimate relationship with their instinctive mating dances, while women in the United States and Ecuador are challenged in the flirting department. Come on, ladies. We've made history by burning bras, we've gotten diaper-changing stations installed in men's rooms, and we've taken public office. You can't seriously expect me to settle for next-to-last place in something as organic as flirting.

We've got something to prove. I need you to get out there and dance. The steps are in you. If you can't find them, lessons are on these pages.

No more excuses.

It's time to get jiggy wit' it.

If you can't remember the last time you've been hit on, there's a reason, and I'd venture to say that you haven't been letting men know that it's safe to do so.

Shyness, as difficult as it can be to overcome, is a poor excuse for slumping into the wallpaper. It can also be misconstrued as aloofness or arrogance, pushing others away.

Even the most timid of singles can start small—with a simple smile, a vulnerable glance in his direction, or an innocent foot point. You won't feel like you're on display, and once you learn how easy elementary moves can be, your confidence will skyrocket.

Incorporate body language cues of interest into your everyday comings and goings. Practice them at the gas pump, the bus stop, a sporting event . . . anywhere that you can find an audience. Once you're comfortable with the basics—smiling, head tilting, holding extended eye contact, easy conversation—your confidence will skyrocket and you'll be ready for big-league flirting. Soon your interest displays will become as natural as breathing; so will their first moves.

Remember, there is a very fine line between friendliness and flirtatiousness. Because of this, you may pick up practice subjects whom you're not genuinely interested in. In this case, count yourself as one friend, or one boost of confidence, richer. You might just make some man's day.

Jan took her evening into her own hands. In the time it took to get a drink, visit the restroom, and admire an atrocious piece of art, she had moved from potential corner slumper to French Impressionist converser . . . and within days of that, to making a "French" impression of her own.

You can be just like Jan; in fact, we all can be.

Move over, Ms. Fifth Avenue. There's a new girl on the party scene. She's learning to speak the oldest new language on earth: the body language of successful dating.

CHAPTER ELEVEN

Is He into You or over You?

SLAYING REJECTION WITH FACIAL EXPRESSION AND BODY LANGUAGE FLUENCY

The evidence is stunning: not only are we programmed to perform facial expressions and body language cues that attract the opposite sex, but those articulations seem to have come prepackaged for us, with unspoken, instinctual instructions for effective use—courtesy of human evolution. How else would a woodsman in the jungles of the Amazon who has never seen a can opener, a stick of deodorant, or a pair of underwear know that placing his hands behind his head and puffing out his chest are cunning methods for seducing his first love? How else would an Eskimo girl, secluded without access to television or magazines, know that gazing into the eyes of her favorite young man would win him over? The answer is simple, yet stunningly complex: we've come with standard flirting features. Our actions, our emotions, our movements . . . are universally similar.

You've looked on as Jan used the oldest language known to humans to communicate her receptivity to Bob, aka Mr. Magnificent. But chapter 10's story was really only half the tale. You see, Jan wasn't throwing signals out, willy-nilly, with a spray-and-pray methodology. Instead she was taking a calculated and focused risk: calculated because she deciphered Bob's body language to effectively eliminate her chances of being rejected; focused because she directed her signs of interest toward one, receptive man.

If you're like many women, you've been there: you mark a man as a romantic possibility simply because the sight of him curls your toes. You approach. Suddenly you find yourself flattened by the rejection steamroller; you're shamed, mortified, and disabled from making any further hookup efforts for the rest of the evening . . . or the month.

If you can relate, what you've been missing is the body language reading fluency necessary for salvaging your pride.

In the preceding chapter, you learned how to subtly tell the hot possibility across the room that your Spanx are boiling over for him, but before you put that performance in motion, I suggest that you first determine if your target is interested enough to play along.

Either he's into you or he's not, and the more quickly you can decode his thoughts about you, the more productive your dating efforts will be. You might wonder about the secrets of girls who never leave parties, clubs, and blood drives alone, and until now, may have believed that they were either irresistibly sexy to men or that they beat their targets' resolve into submission. Not so fast.

Understand that no lone woman is capable of capturing the interest of every man. Women who enjoy success in the dating arena know how to quickly assess situations and move toward dating probabilities. They know that sending interested body language cues to the entire room would be a waste of time and resources, so they begin the process of qualification the moment they, and potential male targets, walk through the party door.

Just like Jan, you can enjoy romantic encounters of the successful kind. In a few moments, we'll travel back to that cocktail party to take a closer look at Bob's behavior. But first, I'd like to introduce . . . *drumroll* . . . the seven universal facial expressions as defined by psychologist Paul Ekman. These facial expressions are products of a synchrony that occurs among forty-three facial muscles, but they are not products of upbringing, of culture, or even of gender.

Ekman found that no matter the civilization or sophistication of an individual, these emotional responses will be displayed on most every human face, including those of trolling single men.

Sadness: Raised inner eyelids and eyebrows, drooping outer eyelids, raised lower lids, wrinkled forehead, downwardly drawn mouth.

Sadness is obviously a negative emotion, but his pessimism may have nothing to do with you. A sweet smile might brighten his day (and your prospects).

Sadness at losing to the Kansas Jayhawks is written all over the face of Illinois's Mike Tisdale.

Surprise: Elevated eyebrows, widened eyes, wrinkled forehead, parted lips.

This emotion is neutral, in that a man could be surprised at your unmitigated gorgeousness, or he could be surprised that the bouncer allowed you through the door. A bit more analysis will be necessary.

Soccer player Russell Penn expresses surprise.

Fear: Elevated eyebrows drawn toward center, raised upper eyelids, rigid lower eyelids, tense lips that may be parted, mouth drawn down.

If a man is displaying fear on his face, chances are that he's been freaked out by someone or something other than you. However, it can't hurt to tone down the leather, remove a few piercings, cover up a few of your tattoos, or soften your voice. You might get a better reading.

This rodeo rider's face tells us that
he fears what may come next.

Anger: Lowered brow, tense lower eyelids, depressed upper lids, piercing stare, flaring nostrils, tense lips, possible jutting lower lip.

If you see this expression—run the other way. You don't need the hassle.

Duke's Mike Krzyzewski makes his anger evident as he argues with an official during a matchup with Georgia Tech.

Disgust: Unwrinkled forehead, lowered brow, wrinkled nose bridge, tense lower eyelids, clenched lips or slight rise on one side of upper lip.

This one is a cruel but clear vote of "hell nay!" If you inspire a visceral reaction of disgust, you'll never get past first base. You won't typically see disgust in the meet-and-greet stage. You're more likely to see lack of interest, or neutrality, as it takes a lot to bring a person to the point of disgust.

Former vice president Dick Cheney's disgust is written all over his face while he speaks at a conservative conference in Washington, D.C.

Contempt: Wrinkled nose, pursed lips, one raised eyebrow, mouth raised at the corners, protruding lips, sneering upper lip raised on one side.

If you're getting this look, you've done something to offend his sensibilities. Depending on the seriousness of the offense, you should either retreat or attempt to demonstrate harmlessness with a show of vulnerability.

The curled lip is a giveaway for contempt.

Happiness: Relaxed forehead, lowered outer eyebrows, narrow eyes, appearance of laugh lines, heightened cheeks, lines appear outward from nose, corners of mouth upturned to show teeth. Caveat: The upturning of the mouth in a smile without the other elements of a happy facial expression should be tagged as suspicious. Only a genuine smile conveys genuine happiness. However, if he's smiling at all (even an artificial smile), it's a good sign that he's interested enough to make an effort.

This is the most receptive of all the facial expressions. If you detect a look of happiness, move on to a more in-depth reading of interest.

At the Santa Barbara Film Festival, a happy James Franco will soon receive the Individual Performance Award.

Context is an indispensable consideration in the reading of facial expressions. For instance, there may be a man across the room who's engaged in a conversation. The expression that sweeps over his face may seem, in a silent-movie-type context, to be genuine fear. But if you were able to change yourself into the proverbial fly on the wall and listen in, you might learn that the exchange between him and his friend is about dating horror stories, and his seeming expression of "I'm urgently terrified for my life" might actually be more like "I'm hoping I never end up on a blind date with a transvestite like you did." Often facial expressions are enacted to seem genuine, but with comic or sarcastic underpinnings, or are products of empathy (a good quality) for the person your target is currently interacting with. Facial expressions are, indeed, manifest as visceral results of emotions, but their other, often overlooked, purposes involve communication. The muscles of the face react to both the unconscious (like those facial expressions you make involuntarily, when you're all alone, as well as the ones you make when you're falling into natural rapport with someone) and the conscious (the ones you make to show others that you're listening, you're mutually disgusted, or you're elated for them).

Some expressions are simpler to read than others. You can easily divide the seven universal facial expressions into happy and unhappy/neutral (one and six, respectively). However, individually identifying the negative and neutral ones can be more difficult than the *Aha!* that accompanies the viewing of the smile. Additionally, the more neutral expressions can lean either way. (For example, do his wide-open mouth and bulging eyes indicate delighted surprise at his finding of a rare breed of poisonous snake, or terrified surprise at the fact it's coiling to strike?)

In general, happiness, surprise, and fear are the easiest to identify because they hold the most contrast to a neutral expression. Disgust, contempt, and sadness, however, are more difficult to discern because they more closely resemble a nonemotive face. Enter, once again, that all-important context. If a man is displaying a neutral face during a lecture, he might either be bored or paying close attention to the speaker. If his face is unresponsive during a rock concert, he's probably either a strict classical music fan or has a splitting headache. If a man is wearing an expression of disgust while chanting and wielding a sign in a picket line, he's probably exactly where he wants to be—speaking out against those whose actions antagonize him. However, if that same expression is worn in the theater, his dramatic sensibilities are likely being wounded.

Combination faces are created when two of the seven universal facial expressions intermingle. Your challenge comes in determining which of the two emotions is the most authentic or significant. That prevailing emotion can then be used to help clarify his interest, or lack thereof, in you.

If a man is experiencing mixed emotions or is being deceptive, facial expressions will blend, sending ambiguous messages. In cases such as this, it's up to you to determine his actual intentions. For instance, if his mouth is smiling but his brows are pressed inward and his nostrils are flaring, he's either attempting to hide his anger or he's excited by his anger (the former points toward self-control while the latter should point you as far away from him as possible). Another example of a blended facial expression is a mouth that seems to fight turning up at the corners while the eyes and brows convey sadness. This man might be feigning sympathy with his eyes, while allowing his delight at your misery to leak from the lower portion of his face.

Interpretation of blended facial expression always rests on— you guessed it—context. Watch for contradictory expressions and emotional masking, then scrutinize what his intentions might be. Generally speaking, the emotion that is most detrimental to the situation you're in is the one you should concentrate on. If he's talking "first date" but part of his face is saying "no date," go with the latter. If it's worth his effort to mask, it's worth your effort to uncover.

Some men's facial expressions will be undeniable. Others will require deeper investigation. That's why it's important to not only take a snapshot of the expression, but to make your observation the moving-picture variety. Look and listen. Make it your goal to see the dating forest for the facial trees.

Facial rejuvenation may be attempted if your target is wearing an expression of sadness. Often, a man's melancholy mood is temporary, meaning that all hookup hope is not lost—at least not for a woman with fluent and persuasive body language.

You can attempt to lift his curtain with a beguiling jugular display, a sweet smile, or a glance up, down, and back up. If his countenance changes from grouch to grin, you've not only offered a welcome pick-me-up, but you're telling him you'd like to be picked up.

His facial expression may not jump from sadness directly to happiness, particularly if he's shy or if his negative emotion is profound. Instead it might gradually slip into the positive. Maybe his brows or the corners of his mouth will rise at first, causing a blended facial expression to be displayed. Any movement toward happiness should encourage you.

If his face remains sulky or converts to fear, anger, disgust, or simple annoyance after your stab at rejuvenation, abandon all makeover attempts. Abort mission. I repeat: Abort mission.

"I See," Said the Blind Woman . . . Watching the Happy Man Frown.

If you're at all worried about your competence for reading facial expressions, relax. Much of the skill involved is learned by more than your visual cortex, or the seeing part of your brain.

To prove this point, one only needs look toward blindsight patients. Though their ability to "see" in their brains no longer exists, their eyes still function and gather information in other ways. A blindsight patient can still unconsciously read facial expressions, even though he or she can't see them.

One blindsight patient, T.N., rendered cortically blind by multiple strokes, is able to navigate through an obstacle course and identify facial expressions, even though he cannot identify gender or individual identities. Researchers believe this unconscious ability is a result of humans' early evolutionary needs for emotional decoding, for survival purposes.

This means that you can rely, at least partially, on your own visceral reaction created by the expression that's smeared across Mr. Magnificent's face.

Take it easy. Sit back and enjoy the view. It seems that your vision of him, as splendid as it is, is just a fringe benefit in the field of facial expression reading.

Facial expression fluency will give you the data you need to determine your next move: to retreat or to stick around and give him a little more time to gather his nerves into a brave bundle.

Jan's first step involved decoding Bob's emotional state. (Would he be accepting of her signals?) This will also be your first step. If you decide that your target's emotional state is either receptive or neutral, you can move on to establish his level of interest in you.

In order to demonstrate the subsequent steps, let's take a behind-the-scenes look at Jan's Oscar-worthy chapter 10 performance. We'll go inside Jan's eyes, to see what was happening on that hot pink ottoman to encourage her to forge ahead with her half of the mating dance.

SCENE ONE

When Jan first laid eyes on Mr. Magnificent, she noticed his optimistic expression in the form of a diminutive smile. That subconscious cue was her green light to embark upon her performance of interest. As she moved toward the bar, Bob's eyes met hers. His brows darted upward, his eyes opened wide, and his lips parted slightly. Bob's gaze then fell downward, toward the glass of beer he balanced on his knee.

As Jan performed her chest thrust with erect posture, Bob looked at her again, this time allowing his eyes to travel over the topographical map that was her, stopping to vacation at his favorite spots.

The Jumpin' Jack Eyebrow Flash: When a man is fascinated with a woman, his eyebrows will activate with up-and-down motion—they'll jump, even if only for a split second.

This man's animated face and raised eyebrows denote interest in her.

Shock and Awe: This expression can range from a slight parting of the lips to a look of absolute surprise. Parted lips show disarmament and a man's willingness to accept new information. Often accompanied by flash-bulb (large, astonished) eyes, this expression might eventually give way to a quizzical, curious one, which a woman can count as a plus (he wants to learn more).

This man's brows are raised, his eyes widened, and his jaw suspended— he's in awe of something.

Southerly Eye Flow: Looking down after initial eye contact is a good sign that a man is interested in pursuing a woman. When his eyes lower, he's collecting thoughts and grappling with emotions in preparation for his next move. Evolutionarily speaking, this behavior stems from the brain's automatic protection of the eyes and trans-

If a man looks downward after eye contact, he might be interested in you.

lates most precisely to submissiveness. The woman should wait for it . . . he's going to look at her again.

The Reshoot: If a man's first look wasn't enough, he'll take a shameless double take, as if to indicate that he's doubly interested.

The Full-Body Scan: Assuming that a man isn't employed in airport security, the blatant ogling of a woman's every curve is a sure sign that he'd like to fly with her.

Men are often blatant when taking in the sight of a woman whom they find attractive.

SCENE TWO

Bob couldn't help but stare as Jan presented her perfectly executed leg-crossing performance. The Fifth Avenue women gathered to admire a piece of art on the wall next to Bob, but he seemed oblivious. His gaze toward Jan remained unfaltering.

The Steadfast Stare: When a man's head doesn't whip around at the passing of fine female specimens and he avoids looking toward the door every time it opens, the woman he's looking at can presume that she's captured his undivided attention and interest. Maintaining eye contact is difficult when humans, especially men, are uninterested.

SCENE THREE

Bob knew he shouldn't stare, but the way Jan bared her neck and exposed the feminine, fleshy underside of her wrists made it difficult for him to maintain any appearance of politeness.

Jan's acute peripheral vision didn't miss his ogling, or the seductive way Bob treated his beer glass.

Handling with Care: During the early stages of the mating dance, a woman is fragile. By noting how a man treats his beer can, bottle, or glass, a woman can presume with high accuracy how he'd like to treat her. This display not only divulges his desire to touch, but divulges the way he'd like to do it.

SCENE FOUR

Something primal engaged in Bob's brain when Jan took on the look of a young girl—twisting a lock of hair around her finger and batting her eyelashes. During the next moment, when Jan finally looked in Bob's direction again, she noticed his flaring nostrils.

A Metabolic Flare-up: When a man's hypothalamus (the brain's sexual center) is stimulated, a series of electric and chemical reactions trigger an elevated pulse, a more rapid heart rate, quicker breathing . . . in short, a heightened metabolic rate. Because taking a man's pulse isn't something most women are prepared to do, they can instead look to the nose. If a man's nostrils are flaring, his body is calling for more oxygen to fuel the metabolic storm his eye's apple has created.

SCENE FIVE

When Jan delivered that generous eye contact to Bob, he could barely help but smile. His low seat on the pink ottoman made it easy to look up at her on her high bar stool perch.

As he placed his drink on a table, stood up, and walked with swagger to strike up a conversation with his old college buddy, he hooked his thumbs into his front pockets, allowing his other eight fingers to point toward his crown jewels. He kept his arms out to the sides, leaving his chest unobstructed and inflated. With his abdomen pulled in tight, he stood tall.

Bob alternated sideways glances in Jan's direction with wardrobe fix-ups: he brushed lint from his pants leg; bent to pull up a sock. While laughing with his friend, Bob ran fingers through both sides of his hair. He subconsciously copied Jan's behavior and watched her copying his. When his friend made him laugh, he threw his arms into the air with a flourish, temporarily backing up to remove himself from the crowd that had gathered to join in the conversation. Despite the fact that his torso was pointed toward his friend, Bob's feet pointed in the direction of the bar . . . and Jan.

The Coy Boy Grin: If a man shoots a woman a closed-mouth smile and tilts his head so he seems to be looking up toward her, he's demonstrating innocence, modesty, and harmlessness—in other words, interest. This grin can be simple for him to execute if he's shorter than she is or if he has remained seated while flirting. However, this effect can also be accomplished with a simple depression of his chin toward his neck.

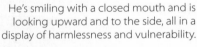

He's smiling with a closed mouth and is looking upward and to the side, all in a display of harmlessness and vulnerability.

The Swagger: We touched on the swagger in chapter 2 and nothing has changed. Men know that if they slow their gait and exaggerate and smooth their shoulder movements, they'll grasp a woman's attention more quickly. If a man swaggers past her while making eye contact and smiling to any degree, he's interested.

The Package Point: Will his package point? I don't know, and frankly, I'd like to leave that between him and the woman he's interested in. What I am certain of is this: if a man wants to let a woman know that his jewels are valuable and worth sharing, he'll put his hands in his pockets or hook his thumbs into his belt and point to his genitals.

His thumbs are pointing to what he'd like you to notice and his body is open— both signs of interest.

Open for Business: If a man's chest and torso are unobstructed by his arms, he's feeling open, both physically and mentally, to the woman he's looking at or interacting with. This usually means that his arms aren't crossed. They might be hanging relaxed at his sides. They might also be perched on his hips to make him appear larger and more attractive/intimidating.

This man's torso and chest are open and inviting. His arms are held out to widen the look of his chest.

Buff Behavior: When a man sucks in his stomach, puffs out his chest, stands as tall as his stature will allow, and flexes his muscles, he's doing his utmost to appear as robust and buff as possible. This is his attempt to seem fit for doing business with the woman he considers to be a hot item.

> GENDER ENLIGHTENMENT: Chest inflation, stomach tucking, shoulder squaring, and swaggering indicate sexual interest in a flirting context. However, if a man is displaying this behavior in a room full of men or in a professional setting, it could be accurately assumed that he is demonstrating alpha dominance.

Preening to Perfection: If a man is pulling up his socks, straightening his tie, tucking in his shirt, brushing lint from his shoulder, pulling his sport coat into alignment . . . he could be attempting to look good for a woman. Couple these physical fix-ups with other interest cues and a woman can confidently assume that he likes her.

The Comb-Through: Whether a man is checking the altitude of his spikes, shaking out his curls, giving his locks a look in the back of a spoon, doing the Fonzie, or running a pocket comb through his mullet, he's preening his coat for the woman who's been interacting with him—either from afar or up close. Even if the man's hairstyle is the worst of news, the good news is that he's into her.

The Magic Mirror: If he's mirroring, or imitating, a woman's actions, he's feeling as close to her as a crowded room will allow. Following a person's cues creates a commonality between two people and indicates intense interest. If a woman wants to see if a man will copy her, she should allow him five to thirty seconds to act like a copycat.

Human See, Human Do

"Monkey see, monkey do" is no longer the measure by which imitation is appraised. It seems that it may soon be replaced by "Human see, human do." Thanks to a new study at the University of California, Los Angeles, it has been proven that mirror neurons, our brain's mechanisms for subconscious imitation of others, do exist.

For years, scientists suspected that mirror neurons were viable entities, and used that "existence" as an explanation for empathy and for our tendencies to copy others whom we feel close to. More recently, researchers at UCLA have found that neurons in areas of the brain responsible for movement, vision, and memory lit up when a person performed an action, but in tantalizing similarity, they also lit up when a person watched that action being performed. Interestingly, they found that mirror cells were more active during actual activity and less active during watching. This could be the brain's method for separating empathy from action—a sort of brake that keeps us from random imitation . . . unless that system is overridden by intense attraction.

This study breaks some pretty tough ground and goes miles in proving that when Hot Stuff sips from his drink, scratches his head, or shakes his tail feathers in brilliant imitation of you, any resolve he has is breaking down like the ozone layer.

Maybe now when someone asks, "If he jumps off a cliff will you do it, too?" you can say, "Only if my mirror neurons tell me to."

The Stick Out: Being swallowed by the crowd is no way to get noticed, and a man who wants a woman's attention knows this.

He might step away from his group to catch her eye so he can more effectively demonstrate the heat that's building for her.

The Bust-a-Move: Often an interested man will make a quick, boisterous, or out-of-context movement in order to attract a woman's attention. He might talk with animated hand movements, laugh loudly, break into a game of shuffleboard, or hit the dance floor without shame. Even if he's not Fred Astaire, his attempt at cutting the rug to shreds marks him as an interested prospect.

The Pointer Brothers: A man will point his feet in the direction that he'd walk if unrestrained. Therefore, if his feet are pointed toward one particular woman, she's his destination of choice.

SCENE SIX

Jan's hair tossing, self-touching, and olive eating obviously inspired Bob's sense of sexuality. After his conversation with his buddy ended he resituated himself on the ottoman, but this time sat with his legs spread widely and his rear end taking up only half of the stool, as if readying to get up and head in the direction of the bar. His beer was back in his right hand, held low. He used the fingers of his left hand to stroke his left earlobe—all the while, his attention firmly fixated on Jan. When another party-goer stopped to have a few words with Bob, he turned toward the lady, centered himself on the ottoman, and placed one ankle on a knee so that his propped foot pointed toward Jan. His legs remained spread.

The Crotch Display: If he drops his pants, he's interested (he might also be arrested), but this one isn't quite that obvious. If a man is sitting or standing with his legs spread, he not only feels safe in a woman's presence, but is also showing off what he considers to be noteworthy assets. This is also a show of dominance. If his legs are crossed at the onset of a verbal or nonverbal exchange with her, but he then uncrosses them, he's opening up with building interest.

The Edge of His Seat: This body language cue relies heavily on context. If a man is occupying the edge of his seat while leaning toward a woman—even graciously invading her personal space with his hands or feet while maintaining eye contact—she might as well be his favorite James Bond flick. However, if he's on the edge of a seat with his hands on his thighs, and not directly facing her, she can reliably assume that he's preparing to get up and make tracks.

Wishful Touching: Women do it, and so do men. If a man is becoming aroused by the sight of a woman, his ears, lips, cheeks, and neck will scream to be touched. Since it's too soon for her to touch him, he'll touch and tug on himself in those engorged, highly sensitized areas. He might even drink, eat, or smoke more in an attempt to satiate this desire. If he can't keep his hands off himself, his greatest wish is for her to feel the same lack of restraint.

A Perfect Four: He might be a perfect ten in a woman's estimation, but if he's sitting in a figure-four position (one foot on the floor, opposite ankle resting on his knee) with the toes of his top (crossed) foot pointing toward her, he might be giving her a pretty generous score, too. This position also displays his crotch, which can be a blatant invitation to play. Though unreliable as a solitary cue, this position can work with others to signify interest, particularly if he places his legs in a figure four after becoming aware of a woman's presence.

GENDER ENLIGHTENMENT: If a man takes on a figure-four position in a professional setting, his intentions may be more about domination than attraction. Location, context, and supporting cues are crucial in reading this one.

The first man's perfect four is about domination.
The second man's is about flirtation.

SCENE SEVEN

Though Jan couldn't see Bob or read any of his signals while she was moving toward the bathroom (taking the extended route), she knew that he was watching her. She knew that he would recognize her efforts to be noticed because men often use the same tactics to put themselves on women's radar.

The Drive-by: Like women, men will often veer off the most direct path just to walk past an interesting woman.

Gravitational Pull: Just as women seem powerless against the pull of an attractive man, men also gravitate toward the objects of their desire. This can be a conscious or subconscious indicator that an approach is imminent.

SCENE EIGHT

Bob's first words to Jan came in the form of a whisper, and while he asked the question about the painting, he pointed toward it with his beer in hand, pushing it into her personal space. Bob took Jan's hand, but didn't just shake it—he squeezed it, too. As the two continued to speak to each other, Jan noticed Bob's authentic smile, dilated pupils, rapid blink rate, intense eye contact, tilted head, and the buttoning and unbuttoning of his jacket. He shrugged ever so slightly when she expressed interest in his vocations as uncle and art instructor.

As the exchange continued, he blocked Jan from the rest of the people in the room with his shoulder.

The Mighty Murmur: If he's speaking in a soft voice, she'll have to move in closer to hear him, right? This is an interested man's scheme. Caveat: This puts him in control because it compels her to come toward him. *Psst . . . I'll bet it works.*

He's whispering so she'll come closer.

Gracious Space Invasion: If a man moves his cell phone onto a woman's piece of the bar or stands with his foot protruding into her circle of personal space (eighteen-inch radius), he is asking for permission to enter. If he's leaning in her direction, he's demonstrating a wish to move closer. She can oblige by allowing the intrusion to occur.

Body Watch: If you'd like to test his interest in you, move one of your belongings into his personal space. If he doesn't chuck it back at you or show some other sign of displeasure (like a scowl or cold shoulder) he's probably open to an interaction.

The "Nice to Feel You": Shaking hands is an unspoken way of saying, "Nice to meet you," but when that handshake lasts five seconds or longer, is accompanied by a finger squeeze of the palm and/or a slight tug in his direction, he's not just meeting her, he's feeling her (and would like to continue).

Body Watch: A handshake is often the first contact we share with a person. When a man takes your hand into his, take note of the visceral reactions that bubble up within you. Emotions surface more quickly than cognitive thought (and they can be surprisingly reliable).

The Genuine Grin: As we noted in the beginning of the chapter, true happiness is indicated by a genuine smile that alters the features of the face. It's important to note that an authentic smile's effects will linger on the face after the corners of the mouth have fallen. If his upper teeth are showing, his lips are stretched but relatively relaxed, and the outer corners of his eyes are turned downward, he's displaying some level of interest in a woman who's been under his scrutiny. Any woman who is the recipient of the Genuine Grin can deduce that the smiler is genuinely happy to see her.

Peeper Dilation: Pupil dilation indicates mental arousal and is a reliable indicator of a man's fascination with a woman. Ladies should be careful when using this body language reading technique in dark rooms, though—they might end up with goddess complexes because pupils automatically dilate in low light.

Pupils dilate when humans are mentally stimulated.

Stuck on Blink: Not as annoying as the driver who forgets to disengage the blinker, but just as subconscious, is a man's increased blink rate. If he is stimulated by a woman, his blink rate will likely exceed the average of fifteen to twenty blinks per minute, in harmony with other body language signals of interest. However, there's no need for her to count. She can take note of his general speed, and watch to see if it increases from there.

Body Watch: An increased blink rate is highly subjective. It indicates heightened mental activity, but there's no way to determine from the blink alone if that activity is slanted in your favor. Decode the situation. If the blink is accompanied by body language signals of interest, such as an animated face, a foot point in your direction, and dilated pupils, you can bet that his blinking is working in your favor. If he's fidgeting, looking around the room, and closing off his torso with crossed arms, he's either blinking because he feels stressed and uncomfortable or he's creating a shield in the form of a blinding flutter to block information absorption.

Body Watch: Research conducted at St. Elizabeth's Hospital in Washington, D.C., under the auspices of the National Institute of Mental Health, has assigned the following average blinks-per-minute rates to common tasks: 19 when at rest, 12.3 when reading quietly, 24.7 when speaking, and 27.6 when listening with the intent to repeat what was heard. As you can deduce from these findings, blink rate shifts into high gear when mental momentum demands it.

GENDER ENLIGHTENMENT: Though a man's blink rate will unconsciously adjust itself in relation to the task or attraction at hand, there are men out there who are wise to the blink rate's disclosures and might try to consciously control it. Studies have found that men are more adept than women at slowing down and speeding up blink rates at will (for example, when lying or attempting to hide discomfort).

Athletic Listening: Silver medal active listening involves maintaining eye contact, allowing her plenty of time to speak, and giving verbal and nonverbal cues that he understands what she's saying. Beyond this, if a man is animated and outrageously entertained by a woman's verbal offerings, his interest level is gold medal level.

A Titillating Tilt: If a man's head is softly angled to one side while he's listening to a woman, he's very receptive and interested. A head tilt also displays his jugular, indicating that he feels comfortable with the idea of being with her. She should keep doing or saying whatever she's doing or saying.

Fickle Clothing: A man who buttons and unbuttons his jacket obsessively while engaging in eye contact, active conversation, or any other conjunctive signs of digging a woman has made his deepest inner thoughts public: he wants to get naked (preferably in her presence). However, socially acceptable behavior dictates that he cannot (that explains the rebuttoning).

Steamed Under the Collar: When blood pressure or arousal is high, heat is generated in the neck, causing it to sweat. Manifestation of this phenomenon comes when a man pulls his collar away from his neck, as if attempting to let some steam out or circulate some air. If he becomes hot under the collar, tugging and pulling, he's silently wishing to undress for her.

The Submissive Shrug: Since the beginning of human bodies, the shrug has been used to show harmlessness and submissiveness. A man who is interested in meeting a woman will not generally use the full-blown variety, complete with upturned hands and obscured neck; but a slight and speedy lifting of the shoulder(s)—aka "shoulder flash"—will convey the same message to the astute viewer. The majority of men will opt for this less risky, nonthreatening approach, the seeming opposite of puffing up and peacocking.

Body Watch: Oftentimes a mating dance can be detoured when body language indicates shyness, submissiveness, or overt harmlessness. Body language like shoulder shrugging, pigeon-toeing, and nervous fidgeting doesn't always indicate a wish for an end to the dance, but rather a switch from a fast dance to a slow, seductive waltz.

The Blinder: If he stands directly in front of her gaze, he's not only trying to be the focus of her attention, but is also trying to shield her from the advances of other competing males. He's effectively blocking her from seeing them, and them from seeing her, with his shoulders.

SCENE NINE

This scene goes beyond what we witnessed in chapter 10. Jan's exchange with Bob continued past their initial meeting, well into the night. Bob extended his open, upturned palm to Jan as he invited her to walk with him in the apartment complex's courtyard. He placed his hand at the small of her back, steering her toward the door. They descended the stairs together with fingers interlocked in a handhold. Bob tripped once, pulled on the exit door instead of pushing it, and forgot his dog's name while telling a seemingly pointless veterinary treatment story.

Bob seemed unable to resist contact with Jan, touching her hand, her arm, and her shoulders repeatedly while speaking. As the chilly night air descended on them, he offered his jacket. She accepted.

Jan and Bob's attraction story didn't end with their initial meeting. Jan continued to take notice of Bob's cues of interest to ensure that his attraction was building and not diminishing. Often feelings can change. Jan could have revealed that she was a vegetarian to a meat-and-potatoes Bob. She could have insulted his niece or his political views. The fact that Bob continued to show signs of interest, right up until the end of the night (when, by the way, he asked for Jan's number), meant that his interest in Jan was compounding. Those cues included:

Palm Offering: Akin to the offering of an olive branch, a man's offering of his hand(s) with palm(s) turned up provides a woman a glimpse into his personality. It telegraphs that he is not trying to dominate her and is open to new ideas. Additionally, he's virtually reaching out and inviting her to come over to his side.

The Calculated Steer: If a woman has met a man and he takes the liberty of leading her through a crowd by her elbow or the small of her back, his gentlemanly ways have possessive underpinnings. Not only does he get to innocuously touch her, but he gets to show other men that she's spoken for. In short, his interest level is significant.

Locked Up: He's holding her hand. This alone signifies a basic level of interest in that, like Mickey, he's attempting to take her by the heart when he takes her by the hand. Even if he's simply being polite by guiding her through traffic, he's touching her, which is a strong signal of interest. If he has interlocked his fingers with her, he has a romantic personality.

Body Watch: A man's hand-holding method is indicative of his personality as well as his level of attraction to you. If he starts with closed-finger palm-to-palm holding and progresses to interlocked fingers, his attraction is intensifying.

The first type of hand-holding is less intimate than the second.

Awkward Admiration: This one might not be the sexiest of displays, but it's worth its weight in interest. If a man is stuttering, struggling with uncomfortable silences, tripping over his words, spilling drinks, or tripping over table legs, chances are the woman he's interacting with has his resolve shaken up. She should protect herself from flying objects and enjoy this awkward display of admiration.

GENDER ENLIGHTENMENT: Studies show that when a man sees a woman he views as attractive, his brain loses a significant amount of cognitive ability. Evolutionarily speaking, there's little brain power left over for grace, memory, or calculation—it's largely devoted to devising a plan for his gene propagation. Interestingly, the same doesn't hold true for women. We're just not as affected by physical appearance.

Touchy Dealings: If a man is interested in getting to know a woman, he won't sabotage his chances with impolite touching. Rather, he might accidentally graze her arm, bump into her, meet her in the peanut bowl, or pluck an eyelash from her cheek or lint from her clothing in an effort to get his fix without being slapped.

The Goodwill Offering: Hand-me-downs don't always carry a positive connotation, but this type couldn't be better for an interested woman's dating prospects. When a man donates his jacket to her, he's not only being chivalrous, he's laying claim to her. She's now attached to him, at least until she warms up. Additionally, when she gives that jacket back to him, it will smell like her (and she'll smell like him).

GENDER ENLIGHTENMENT: Two-thirds of men admit to smelling articles of clothing that the objects of their desire have worn— and that's only the ones who fess up to it. If the weather is warm or he has no jacket to offer, you can still gift him with your lingering scent. While interacting with him, snatch opportunities to rub your wrists or neck, where perfume has been applied, onto his clothing.

Women aren't the only creatures who display interest signals in clusters. Here are some examples of how men do it:

Eye contact, slight smile, preen.

Smile, head tilt, jugular
display, touch, leg spread.

Open body posture, hand and leg
protrusion in her space, upturned
palm, wrist display, smile, eye
contact. (Note: Most of his weight
is on the leg farther from her—this
indicates some indecision.)

Personal space invasion, touch, glass
fondle, smile, upper body turn.

Leg spread, thumb display, open body posture, self-touch,
fixated stare. (Notice that she's sending mixed signals: her
leg is crossed away from him, but she's displaying her wrist
to him. She may be undecided about her attraction level.)

Body Watch: Which man is more interested in one of the ladies? *Take a good look at the photo before continuing.* If you guessed the gentleman on the right, you're correct. The man on the left is holding his beer high, closing off his chest and torso. His upper body is also angled away from the others, and he is shielding himself with his shoulder. Additionally, his elbow is drawn in, so as not to interject himself into anyone's personal space. The man on the right has a more open body posture and is introducing his leg and left arm into the woman's personal space.

Body Watch: Which man and woman would you expect to interact later? *Take a good look at the photo before continuing.* If

your answer is the two in the foreground, you're a grade-A student. Not only are their body postures more open, but their bodies are angled toward each other. Her hand is either touching her
heart, preening, or engaged in self-touch—all of which indicate
interest in the man she's looking at. The two in the background
are looking more reserved with closed postures and their bodies
angled away from each other.

Jan was not only able to decipher Bob's level of interest; she also
passed over a number of men in the room whom she recognized as
unavailable. In order to avoid rejection (or indifference) and save
your precious time for more productive interactions, you can do
the same—learn to recognize and navigate away from men displaying uninterested body language. Even if he was into you from
the starting gate, nonverbal manifestations of his lack of interest
will prove that he has no intention of crossing the finish line.

In many cases, **the absence of interest signs** is enough to indicate his lack of fascination with you. For instance, if his feet are
pointed away from you; if his face is unanimated, or his pupils are
constricted; if his attention lies elsewhere; if he's making no effort
to correct his messy clothing; if he's leaning away from you, or
he's not mirroring you, you can accurately assume that he's not
feeling you (or not wanting to feel you).

There are also some other uninterested signals that are more
detailed contenders. They include:

Disgruntled Eye Contact: After initial peeper contact, a woman
should watch the direction in which his eyes travel. If he looks to
the side or up after leaving an eye lock with her, he doesn't want
to try out for her team.

Rude Revolvers: An eye roll can be the epitome of disrespect,
passive aggressiveness, trivialization, frustration, condescension,

disagreement with beliefs, indifference, superiority, and sarcasm, and a clear indicator that a man's not only uninterested in a woman, but also would rather be anywhere else. Seriously, the eye roll can be so offensive that I can't believe it's taking up ink on this page. If a woman finds herself the intended receiver of one of these ocular revolutions (accompanied by a snide remark, no speech at all, or one of the negative facial expressions), she should take her own revolvers and roll on to other prospects—pronto.

Body Watch: There are a few exceptions to eye rolling's overwhelming negativity. First, if he rolls his eyes playfully while smiling, maybe you're not being completely dissed. Or, if he's rolling his eyes at something he did or said, he's simply using self-deprecation to disarm and charm. In either case, you can cautiously assume that if the eye roll is aimed at himself or someone other than you, he might be interested. Support this tricky display by reading other cues of his interest.

The Bored Stiff: If a woman's dating prospect is scanning the room, yawning, resting his chin on his palm and his elbow on the table, praying to Father Time through his wristwatch, drumming his fingers on a tabletop, or otherwise silently screaming that his mind is numb, she's in the presence of a Bored Stiff. I recommend that she put a Do Not Resuscitate order on this one. He's not intrigued.

Dead on His Feet: Maybe he's worked so hard today that he can barely keep his eyes open. Maybe he has an early meeting in the morning and should get home to bed. Please! If she was bleeping his radar, he wouldn't think twice about pulling an all-nighter followed by another double. A sexually interested man can put the Energizer Bunny to shame.

The Clown Face: Smiles only indicate happiness when they're genuine. Without an eye squint, laugh lines, dipping outer eyebrows, and rising cheeks, a smile is halfhearted, tentative, or deceptive. One phony smile is okay, but once a woman determines that all of his smiles are snake oil, it's time to admit that while he might be polite, he's certainly not interested in raising the big top at her place.

Specifically, there are two types of smiling mouths that indicate a lack of sexual interest. When the lips are closed and there is no shine or smile from his eyes, he's just being polite; maybe just saying hello with the intent to keep on moving. If his lips are stretched tightly over his teeth, with both rows of choppers tightly clenched, he's either feeling fearful or defensive—neither of which is conducive to romance.

Furthermore, if he's making no effort to smile at all, even when she throws a sweet one his way, he's mourning the time spent under her gaze, and may be flirting with insolence. She should release him.

Body Watch: Visit http://www.bbc.co.uk/science/human body/mind/surveys/smiles/ to take a smile quiz based on Dr. Paul Ekman's research. Just how good are you at separating real smiles from counterfeit ones?

The Outer Limits: If he's standing so far away from her that he might be in another zip code, or if she's considering continuing their exchange via text messaging, he's effectively removing himself from her personal space (and her grasp). Men tend to use any excuse (loud music, quiet conversation, etc.) to move closer to women they're interested in, so there's no reason for his drifting away except his uninterested disposition. He may not even realize he's retreating, but she will.

The Un-Kiss: Though the early stages of flirting don't include the kiss, the lips will involuntarily hint about their desires. When he's not receptive to how she's looking or what she's saying, his lips will purse like a Louis Vuitton.

The Blockade: Crossing of the arms is not just an effective way to say, "I'm not willing to hear you"; studies have shown that crossed arms actually block the brain's absorption of information. If he's built a blockade with his arms, she should hand him a drink, a brochure, or a bar menu to open him up. If he moves to uncross his arms, he's at least partially interested. If this doesn't work, I recommend that she retreat.

GENDER ENLIGHTENMENT: If a man places his hands under his biceps and pushes them outward to make them appear larger, the uninterested arm cross converts to a sign of interest. Studies suggest that women are unlikely to fold their arms in the presence of men whom they find alluring. Men, however, are more likely to fold their arms even if they're interested in a woman.

Even though his arms are crossed, he's using his hands to make his biceps appear larger. He's probably interested in the woman he's looking at.

The Butt-in: Interruptions in a woman's monologue (unless a lively debate is in progress) or abrupt subject changes (on his part) indicate that her next move should include changing her object—the object of her affection, that is.

Institutional Inquiries: There are two types of questions: filler and fanciful. If his questions are asked without passion or without an "I've gotta know" attitude, he's simply attempting to sidestep an uncomfortable silence. If he asks a question like "What's your favorite ice cream flavor?" with as much enthusiasm as Ben Stein, eating it with (or from) her is the furthest thing from his mind.

Stroke of Modesty: If the room is warm and he's sweating, yet making no move to ditch his jacket, he would rather die of heat-stroke than remove one article of clothing. He's effectively saying, "I'm outta here soon, so don't get too attached."

Dating ADD: If a man searches the room for conversation salvation, noting the number of mirrors on the disco ball or speculating about the grams of sugar in the punch, the woman he's talking to should move on to someone who's more interested in talking about what's right in front of him. If he seems preoccupied with checking the door, he's probably waiting for something better to walk in. And most blatantly, if his head spins every time a woman walks past, he's telling the woman he's with that he's not interested enough to fake fixation on her.

Encino Man: Active listening includes leaning in, tilting of the head, and fluidity of neck movements. If a woman's hot possibility isn't performing as such, he's freezing her out because he's uninterested in continuing an exchange with her. She should refrain from attempting to thaw the man who's answering her questions curtly, stiffening his body posture, giving her the cold posterior of his shoulder . . . or she'll get burned.

Equipment Storage: There aren't a lot of men who fully cross their legs when sitting, but when they do, there's a good chance that the plow and planters are being stored away for use in another season or in another field. If he crosses his legs tightly after he's become aware of a particular woman's presence, he's probably not interested in an exchange. The woman should take note of the direction of his top (crossed) leg. If it's pointed away from her, so are his mind, body, and spirit.

The Untouchable: If he jumps back when she attempts to casually touch him, he's either consciously or subconsciously letting her know he doesn't have a hankerin' for interaction. Either way, I suggest that she save him the trouble.

The Cold Thigh: If a man's legs are pointed away from a woman, he's not only shielding his manly bits from her, he's protecting his sensibilities with a large part of his body: his thigh. To eliminate the possibility that he's shy or avoiding being overbearing, she can give him two to five minutes in which to open up. If his thigh remains frigid, a sensible woman will not attempt to defrost it.

The Great Fade: A man will go to great lengths to blend into a crowd if he doesn't want a woman's attention. If the apple of a woman's eye is doing his best to bury himself in the applecart, she might want to patronize a different orchard.

Missing Person: I hope this one is obvious. If a man whom a woman's been interacting with suddenly cannot be found, she can reliably predict that it's intentional. True, he could have been clubbed over the head and kidnapped for ransom, but chances are that if she's lost this man, she's actually been set free.

Body Watch: Is he interested in her? No way. She is displaying plenty of interest, but she's probably wasting her time. He's got his equipment stored in closed legs, he's looking away from her, his feet are pointing straight forward (not at her), his body posture is closed, and his face is demonstrating fear.

Baselining: These facial expression and body language reading tips assume that you haven't already made the acquaintance of the man whom you're reading. Some human faces are naturally more animated than others. It's important to observe your target early on, so that you can baseline, or norm, him. Notice how he acts when relaxed and not under pressure. Take note of his hand-shake, the way he stands, the positioning of his torso, his typical gestures, his neutral facial expression, and his comfort with eye contact.

Now watch for any change in his behavior. Is the shift positive, with an increase in interested body language? If so, continue on with your own displays of interest. If he's cooling off with unin-terested facial expressions or body language, pack up your display and retreat.

There you have it. The secret to making connections with men is first finding those men who are most interested in making a connection with you. When you pinpoint someone who's display-ing at least four signals of interest, half the work is already done for you. These signals make your hookups seem relatively effortless, as they do for the most successful of dating women.

Remember that a significant portion of the male population is shy or has been taught not to come on too strong or to be too pushy. This can interfere with the reading of a man's body lan-guage cues. Be patient. As your signals of interest are received, his comfort level will increase. Not all interest is evident immediately.

Venue is also a consideration in reading his body language. If you're at a funeral, his displays of interest will (hopefully) be more subtle than they would be at a cocktail party. This is one similar-ity between the sexes. We naturally adjust our behaviors to match the context of the location and the situation. Those who don't have that innate sense are generally deemed to be rude or socially challenged. Though flirting in church might be more subtle, that subtleness will give good clues to his social adeptness and respect for socially acceptable behavior.

If you've been largely disappointed with the number of approaches you receive from men until now, you may have been pitching to an unreceptive audience or sending incorrect signals. Even if you haven't heard the words "No thanks" or "Bug off," body language was sending reliable clues that would have said the same things to your psyche, had you known how to listen.

But this is a new dating day (or night). You no longer have to wonder what's wrong with you. You need only ask, "What signals have I been missing?" or, "What signals have I not been sending?" If you can learn to speak nonverbally to men, you might find that even those who were not initially interested in you suddenly are. In fact, most men might now think of you as close to ideal in their eyes. A perfect ten is not just about looks—it's about using body language to take possession of the room and transform yourself into that coveted number.

Mastering the reading of dating body language will take practice. You'll need to study the outward signs of interest, along with the signals that indicate a lack thereof. Then you'll need to take that knowledge into the field. Watch people closely no matter where you are. Notice how men react to your friendly smile, a glance over your shoulder, or any of the other signals of interest that you've learned to orchestrate. Something as simple as a trip to the supermarket should result in a mental tally of how many interested and uninterested parties you encountered.

Once you master the art of reading the body language of dating, time invested in indifference and rejection will be nothing but bad memories. Failure won't be an option.

It's true.

It's that powerful.

Just ask Jan.

CHAPTER TWELVE

When It's a Fling Thing

RECOGNIZING THE PICK-HER-UPPER AND HIS SCHEMES

You've learned to identify the facial expressions and body language that speak of his willingness (or not) to play, so you should have everything you need for zeroing in on your target at the cocktail party, right? Not so fast. Sure, we could stop here and consider the scene at your friend's cocktail party a cut-and-dried one in which all signals convey either a solid "Yea" or "Nay" but that would be reckless of me. The subject of deceptive schemes must be addressed.

There is a portion of the single male population that will, without remorse, engage your sensibilities with games that teeter on the verge of cruelty and leave you wondering at which station you boarded the "stupid train." If you've ever fallen for or been misled by a man's dating (or bedding) tactics, you'll be interested in learning how to recognize them should they come calling again. If you're interested in a fling, there's no harm in playing along. However, if you're looking for a relationship with more durability, the disposal of the serial Pick-Her-Upper is of paramount importance.

The pickup scene has changed. Cheesy pickup lines like "Heaven must be missing an angel," "Where've you been all my life?" and "Put 'em up. You just stole my heart" are as antiquated as hoopskirts and handlebar mustaches. Instead, they're systematically being replaced with lines like "You're fugly," "Do you like my ass?" and "I usually date perfect tens, but I'm looking for a change."

Confused?

Sure you are, and you're not even in the club yet. Because modern women are taking the time to educate themselves in the tactics that men use to score, those men must switch it up in order to continue enjoying success. Men's secrets are being uncovered and they must incorporate elements of surprise and trickery to preserve their chances of hooking up with the most attractive women.

Be ready for the games they play. Study these tactics of the practiced player and note how each one is used to confuse and disarm:

The PROD: The PROD, or *Playful Rip Or Dig*, is a statement that makes us question our own worth and the worth of others. I can remember an instance in which I was the target of one of these declarations. I had been taking an online class with some phone conferencing involved and quickly made friends with a wonderful guy. We would chat weekly and email daily but we had never met or seen each other. During a conference a few months later, a man walked up to me and said, "I know that voice. You're Tonya." I instantly recognized the voice of my online friend. Although it was awkward to meet in person, he made it quite easy to hold a conversation, and it didn't take long for him to invite me to lunch. While ordering he said, "My future ex-wife will be having the Caesar salad."

By excluding me with a PROD, he employed a tactic that is often used to gain a woman's attention. We're always attracted to a challenge, and most men know it. His approach was effective because he wasn't falling all over me; he didn't come across as needy.

A man might use this type of statement in a casual social conversation to attract you, as my friend did. That was his way of sending the innuendo that a relationship between us would never work out. He was indirectly disqualifying himself in order to pique my interest, lower my self-esteem, and intensify my attraction to him by causing me to wonder, *Who is this man who has absolutely no curiosity about me?*

Men will use PRODs such as "I don't date women like you," "My weekends are reserved for my buddies," or "I have bad memories of blondes" to turn you into the pursuer. Suddenly you have something to prove. Remember the instances on the middle school playground when boys would insult your clothing, make jokes about your hair, or tell you that you smelled bad? Sure you do. We all do. Remember returning home to complain about it and your parents surprising you with statements like "He probably has a crush on you"? Well, not much has changed. If you're being PRODded, you're probably on his sexual hit list.

> DEFINITION: PROD *(noun)*— Playful *Rip* *Or* *Dig*; a negative comment that seems to reject or exclude a member of the opposite sex as a dating possibility, but is actually intended to incite sexual competition, expression, and attraction; *(verb)*—the act of prodding.

Work-Only Bonuses: Men are taught by modern pickup artists not to shower women with compliments unless they're first earned. If you find yourself on the receiving end of this tactic, you might be greeted with something like "That dress is okay, but you'd look better in something like that," as he points across the room to a replica of Marilyn Monroe's infamous white dress. A simple statement like "What's that smell?" accompanied by a wrinkled nose might make you want to get closer to prove that it isn't you stinking up the place.

Every time you do what he wants you to do (like express a desire to try on the white dress or move closer to allow him to smell your perfume), you will be rewarded with a compliment.

For example, "Yeah, only women with figures as nice as yours could get away with something Marilyn wore," or "Is that Obsession or Eternity?"

If you choose to keep score in this game, be prepared; the compliment count will never exceed the statements that urge you to earn them.

Interest Level Mix-ups: He might show interest with touch, conversation, or body language only to then push you away with a PROD like "You're nuts. How do you function in society?"

Stick around. It won't be long before he attempts to lure you back in with another positive signal. What he's doing is creating an environment in which he's teasing you with attention, hoping that you'll switch from the hunted to the hunter. When a cat's stalking a mouse, she's completely engrossed in the pursuit: this is a metaphor for the provocation tactics the Pick-Her-Upper uses. Once the mouse stops moving, the cat loses interest.

Serial Touching: A man who uses frequent touching is doing three things: he's paying close attention to your reactions in order to gauge your reception to his touch, as well as measuring your willingness to jump through hoops in pursuit of him. In addition, he's establishing himself as a touchy-feely person. When it comes time for the kiss, it will seem like a natural next step for the Pick-Her-Upper (rather than an awkward moment under the front porch light).

The Socialite: Veteran Pick-Her-Uppers do their utmost to ensure that they're not seen standing alone. Just as a restaurant with a packed parking lot gets more subsequent customers than one with an empty parking lot, men who seem more social get more resulting attention.

If he jumps from group to group, publicly socializing and drawing attention to himself, he's hoping that by the time he gets to you, you're thinking, *This guy is well liked; I can't wait to find out why.*

Caveat: Don't get your hopes up too soon. You could be part

of the "social proof"—only a pit stop on the way to the object of his interest.

So, what's the best way to determine whether you're his target or just another pawn in his social proof scheme? If he's PRODding you, you are the end result that he desires. If the Pick-Her-Upper is simply being polite, he's either getting ready to make tracks or you're an accessory to his crime.

Monologue Absorption: When a man strikes up a conversation with you that's more like a monologue, don't jump to the conclusion that he's self-absorbed. He could be attempting to steer you with mental images and social proof, seeming more interested in the words coming from his own mouth than in you—but that could all be part of the ruse.

No woman likes to sit still while she listens to a man drone on about himself. However, listening to a man talk about the things that define him and his life without his inclusion of the word *I* can have a distinctly separate effect.

The Pick-Her-Upper will often use descriptive words that seem to take you to another place and cause a positive emotive reaction in your mind. He might talk about a recent vacation he took to a private beach or his childhood wish to Rollerblade through the mall after closing time. He might talk about singing karaoke with Lady Gaga when she was still Stefani and having drinks with Steve Carell after he'd had a hard day at *The Office.*

He's busy creating feelings that you'll want to duplicate. This is genius, really. He knows that he'll accomplish much more than he could with general, interview-type conversation because it causes you to want to become part of his exciting world. He creates social proof by showing evidence of why he's well liked, instead of by saying, "I'm well liked."

He'll show instead of tell.

And once again, you become the pursuer.

Hurdle Elimination: The masterful Pick-Her-Upper is not intimidated by groups. In fact, he'll use them to his advantage.

If you're the prize he's after, he might start with your friends. By complimenting them or simply engaging them in conversation, he's gaining their trust and keeping their attention so they don't steal you away before the deal is closed. He may whisper nice things in their ears or throw PRODs your way to disguise his true intentions and to win them over. If they like him, they'll stick around to unknowingly play gate guards for the hookup. This move is complex, and will require some scrutiny to determine his true intentions. If you're the first one he approaches, he might have his eye on one of your friends. If you're the last one he speaks to, or the one he speaks to the least, you're almost certainly the target. I know, this seems to make little sense, but unfortunately, we can be complex creatures and the best Pick-Her-Uppers have solved the riddle. Remember, these moves are generally executed by semipros and professionals. Amateurs usually get this all wrong, reversing nearly every play.

If there are other men in your group, the pro will befriend them, too. Tradition would suggest that he try to "outman" each one, but nothing about this new style of courting has to do with tradition. Instead he'll gain their trust with things like fist bumps and storytelling. He may also request to know (as one major player suggests) "how every-one knows one an-other." This will alert him to any boyfriend-girlfriend situations.

Also note that if he shows up at your group with women, he has cunningly come equipped with proof of his social capabili-ties (in other words, if these women think he's intriguing, you and your friends will, too). Keep in mind that he's probably going to attempt to pair them off with your guy friends, in order to open a clear pathway to you or one of your girlfriends.

Dynamite Duos: The best Pick-Her-Uppers are all about team-work. They travel in groups of two or more and celebrate cumulative successes. They cheer each other on.

You've probably already heard of the wingman, but are you clear on his responsibilities? He will help his trolling partner spot targets, engage potential hurdles in conversation for the sake of the team, provide social proof for his friends, offer backup evidence for the Pick-Her-Upper's incredible stories, and deliver play-by-play commentary on targets' movements.

Members of pickup groups are great planners. They'll pinpoint their targets before approaching and the experienced ones will have canned scripts on hand to handle objections, rejections, and interruptions. A talented wingman will never seem surprised at a story told by his cohort(s). Instead he'll have already heard all the tales that are used to engage and attract.

Men don't instinctively travel in packs like women do. If two men are approaching together, you can bet they're running interference for each other; and if one is more than ready to defend the other's wild and crazy stories, you've been targeted.

The Brag Switch-up: The days of men bragging their ways into women's hearts are over. Apparently they've learned that it annoys us and therefore doesn't work. Instead it seems that men are turning the tables and cajoling us into bragging about ourselves.

The masterful Pick-Her-Upper will use emotional soliloquies to give you a taste of how he lives, instead of just listing off a bland catalog of his good qualities. This takes care of his bragging. But then what he might do is ask you to list your best qualities. See what's just happened? All of a sudden, you're selling yourself to him.

The "Hold This Please": If a man hands you his cell phone, his camera, his drink, or any other personal object and then takes off to engage in conversation with another woman, he's set you up for a devious, but effective, trick.

Not only is he using jealousy to fuel your fire for him (because you have his personal item, you'll feel naturally compelled to look in his direction while he's flirting with her); he is using the item as a placeholder. He's assuming that you'll stay put while he's off doing God-knows-what, and if you're approached by another man, his personal possession will be right there in full view to remind you of his imminent return.

Different women will react in various ways to these games. You might be charmed, beguiled, relieved that he's taking the wheel . . . or you might be insulted at his belief that you can be swept up like a feather in a stiff breeze. You might be pleased that he's mistaken your chest for your eyes, or you might be insulted beyond belief. No matter your educated reaction, know that dating games aren't reserved for the male sector. There's no reason that a woman who's either looking for a fling or a long-term thing can't turn this male medicine right back on the doctors who prescribe it.

I intend in no way to demonize men. In fact, I think these games are rather ingenious. Men, especially those who feel that their looks alone aren't enough to elicit attention from women, have recognized a problem and are setting out to solve it. Additionally, there are men out there who are looking for something more than one-night stands, and are using these techniques as routes to their goal because they lack the necessary tools to aid them in the first approach. Remember that their hypothalamuses put ours to shame, their sex drives are commendable, their desires to propagate the globe with their spawn are impressive . . . and thanks to all these forces, our species has proliferated on a scale that has contributed to its longevity.

If you fall victim (or willing participant) to any of these games, he can easily swoop in under your newfound body language radar to tweak the situation to his advantage. In a matter of seconds, you might find yourself on the pickup or drop-off end of these tactics, but knowing which way he's headed can be invaluable in keeping your evening on track.

Sure, one-sided dating games might piss you off. But the remedy for that is simple: learn the tactics, know what's coming, deny or accept it based on both your dating expectations, and then silently commend him for an admirable effort (even if it failed).

There's no denying that a perfect ten will be hit on incessantly, either to her delight or her disgust. But for those of us who teeter right around that six or seven mark, being proactive (even if it involves a bit of psychological warfare) can round up some opposite-sex interest. In fact, with the proper strategies, a six can be just as sexy as a ten. By employing these tactics, you can gain the attention necessary for steering any interaction in the direction of your desires.

If you're the kind of confident girl who can't sit back and watch it happen *to* you, get up, interact, play, and make it happen *for* you. Just as men use conversation and carefully conducted actions to elicit pursuit by women, you can quickly create a scenario in which you are the pursued. Don't fall into a role of dominant alpha woman, but rather, remain playful. Gather your cast, complete with supporting actress(es) to imitate the wingman's role. Practice disqualifying phrases, bragging switches, and emotional engagement to turn the tables of pursuit. If a situation is progressing before your eyes—if your target is being targeted by other women—acting quickly with a few of these dating games might be just what's needed to point the possession arrow toward Team You.

Don't be unknowingly played by a Pick-Her-Upper—ever again. Either play because you want to, say no because you recognize a fling attempt when you see one, or take possession of the ball and throw passes to the receiver of *your* choice. You have more power than you think.

CHAPTER THIRTEEN

Real, Manufactured Confidence

SELF-ASSURED BODY LANGUAGE: A SELF-FULFILLING PROPHECY

I want you to try this dating experiment: Walk into a coffee shop, a church social, or a nightclub, go directly to the first seemingly single man you see, and say, "I've had a rough life. I have too many problems to count and I can't remember the last time I've smiled." Then look into his eyes with as little enthusiasm as possible and ask, "Would you like to take me out sometime?"

Let me know if it works. I'd like to study the man who jumps on that.

The negative body language that women sometimes use can be even more powerful than those words. Albert Mehrabian's often-cited study of decades ago stills hold true: communication relies more heavily on nonverbal expressions than it does on verbal ones. A person's true feelings can be predicted only by scrutinizing their facial expressions, body language, and ways of speaking. If you enter a room with forward-curling shoulders held high to protect the neck, a furrowed brow, darting eyes, folded arms, a rigid jaw, pursed lips, and tightly clenched fists, you are saying the same things as spoken in the monologue above—except that the message will be stronger. When you're worried, depressed, or insecure, your body rarely lies.

Body language that speaks of insecurity invites no one to approach. When you enter a room using body language that says, "I have problems," you literally discourage others from even looking in your direction.

Of course, this raises the question of what to do if you really *are* worried, depressed, or suffering the confidence level of a rabbit in a wolf's den. This is the beauty of confidence: if you don't have it, you can learn to fake it—and once you get good at faking it, your confident body language will teach your brain to feel confident. Yes, it's true: even if you're notorious for ditching parties and nodding out of high-pressure dating situations with excuses like "My mother called—our bridge game is about to start," or "I'm feeling lightheaded—I'm allergic to the pleather on this booth," you can learn to not only own a room, but to captivate nearly everyone in it.

Confident Perceptions

Confident people think that everyone likes them, right? Wrong.

It's tempting to believe that confident people are successful (socially and romantically) simply because they convey feelings of self-adequacy and contagious happiness. That's true, but there's more.

An exciting study conducted at Washington University in St. Louis has found that confident people are better at gauging others' visceral reactions to them. Researchers asked people of all confidence levels to determine whether they "struck out" or "hit home runs" upon meeting other participants. The most confident people were right most of the time about what kinds of first impressions they made.

This study tells us that if a man is interested in a confident woman, she'll not only pick up on that interest, she'll feel confident enough in her perception of his feelings to run with it like an Olympian. Likewise, if she detects that he's less than interested, she can walk away with the assurance of knowing that the right decision was made.

Much of the time, an insecure woman will feel assured in her assessments of a lack of interest and shaky on her readings of interest—bad for her dating prospects, when you consider that she's glossing over a significant portion of her most receptive market.

Women are more prone to low self-confidence than men. This is due in large part to the fact that our brains (as discussed in chapter 6) ruminate on problems. In other words, we worry. It's a negative circle, really. Self-doubting women have fewer friends. Women need to talk about their problems. If we don't have the support system (friends) to talk to, we continue to worry until our already insecure natures start to put strain on our faces and bodies. This strain then manifests itself in poor posture, wrinkles, and a habitual scowl . . . making it even more difficult to attract new friends.

In order to increase your own confidence level, practice these body language exercises in every public setting:

Belly Breathing: Take a yoga class and you might learn that you've been breathing incorrectly and adding to your own anxiety. When you breathe, push your belly out and your diaphragm down, allowing more room for the bottom of your lungs to fill with air. Your chest should not rise when you breathe, unless you're attempting to exude confidence on a treadmill.

When you breathe deeply, using your diaphragm, your nervous system's firing is slowed, resulting in a relaxed feeling that shallow breathing could never accomplish. When in control of your breathing, you'll be more likely to detect your own heartbeat, which, studies suggest, helps to create a positive whole-body image, which will in turn boost confidence. Additionally, when your chest isn't pumping in near hyperventilation style, others will believe that you're confident and in complete control.

The Acquaintance Wave: What if you ran into your friend, Josephine Schmo, everywhere you went? What if you could walk through the door of every bar, retail store, party, or bakery with a wave at Ms. Schmo? You'd seem instantly popular and friendly, and your social proof would precede you.

Knowing someone when you enter strange territory is always a plus. Your anxiety is relieved. But here's the beauty of this phenomenon: you can fake it and get the same result. Whenever you enter a public place, pause in the doorway and throw a bright smile and friendly wave toward the back of the room. Those who don't know you will assume that you're waving at someone else. If someone does assume that you're waving at him, move your eyes just slightly so that he believes he's been mistaken. Your confidence in the interactions that follow will balloon, along with others' desires to get to know a woman who has friends and a fantastic, friendly nature.

Caveat: Only attempt this move if you're entering a crowded scene. If there's only one table of people in the room, and none of them know you, you won't find Schmo and you'll look like a schmuck.

Who is Angelina waving at? We may never know.

Clear for Landing: Confident people walk into a room immediately ready to accept approaches. They don't fold their arms over their chests or abdomens and they don't cover their throats with their hands.

Keeping your hands at your sides or otherwise occupied leaves your core open and inviting for others to approach. Covering your body with your arms tells others that you anticipate an attack or that you'll view even an innocent approach as an attack.

Body Watch: Placing your hands behind your back can work to open your midsection, but only if you send the right hand signals to those at your posterior. Tightly clenched hands and rigid arms give the impression that you're forcing your arms to stay in place because they're aching to snap forward like built-in security blankets. However, loosely held hands and fluid arms at the rear say "relaxed" and leave the torso open and inviting.

The Loftiest You: In chapter 9, we talked about how tall men generally earn more trust, credibility, and money. The same concept applies to women. Straightening from a slouch can add as many as four inches to your height, enhancing both your social authority and your sexual appeal. The simple act of expanding the chest, holding back the shoulders, and stretching tall not only affects the appearance of power and confidence; it changes the way we think, which will manifest positively in our behavior. Remember that tall is good in evolutionary terms. Men will be attracted to tall women for the built-in indication of past health, for the propensity to bear big, healthy babies, and for the chance at fathering a brood of tall, authoritative children.

Body Watch: Ask your shortest friend to stand tall and your tallest friend to slouch for one evening. Who looks more confident and authoritative? Whose posture says "tall," regardless of measurement?

The Air Head: A confident woman walks as if her head is filled with helium. An insecure woman walks as if her head is filled with rocks. In this instance, the Air Head is the smartest way to roll.

By holding her head high, a woman can effectively look taller, more approachable, and more confident because her line of sight is higher in space, creating an air of authority. Additionally, her neck is fully exposed, demonstrating that she is fearless.

Caveat: Holding your head too high (looking down your nose) will give you a condescending air and discourage others from approaching you.

The Straight-Stack Walk: No one would feel confident entering a leaning building. Likewise you'll convey your lack of confidence if you walk without maintaining a straight, stacked posture. If you're not walking in an upright manner, the part of your body that enters the room first will hint at your insecurities. If your shoulders precede you, you'll look like a defensive or fearful boxer or a narcotics squad cop who's ready to bust down a door. Either way, you won't be warmly welcomed. If your legs come first, you'll look as if you're being taken for a ride. You might remember from chapter 10 that feet point in the direction of inner desire. If your inner self would like to make a nervous run for your life, your legs will seem to want to carry the rest of you right out the door.

When entering a room, balance your body so that all of you enters at once. That way, all they'll notice is the whole package.

The Certain Saunter: When you're certain about where you're going, your intentions for when you get there, and your ability to accomplish your goal, your gait will prove it.

If an overtly sexy walk is a milk shake, then a confident walk is extra-rich chocolate milk. Confident people don't imitate sticks, nor do they overemphasize the sexual nature of the girly hip swing (unless the situation demands serious flirting). In most situations, a walk in which you swing your arms comfortably, hold your shoulders down and back, and swivel your hips just enough to differentiate your gait from that of your male counterparts will boost your confidence in yourself and others' perceptions of you.

This confident woman is walking with rolling hips, relaxed arms, shoulders pushed down and back, head held high, neck exposed, open torso, eye contact, and upright posture.

The "Eye'm" Here: Confidence invites other people to look in your direction. Eye contact from you lets them know that you're aware of your surroundings and that you're available for communication.

This tactic also builds confidence. When you spend all night looking at the carpet, it's easy to believe that no one's looking at you. Raise your eyes and conduct some optical lockup with a few willing participants and you might be surprised at how many people are looking at you.

The Low-and-Exposed: Whether you're holding a cell phone, a drink, or a purse, keep it low or to the side of your body (which gives you the added effect of taking up more space). This opens your body up and shows that you're confident enough to showcase your physical goods while laughing in the face of that "impending" danger. An item that's held high, over the chest, is essentially being used as a shield for an anticipated attack.

The Product Pose: Confident people are not only self-assured about their abilities and their social skills; they're also confident about the package in which it's all wrapped. By facing people head-on, putting your hands on your hips, and casually resting the majority of your weight on one leg, you're letting them know that you're happy with your packaging, and that you think they'll like it, too.

Taking Up Space: Shy and insecure people try to take up as little space as possible—as if they don't deserve it. You can increase your self-confidence by moving your arms while you talk, standing and sitting with your legs spread slightly, and being generously mobile within a group.

This woman's pose tells us she's confident.

Caveat: Be careful not to take your chunk of personal space out of others'. Often they will view this as an unwelcome invasion. Remember, "too confident" can easily drift into "cocky."

Introversion: An Evolutionary Relic

About 20 percent of the world's population is estimated to be shy, reserved, quiet, introverted . . . and if that includes you, you may have grown to believe that because you are shy, there's no hope for you in the confidence department. Therein lies a glaring misconception.

True shyness, scientifically dubbed *sensory perception sensitivity*, does not equate to a lack of confidence. Instead, introverted people are particularly sensitive to loud noises, take more time than average to become comfortable in new situations, are moved to tears easily, resist idle conversation, tend to be more philosophical and contemplative than average, are startled easily, hold particular sensitivity to caffeine, and as has been more recently discovered, are more meticulous in the performance of tasks and show more brain activity when presented with visual stimuli.

If you're introverted or shy, that doesn't automatically mean that you're underconfident, snobbish, or unapproachable. Instead it simply means that your brain is designed to effectively take in experiences and sights without being hurried. Fruit fly, fish, dog, and primate species all include individuals that demonstrate shyness, giving credence to the belief that this personality trait serves a purpose in an evolutionary sense. As humans developed, those who looked and listened first, rather than diving into danger, would have enjoyed longer lives under the auspices of their introverted natures. However, when danger or fleeting opportunity presented itself, the daredevils would have benefited. Even in cave huddles, the need for both thinkers and doers was prevalent.

If you do experience some level of shyness, know that you can still effectively exude confidence. Shy women are not automatically underconfident and shyness isn't necessarily something that needs to be "fixed." Authentic self-assurance does not come in the form of loud speech or a partying personality. Instead it's all about feeling comfortable in the quiet, yet confident, role that evolution has chosen for you.

Master-Touching: Socially acceptable touching can be used to gently control, and when you're the controller, your confidence will build. Momentarily lay a hand on someone's hand, arm, or shoulder while you're speaking to them and you'll establish your-self as a confident and playful individual.

No Digit Fidget: As a serial fidgeter, I can tell you that leg jig-gling burns calories in home offices, but it also holds the potential to burn confidence bridges in public settings. If you fidget, make it a habit to ask yourself, "Am I being still?" Foot tapping, finger drumming, hand wringing, lip biting, eye darting, nail picking or chewing, and NASCAR-speed leg pumping are all outward signs of inward anxiety.

Confident people aren't anxious. They sit still. Often.

The Thumb-body Special: An insecure woman will hide her thumbs, tucking them against the palms of her hands or stuffing them into her pockets. I like to call the thumb "the power digit" not only because it has helped hu-mankind to accomplish all things mechanical, but because display-ing it tells others (covertly) that we are in charge of ourselves and of the situation.

The farther from the palm the thumb is held, and the more up-ward it's pointing, the more pow-erful and confident the thumb's proprietor is feeling. Additionally, the more exposed and vulnerable the thumb appears, the less vul-nerable the user of that thumb is feeling. It's a paradox, but so is the thumb—an overlooked but powerful digit.

A powerful, confident thumb.

The Shake-It-Up: A confident greeting shakes up people's per-ceptions of you without shaking up their rotator cuffs. Your hand-shake should be firm. Too clammy or weak and you'll be perceived as . . . well, clammy or weak. A bone-crushing handshake or one that knocks eyeglasses off faces tells people that you're trying to compensate for a weakness.

When it comes to handshakes, follow the golden rule: Shake as you wish to be shaken.

Body Watch: If you want to show confidence or control of a situation, manipulate a handshake so that your hand is on top.

The Right Register: In business and other nonsexual situations, when power is an irrefutable asset, a deep voice shows confidence. Remember that long ago, people used low, growly bear tones to scare away wild predators and scavengers. (Now, that was confidence.) You don't want to scare your target away, but you do want to leave him with the impression that you're not afraid.

When interacting with the opposite sex for sexual or affectionate purposes, you can take your sexy pick: a pitch that's slightly lower than your norm, in imitation of a raspy, sensual voice like Demi Moore's, or your natural speaking voice. Either way it should be melodious, not curt and snappy. Avoid a tight, high-pitched tone that gives away your rattled nerves. When you're not confident in the words that are spewing forth from your mouth, your vocal cords will tighten, elevating the pitch of your voice. Therefore an insecure speaker will use the upper register of her voice, sending reliable cues that she's unsure of her own words and causing doubt to blossom in others' evaluations of her.

Find your head voice (nasal), your middle voice (between the nose and the throat), and your chest voice (feel the vibration in your chest). You can do this by humming a scale, starting with a high note and sliding down to the lowest note you're able to sing. Take note of the vibrations and how they move downward, into your chest. Practice duplicating that chest vibration with your speaking voice. Use it enough and it's likely to become your comfort zone.

Taking some deep, diaphragmatic breaths before speaking will calm your nervous system and help to relax those uptight cords.

You Are What You Wear

As Dana from the sitcom *According to Jim* attests, confidence starts from the outside in. Though seemingly shallow, this statement does carry some truth.

If you feel that you look good, others will pick up on that vibe and stop to take in the scenery. In a Finnish study published in 2009, researchers asked twenty-five women to exhibit neutral facial expressions while wearing different outfits that made them feel attractive, unattractive, or comfortable. When men were presented with the photographs, they almost always rated the faces of the women who were wearing nice clothing (as rated by the women themselves) as more attractive. Not surprised? What if I told you that the men couldn't see the clothing but saw only the faces? Now that's remarkable.

Even though we may perceive our own expressions to be neutral, underlying emotions still leak out—so we'd better make them good ones. Attractiveness increases your chances of interaction with everyone (not just men), and with every encounter, confidence will bloom.

Brake Application: If you're operating at a caffeinated pace, your demeanor exudes anything but confidence. Confident people move a bit slower than the speed limit, forcing others to decelerate in order to interact with them.

Walk into a room slowly. Pick up your drink and stir it with purpose. When you speak, allow every word to form on your lips, rather than crunching them all together like a verbal pileup on the highway.

Taking your time says, "What I have to say is worth waiting for." When you apply the brakes to your behavior, you will appear to be purposeful, content, and confident while in motion.

Face-Aching Smiles: A smile is the single most important thing you can do to build and convey real or faux confidence. It tells others that you're a joy to be with, that your outlook is positive and relatively problem-free, and that you have plenty of happiness to share with them.

Going back to mirror neurons, you can ask any psychologist about facial feedback and he or she will tell you that not only are facial expressions the products of emotions, but emotions can be affected by facial expressions. That means that by simply plastering a smile on your face, you can improve your mood and your outlook on your day and your life. In fact, research has shown that one smile does more for the human brain than $25,000 in cash or $2,000 worth of chocolate bars.

When you smile, allow it to slowly spread over your face (as opposed to making eye contact and "slapping" on a quick grin). This will be seen as more authentic. Tilt your head toward your target or in the same direction as someone you're talking to: this will increase the impact of that confident smile. Finally, don't forget to allow your smile to transform your entire face. Your lower eyelids should raise, your cheeks should elevate, and a generous portion of your teeth should show.

Remember to always buttress your new confident body language with a smile. Your face might begin to ache, but you'll find that your confidence has never felt better.

Body Watch: Smile at everyone you see in a single outing. Commit to counting the number of people who smile back.

Contagious Confidence: A study conducted by researchers at the University of California, San Diego, has shown that people who are near the center of social circles are happier. Furthermore, the happiest people spread their feel-good ways to their friends, as well as to friends of those friends.

Thanks to our mirror neurons' propensity for imitation, it seems that happiness and confidence have strong tendencies to go viral. Make confidence one of the factors you use to choose your friends. Imitate them. It will prove to be infectious.

Plaster Your Brain with a Smile

As far back as 1872, Charles Darwin introduced the idea of facial expressions intensifying emotions, and it appears that recent studies can find little fault with that hypothesis. At the University of Cardiff in Wales, psychologists studied twenty-five women, half of whom were injected with Botox, administered in a manner that decreased their abilities to frown. At the conclusion of the study, the women who couldn't frown reported having reduced levels of anxiety and increased feelings of happiness and well-being. They felt that their personal attractiveness levels remained constant, proving to researchers that their feel-good attitudes had nothing to do with enhanced beauty. Similar studies demonstrated that when pain was inflicted on subjects (in the form of heat), those who wore smiles rated the pain lower in intensity than those who wore frowns.

It's enough to make a person wonder: Is Botox popular because it affects the view in the mirror or because it transforms the outlook in the mind? No matter the reason, it seems that an act as simple as turning a frown upside down can turn a crummy emotional, social, or dating life on its head.

Body Watch: This is going to seem like a strange one, but just humor me. Grab the nearest pen or pencil and put it between your teeth (sideways, touching both corners of your mouth) and smile so that you're exposing as many teeth as possible. Hold this position until the end of the chapter.

Building confidence can be as simple as adding one confident body language demonstration to your repertoire every few days. Within a month you'll know how to walk into a room and make an impression that invites others to approach. Confidence is a highlighter. It draws attention to all of your best qualities. According to a recent study in *Journal of Personality and Social Psychology,* men find confident women more attractive than insecure ones. So, if you want to play to your market, which is, in general, men, you must give them what they're looking for.

Thinking about building confidence is about as effective as thinking about putting gas in your car or thinking about going to work. *Thinking* doesn't affect anything but your anxiety levels . . . for the worse. Instead you need to get *moving*. Get out there and put your new body language to work. Practice your new confident posture while smiling and talking with friends, waiters, and bank tellers. Walk everywhere, even to the bathroom or to get the mail, using your new stacked and upright saunter. Slow the speed with which you eat, talk, walk, and interact with pets, family, and friends. Practice making a confident entrance at a family dinner, then at a convenience store, then a restaurant, then a bar.

When the time comes to try out your new confident body language in a potential dating situation, your poise will have grown.

Remember the disheartening scenario presented at the beginning of the chapter? Now forget about it.

With your newfound confidence, you can walk into any venue and communicate self-assurance as effectively as if you were to hijack a podium and make this announcement: "I have an exciting and interesting life that I know you'll all want to be part of. There's no problem I can't shoulder—mostly due to the fact that I can't make myself stop smiling. What's that? You'd like to ask me out? Surely. The line forms here."

Your outward appearance will communicate what you feel inside, which will likely go something like this: *I am an amazing person. I have an interesting and enjoyable life. I have a lot to share and love to make friends. I'm confident in my abilities. I like the way I look. I smile because I can, because I want to, and because it makes me feel good. Join me, won't you?*

And you can do it all without uttering a single word.

Body Watch, cont'd.: Still have that pencil between your teeth? Still smiling? Feeling pleased, contented, happy, and amused? Studies have shown that when people place objects between their teeth and simulate a smile, life takes on a more lighthearted undertone. Why? Because the combination of the contrived smile and the muscle engagement enacted by the holding open of the teeth sends "happy" messages to the brain. This proves that you need not wait for outside influences to make you happy. Instead you can help yourself along by ensuring that you have plenty to smile about (or even by faking a few). The moral of this pencil tale? For a better and more confident outlook, smile if you're happy . . . and if you're not.

CHAPTER FOURTEEN

Talk Is Cheap . . .

AND THEREFORE A GOOD INVESTMENT

Define a good investment.

Is it a two-dollar lottery ticket that pays out millions?

A three-dollar-a-month life insurance policy that can never be canceled?

A sheriff's sale house that you can flip to triple your money?

Or might it be a no-cost exchange with another in which you connect your way to synchrony, rapport . . . and a first date?

Conversation, or the harmonized coordination of words, sound, and body language, offers such an investment. For no initial outlay other than time, we can build friendships, professional connections, and romantic relationships that span careers and lifetimes.

Are you in? Would you like to take advantage of this once-in-a-lifetime opportunity?

Let's talk.

Your body says more than your mouth. Along the timeline of evolution, speech postdated action, and therefore the subconscious mind was shaped to recognize the language of the body before the cognitive mind learned to create and decipher speech.

When you think of conversation, you might think of the exchange of words alone. While a friend recounts a conversation, you might ask her, "What did he say?" But maybe what you should ask is "How did he say it? What were his eyes doing when he said it? What did he emphasize? Was he leaning in?" That's because the subconscious mind makes the conscious mind look like a slacker (when it comes to conversation). Sure, words are important, but how they're spoken and the body language cues that accompany them make up the genuine basis of human interaction.

Let's embark upon a conversational journey that will empower you to make connections and gently control the direction of your psychological seduction.

A monotonous voice is an effective sleep aid. To hell with counting sheep; if you're feeling sleep-deprived, open a conversation with someone who uses no pitch changes when speaking. Not only is a droning voice boring, but it slows information absorption by up to 10 percent.

Pay attention to your pitch variances when you speak. If your natural speaking voice is low in timbre, highlight words that you'd like to emphasize with a higher pitch. Conversely, if you're a soprano, use deeper tones to stress words of significance.

For instance, "I can't believe he didn't win," when spoken with the *I* a few steps higher on your low vocal scale, will send the message that you recognize that others saw the contestant unworthy, but you were a fan. Likewise, if you deepen the word *win* from your typical high-pitched voice, you send the specific message that your greatest hope for him was to win.

Pay attention to the inflection that he uses, too. A statement as simple as "Your hat rocks" can take on three different meanings. "*Your* hat rocks" means that your friend's hat looks like roadkill. "Your *hat* rocks" hints that he can't say the same for the rest of your outfit. "Your hat *rocks*" means he's simply smitten with your headwear.

Pay attention to the inflection and pitch variances in his voice
to get a feel for what he is *really* saying. Practice using your own
voice variances. Convince yourself so that you can learn to convince others.

**Upspeak is the practice of raising intonation at the end
of a** statement, making it sound like a question. Though this can
become annoying if used in everyday conversation, as Michelle's
band-campitis voice in *American Pie* proves, it holds powerful connection potential if your conversation turns down a melancholy
road. Researchers have recently pinpointed a correlation between
people who use upspeak and those people's empathetic capabilities
(more upspeak equals more empathy). Similar to the type of voice
you might use to speak to your pet, it can be used in conversation to show compassion if he's talking about something painful
(followed by your steering of the conversation in a more positive
direction).

Watch his eye movements to determine the words you should
use. A person who looks up is a visual learner, to the side an auditory learner, and down a kinesthetic learner. By determining the
communicatory preferences of your target, you can use words that
appeal to his unique psychological operation. This will establish
rapport and prompt him to invite you into his conversational
circle more readily.

If he's visual, say things like "I can *see* where you're coming
from," "*Look* at this," and "From my *perspective* . . ."

If he's auditory, use phrases like "Have you *heard*?" "*Listen* to
this," and "I've been *told* . . ."

If he's kinesthetic (or tactile), say, "I *feel* like . . . ," "I'd love to
touch on that subject," and "I could *sense* something was going to
happen."

When you use words that speak to his natural information absorption pathways, your words will hold more connection power.

Body Watch: Want to know if he's being truthful? Ask him a few innocuous questions and pay close attention to the direction his eyes point when he's calling up his answers. "How many years have you played soccer?" "Can you remember the name of your kindergarten teacher?" or "You have long fingers . . . any pianists in the family?" will work. Now, ask him the bombshell and watch to see if he looks up in the same direction. If he doesn't, he's probably being untruthful to some degree.

This man is innocently remembering a detail from his past. If he looks up to his right when you ask him the next question, he's probably being untruthful. If he looks to his left (as he is here), he's credible.

Caveat: Unless you've undergone interrogation training or have already baselined the eye movement behavior of your target with consistency, this method could easily be spoiled. For instance, if the person has to reach into his imagination to create a picture of his kindergarten teacher, his eyes might move in a direction that seems to indicate deceptiveness—when actually, he's just trying to paint a mental image of her using the creative part (also the lying part) of his brain. This is a fun tool that can be used to support your perceptions of a man, but should not be used alone, in situations of a serious nature, or on a man whom you haven't yet baselined.

The icebreaker has evolved—and continues to evolve—from the cheesy pickup line to a statement that's relatively neutral, requires a response, and uses mutual experiences to create connections. Try talking about things you're both simultaneously undergoing. This will draw you into a mutual experience, even before his response is delivered. "Did you see the size of that bouncer?" "I love this song," or "It's a little hot in here, don't you think?" will give him the opportunity to answer easily with his opinion or observation.

If you've been on the sidelines of his conversations with others, and have been able to determine his visual, auditory, or tactile cue preference, use that knowledge to tailor an icebreaker to his unique inclinations. If you find it difficult to think on your feet, plan some open-ended statements in advance. To avoid sounding like an actress in a B movie, plan your phrases, but don't use canned speech that's overrehearsed.

Note the nature of his response. If it's gentle, singsongy, and melodic, accompanied by eye contact, you may continue. If it's curt and obligatory, accompanied by a cold shoulder or the stiffening of his body, retreat.

GENDER ENLIGHTENMENT: Typically, the more powerful of two conversing people will hold eye contact while speaking. As a woman, make sure that when you have the figurative podium you maintain eye contact in order to convey confidence.

Choose his ear wisely. If you're speaking to a man about business or other sensible matters, speak into his right ear. But if you're trying to making an emotional impression, or brand him with your charm, appeal directly to his left ear. Not only does the left ear feed to the right brain, which houses his emotional centers; the left ear is also more capable of delivering cues about intonation and speech nuances to his creative and expressive side.

Researchers from UCLA and the University of Arizona tested the ears of three thousand newborns over a six-year period and came to one startling conclusion: the right ear is specially designed to hear short, curt sounds like words (logic and literal meanings) while the left ear is particularly sensitive to the musicality of tones (intonation, inflection, and other subtleties of paralanguage). Different types of sounds are amplified and converted to vibrations in each ear, making it evident, if not undeniable, that each ear holds its own specialty.

If you're having lunch with a business associate, you'd do best to sit to his right while delivering the fiscal year's numbers. But if you're out to dinner with a promising personal prospect, I'd suggest that you position yourself to his left. His body will feel the underlying meaning of your words before his brain has a chance to deconstruct their literal definitions.

Body Watch: It can be difficult to get your point across in a noisy room or in a crowded bar with music blaring, so opt for his right ear—at least until you can get to a quieter venue, where you should shift to his left.

Studies have shown that in noisy environments, humans generally offer their right ear for listening, while brain scans show the greatest amount of neural firing in the left brain (connected to the right ear) when listeners are required to pick a voice from a noisy background.

Shifting from subject to subject is something good friends do effortlessly, and it's also a tactic that you can use to make conversation flow more easily.

Often two friends might chatter back and forth, jumping from astrological signs to favorite pastas to the best way to fold fitted sheets. The eavesdropper's head might spin, but the friends know that a common conversational thread flows through all of their subjects. Sometimes the end of the conversation will in no way resemble the subject matter of the beginning, and at other times the conversation will come full circle, with the beginning and the ending sharing common subject matter.

A piece of a conversation between friends that's well-sewn with common threads, but ends in a different place than it started, might go something like this:

"Quick—turn on channel three. George Clooney is giving an interview."

"Oh my gosh. Look at him."

"I'm looking. And check out Barbara's jacket. She always looks so cute."

"And what's her hair color? Platinum?"

"I'd say more like ash."

"I've got to do something with my hair. My love affair with red is o-v-e-r."

"I'd try plum. Don't go blond . . ."

"Why not? It's my natural color."

"Yeah, when you were three."

This conversation started at George and ended up in childhood. However, the common thread is the observation of a television program. It flows easily from topic to topic because there's no mechanical finishing of subjects or perfunctory initiation of new ones. One topic segues right into the next, without uncomfortable silences or panic-stricken moments of *what do I say next?*

Other friendly conversations will come full circle. When the common thread is retrieved, everything is pulled together like a novel's plot:

"Did you see those boots she was wearing?"

"Yeah, I tried to get them in red but Foster's was sold out—they're not expecting another shipment for three weeks."

"I was over there this morning looking for new tennis shoes. The owner said there's a new restaurant going in next door. Moroccan, I think."

"Ooh, where's Morocco?"

"The top of Africa, near Europe."

"That reminds me: did you get those Sting tickets yet?"

"Let me do that now. I'll bet I can have those boots in time for the concert."

The common thread here? Boots. This conversation could have easily started and ended with one statement about footwear, making it a virtual "nonversation," but instead a willingness to stray from the given subject contributes to its meatiness and keeps the participants' interest piqued. This conversation will likely move on to other subjects, and might continue for hours without either speaker giving much regard to the passage of time.

When you find yourself on the cusp of conversation with a man, don't handcuff yourself into the opening subject. Be willingly fluid, like this:

"Did you catch that Jets game?"

"What a nail-biter—but they pulled through."

"You like football?"

"As long as *Modern Family* or *Friends* reruns aren't on."

"No kidding. That kid . . . what's his name?"

"Manny or Joey?"

"Hah! That's funny. Joey is such a preschooler."

"Can you imagine a soap opera director putting up with him?"

"No. I can't . . . and I'm a director."

"Really? I'm a marketing director." [*laughter*]

"Would you like a drink?"

From Jets to drinks, this conversation flows easily from one topic to the next. Don't wait for one subject to be entirely closed to introduce another; you'll easily fall victim to the awkward silence. Instead introduce a related thought while the previous one still has life in it. Remember, if you beat a conversation to death, you'll be left with nonversation.

GENDER ENLIGHTENMENT: Women enjoy face-to-face approaches, but men (thanks to their evolutionary roles) view a frontal approach as confrontational. For this reason, early conversation should be conducted from his side. If he's sitting, don't take a seat across from him, but take one beside him at the bar or perpendicular to him at a table. Walking alongside him is also a good way to remain unthreatening.

Establish a positive air by eliciting the word *yes* from him. By asking questions to which the answer must be positive, you will enrapture him in a Yes Set, or a series of yeses in a row, and covertly cajole him into declaring the most important *yes* (aloud or silently).

A Yes Set is simple to enact, once you know how one looks. "Is this the line for drinks?" when you already know it is; "Isn't this weather gorgeous?" when it's sunny and warm; and "Will you please pass that menu?" when it's sitting within his reach are all simple ways to get him on a yes roll. Every time he says "Yes" or a similar affirmative, his level of optimism—and his receptivity to what you want—will increase. By the time you ask the all-important question(s) he'll feel compelled to keep the *yes* train in motion. Salespeople use this tactic to get the answers they want, and so can you.

Body Watch: Match your blink and breathing rates to his and you'll be furthering your efforts to synchronize conversation and mutual attraction.

Use words that evoke different positive feelings in different people and you'll hit your mark with Tom, Dick, *and* Harry. Nominalizations are words colored by personal life experiences and therefore can be interpreted differently by each of us. To a single woman who has worked all week at the office, *tranquility* might make her think of lighting a candle, doing some yoga, and meditating. For a stay-at-home mom, it might be the thought of the few moments after she gets the kids off to school.

Words like *wonderful* mean one thing to me, another thing to you, and yet another thing to the hottie you're attempting to captivate with conversation. Using words like *beautiful, comfortable, friendly, respect,* or *communication* can be hypnotic. They force someone to focus inward and find their own definition, which allows you to slip into their world more easily. Speak about a relaxing day, breathtaking scenery, or an exciting trip and you'll not only take his subconscious to places that relax him, take his breath away, and excite him; you'll move yourself to a similar category.

Knowing when to take your turn will help you to avoid rude interruptions, that uncomfortable feeling of "disconnect," awkward mouth battles, and profuse, mood-altering dialogue: "You go," "No, you go," "No, really, what were you going to say?"

If the speaker ends a phrase with a heightened pitch, this usually invites a reply. Imagine a man asking, "Are you hungry?" with the "gry" holding a slightly higher tone than the rest of the statement. Even if it weren't a question, the higher ending pitch should compel you to speak. You can also give him "permission" to speak by utilizing this strategy.

Most of us speak with accompanying hand gestures. When the speaker's gestures begin to decline in intensity, he's considering a corresponding drop-off in speech. If those gestures are on the upswing, keep your trap sealed . . . he's going to be talking for a while.

Recognize when he's finished speaking; there will be a lull in speech and action. This is his method for showing you that he's ready to hand over the podium.

GENDER ENLIGHTENMENT: As mentioned in chapter 8, dominant men generally prefer women who are agreeable and non-dominant-acting. By nodding slowly while he speaks, you send the message that you agree with what he's saying. This feeds his need to lead and to be right and will shine a favorable light on you. You don't have to concede to his views, only show him that you're understanding and appreciating his statements.

Of course this approach might keep you on the bottom rung of the corporate ladder, but when you're embarking upon a flirtatious journey, appealing to a man's primal mind will help you to tap into one of the oldest forms of attraction. Showing vulnerability doesn't always suggest that you're a weak person . . . in fact, when used intelligently, it can put you in a position of power.

Eating finger foods feeds more than your belly; it feeds conversation. Because the areas of the brain that are responsible for speech and finger movements are adjacent to each other, picking from the snack table both encourages and prolongs conversation.

Their conversation will be aided by the eating of finger foods.

"Thatza Spicy Meatzaball"

Want to enhance conversation and spark attraction? Hang out by the spicy meatballs and hot wings.

A desire for meat is deeply rooted in our subconscious and bonds us when we are eating it. When you gather round the wings, it's like being back around the communal fire. By eating meat together, it seems that humans enliven ancient pathways of survival . . . through nourishment and arousal.

Spicy foods spark feelings of danger (that's their evolutionary defense against being eaten), and fear increases adrenaline, which ignites attraction. Additionally, the capsaicin in hot peppers has an effect on the brain similar to that of opium—pure pleasure.

If you're hosting a party, keep the staples of meat and spice in mind (and don't forget the chocolate-covered strawberries and oysters). If you're a guest, take the opportunity to bring a covered dish that holds the potential to aid passionate, spicy exchanges.

Large spaces are more conducive to starting conversation because they make escape easy. People don't like to feel trapped (even by confident, sexy women), and if you can eliminate that possibility, you can get a better reading on his willingness to converse with you.

Nightclubs, malls, and markets offer plenty of directions to run, and are therefore more conducive to comfortable, escapable, voluntary conversation. A tiny café or the line for the tanning booth isn't going to be as relaxed an environment. Keeping this in mind can help you choose venues that support good exchanges, as well as recognize potential signals of nervousness before disregarding a conversation as a nonversation.

Body Watch: If he's rubbing his neck with fervor, seeming to silently wish for an on-site masseuse, your conversation is probably stressing him out. You're quite literally a pain in his neck.

Additionally, there's a type of ear touching that bids you to back off. If you're conversing with a man and he's pulling on his ear, as if he'd like to remove it from his head, he's indifferent, bored, or wishing he didn't have to bear the fate of listening to you. He's pissed off. He's wishing for silence.

This man is stressed by what he's hearing, and doesn't want it to continue.

Use varying facial expressions to demonstrate that you're listening to his words. Change your expression as you speak, too. Not only will your varying visages draw him into your emotional world; they will help to modify and alter the tones of your voice to match the tone of the conversation.

Hand gestures are invaluable parts of conversation. Besides drawing others into our worlds and working to get our points across, they help us to organize our own thoughts. Often a thought can seem too abstract to grasp, not only for the listener, but for the speaker, but by employing motion, you can literally bring your thoughts into action . . . and words.

Body Watch: If he's using a chopping motion, particularly chopping with his dominant hand, he's showing emphasis about something that is überimportant to him. You can enter his world by combining verbal, auditory, or tactile (his preference) speech with words that relate to his passion.

A verbal matchup will build rapport and make conversation seem to flow easily and comfortably. If the object of your desire is speaking slowly, try to match his tempo. If he's speaking loudly, turn up your own volume. If he uses intellectual phrases with sharp, enunciated words, do your best to squelch your home-fry accent in favor of open vowels, crisp consonants, and words that include all the syllables their creators meant them to have.

If you're not confident in the way that you speak, practice. Listen to a disc jockey or a newscaster who has no discernible regional accent, imitate her, and record yourself to track your progress. Recording yourself, though shocking to the ear, can be a real eye-opener, as it will give you the opportunity to hear yourself as others do. Critiquing your own manner of speaking can help you to make necessary corrections as well as to perfect what you're already doing well.

People who are underconfident in their manner of speech will often have difficulty gaining the confidence of others. Keep in mind that the premise is not to fake a voice, to put up a deceptive front, or to make him believe you're someone you're not. Sure, we're all presenting the best foot when dating, but exercises that improve speech will stick with you and benefit you in all areas of life—personal and professional—into the future.

Pauses are normal parts of good conversation. In fact, a half-second silence between phrases is normal and expected. Inserting fillers like *um* detracts from perceptions of your confidence.

Pregnant, or suspenseful, pauses are powerful tools for ejecting *ah*s, *um*s, and *er*s from conversation. By inserting a pregnant pause (longer than the typical half second), you'll be giving yourself a few extra seconds to collect your thoughts. These pauses also give you the opportunity to demonstrate your comfort with silence and the confidence that it takes to be quiet and relaxed in your own skin while others wait.

Practice speaking without fillers and your phrases will naturally begin to connect to each other in a more fluid manner.

Body Watch: If you wonder if you've taken control of the conversation and his interest, simply pick up a glass or scratch the side of your face. Give him five to thirty seconds to perform a similar movement. If he does, you've got him under your spell.

Some of us talk more than others. Just as some dogs are barkers, some are whiners, and some howl, people engage in different levels of chattering. Women usually speak more than men, but within each gender category are wide variances.

Motorboat talking doesn't make you a great conversationalist. In fact, it may affect your credibility and the enduring attention that you score. On the plus side, you have the innate opportunity to convey *all* of your ideas and to easily fill in awkward silences.

For those of you who hover just above chronic silence, you have a noted advantage: you can display cues of active listening, which make the more talkative person feel valued. When you finally do say something, everybody stand back . . . it's going to be earth-shattering. This is the quiet person's power.

Storytelling evokes emotion and forges bonds. Have an arsenal of ten funny, touching, and triumphant stories ready to further the conversation. Each should be able to be told in both ninety-second short form and four-minute long form, depending on your time constraints, and should be based on your personal experiences. Stories that tell of an embarrassing situation or a seemingly insurmountable obstacle (real or figurative) work to show that you're comfortable with your own humanity but also resilient enough to pull out of problematic scenarios with a positive attitude. Maybe you were stranded in Sicily and convinced a cranky shopkeeper (in broken Italian) to drive you to the airport. Maybe your basement flooded, leading you to spend two weeks living amid makeshift drying racks for all of your precious collectibles. Tone down the fool factor, though. Your girlfriends will appreciate the story about your klutz-trip down the subway stairs, but a man might view this as ditzy and write you off as a one-night stand or a no-go.

Your stories should allow your listener enough freedom to establish an opinion about you. Don't tell him that you're reliable; tell him a funny story about delivering flower arrangements during a Valentine's Day blizzard. Don't brag about your career success; instead recount a tale about three of your clients making friends with one another in your waiting room.

Knowing your stories before going out will give you plenty of material to fall back on. Weave them into conversation when common threads emerge (or use them to start conversation). Feel free to tweak them to fit the situation, or the emotional tone, at hand.

Practice recounting your stories. Record yourself telling them. Ask yourself if you're entertaining and if the stories will make others want to know more about you. Remember, plan them but don't memorize them word for word. A boring story that sounds as if it's being told for the hundredth time is a catalyst for comatose nonversation.

Starting conversation can bring on panic-level feelings in the shiest of singles. However, it's imperative that everyone remember that conversation, especially during the initial phases of attraction, is less about what you say and more about how you say it.

In order to make the icebreaker and subsequent getting-to-know-him talk more comfortable, practice being more attentive when others are speaking, use inflection in your voice to make it more interesting, and look for cues that it's your turn to talk. Use planned, not canned, phrases as openers. Maintain a positive air and remember to smile. Have those ten motivational, funny, or endearing stories ready to tell. Peruse the newspaper daily and stay abreast of subjects that aren't politically or religiously charged— then if conversation stumbles, you'll have a soft, current-event place to fall.

Conversation is essential as a direct follow-up to initial physical attraction. Without it, psychological connections, which are invaluable in human interactions, cannot be forged. For the minimal investment of some well-timed and well-executed conversation, you can welcome people into your world (and it won't be long before they extend their own invitations). You can turn the visceral reaction that drew you and Mr. Marvelous together into something real. You can collect a full return, with benefits.

I'm glad we've had this talk.

CHAPTER FIFTEEN

Touch 'n' Go

USING PHYSICAL CONTACT TO PUT
FLIRTING IN FORWARD MOTION

"Touch me." "Hold me." "Feel me."

How do you react to those phrases? Are you flooded with romantic feelings? Do you suddenly want to snuggle with the nearest warm body?

For most, the feeling will be one of happiness or contentedness, but for a small portion of the population, there will be feelings of discomfort, stress, and even nausea at the mere utterance of the words *touch, hold,* or *feel.*

Touch carries different associations for different people, and a lot of the variance is a result of our childhood experiences. If your parents held you often as a baby, cuddled you regularly, kissed you through adulthood, and used hugs to greet you and to say good-bye, you probably equate touch with affection and welcome it. Conversely, if you grew up with little physical contact, if touching was considered to be a religious or cultural taboo, or if the physical contact you did receive was demeaning or unpleasant, the mere thought of other people touching you (and you touching other people) can spark some pretty uncomfortable feelings. The need to be touched doesn't expire as we grow and age, but our comfort levels with it will vary from person to person, depending largely on our childhood conditioning.

If you're comfortable with touching, the concept of flirting with physical contact will probably come naturally to you; you're already well practiced. People who like to touch have plenty of experience doing so. However, it's important to understand that not everyone enjoys that level of touching ease. There will be times when we touch a person and feel them recoil, flinch, or pull away. At these moments, we hold the unique opportunity to build rapport by displaying sensitivity to it and curbing tactile contact. Touchers also have the opportunity to literally feel receptivity from others. When the one being touched smiles, leans in, or even touches back, the toucher has permission to flirt and build rapport by traveling along infancy-established pathways.

But what if you don't like to touch others? It's simple: you're missing out on building rapport, controlling the speed and direction of dating encounters, and enjoying touch and its happy-hormone-releasing power. There's no doubt that you're losing out. But before you chalk up your dislike of touching as a dating death sentence, understand that with practice you, too, can learn to melt under the heat of touch.

Humans need touch. From the moment we're born, we crave touch. It builds brain matter. A lack of it is invariably detrimental to a human's psyche and general well-being.

Cases have been documented in which orphans who have been virtually abandoned in their cribs have suffered physical and neurological delinquencies. Without touch, a baby's system falls victim to the symptoms of overactive adrenal glands, resulting in elevated levels of cortisol and other stress hormones. Neuropsychologist James W. Prescott found evidence that the most violent of societies are also the most affectionate-touch-deprived.

So why is touching so difficult for so many? I believe there are a couple of reasons why touch seems to be slipping out of our

fingers. First, there's a psychological camp out there that recom-
mends allowing crying babies to self-soothe . . . so parents avoid
spoiling them with too much holding. Millennia ago, while evolution was busy fashioning human bodies and minds that require
touch with more intensity than any other interaction, mothers
were holding and nursing their babies more often than is customary today. There were no baby carriages, car seats, jumpers,
baby swings . . . instead mothers carried their babies with them.
Second, our cyber society is moving in the direction of tweeting
tweeple over touching people, detracting from the power and
frequency of human-to-human tactile interaction.

Touch is a proficient tool for establishing bonds that last much
longer than simple verbal exchanges. Increasing your daily level of
touch can help you spark new relationships, build more enduring
friendships, enjoy better sex, and create dynamic, confident, and
lasting relationships.

Let's discuss the many ways we can use touch in order to build
rapport and make better connections. Even if the idea of touch
makes your skin cower in fear, there's no reason you can't grow
to enjoy it and to deliver it with confidence. But you're going to
have to break the boundaries of your comfort zone in order to
move into a more touchable place. Remember, we all, at the cores
of our most primitive neurological pathways, crave touch. It's just
that some of us have learned to exist without it.

Start small. Briefly touch the hands and forearms of friends
while interacting with them. Cuddle with and hold a niece or
nephew in your arms, even if that's not your typical way of interacting with them. Shake hands. Hug. Pay attention to how
touch strengthens bonds with those you already love. Take note
of the sensations that light, medium, and heavy touches generate
in you—and concentrate your attention on the one that elicits
the most pleasurable response. Women are more sensitive and responsive than men to feather-light touching, and you'll probably
connect this type of touch with sensuality.

The first touch can be the most unnerving, but no matter
where you fall along the spectrum of touch enjoyment, these

touching tactics can transform your flirting from standard to spectacular:

The Touch-Yourself: As discussed earlier, this is a clear sign of sexual interest. If you want him to touch you, touch yourself. By self-stimulating your face, ears, and neck or stroking your arm, you're sending a clear signal of your need to be touched. Likewise, if he's touching himself, you're being invited to do the same.

The Prophecy of Touch: Performing actions that typically come before touch will indicate your desire to touch as well as test his receptivity to the idea. Commonly referred to as intention cues, pushing your hand into his personal space, stretching your legs toward him, and increasing animation with your hands so they come closer to him are all effective ways to prophesy touch.

Their hands are so close that touch is practically inevitable.

Touch Through Association: If you feel that it's too soon to touch, or you're not sure what his receptivity will be, you can touch through association. Pass a bowl of peanuts to him. Hand over your cell phone so he can look at a funny picture. An eager acceptance of the object will tell you of his receptiveness to a real touch.

We all instinctively know that when someone touches something, they leave skin oils, bacteria, and pheromones on the object (hence our fear of public restrooms and phones). Passing an object to the target of your affection gives you a perfect excuse to exchange an almost-touch or an accidental touch.

A Good Excuse: Lay a palm on his back to gently nudge him from your path. Accompany it with a low and slow "Excuse me."

Most men will turn to see who's moving them. This is a beautiful thing, in that you've taken care of the eye contact that's so very necessary for establishing human connections. After you get to your destination, look back at him. My money is on a second ocular lock.

The Deliberate Accident: Oops! You both reached for the same napkin and brushed hands. You bumped into him while shakin' your funmaker under the disco ball. You grazed his finger while reaching for the pen he was extending toward you.

Accidental? In his estimation, yes. Effective? Extremely.

Body Watch: If you feel that you're on the receiving end of the Deliberate Accident touch, watch his reaction just after his skin meets yours. If he flinches, draws back, or blushes, it probably was an authentic accident, rather than an indicator of sexual interest.

Trip His Breaker: If you're not sure of his touch receptivity, or if you're too shy to touch him with your entire hand, start with a slight fingertip touch or brush. The electric shock might astonish both of you.

The Aloof Touch: In chapter 12, we discussed the pickup tactic of mixing interested and uninterested signals to keep the target in hot pursuit. If you touch him during stints of feigned indifference, that play will seem less invasive. However, sparks will still fly freely.

Admire His Piece: Often a timepiece will be the only jewelry a man wears. You can feign interest in its design or the time it tells, but either way, you've got a perfect excuse for gently grasping his wrist and turning his watch's face toward yours.

GENDER ENLIGHTENMENT: Studies have shown that the gender that most actively avoids same-sex touching is male. In other words, a man is more likely to pursue touch when a woman is involved (especially one he's sexually interested in). Conversely, women are more likely to avoid touch with the opposite sex. This translates to women usually being more comfortable with touching a female acquaintance than a male acquaintance.

This information can be beneficial for you if you play it right. When you first meet a man, touch him. This not only speaks to his preferences; it tells him that you're willing to break away from the norm in order to show interest in him.

Classic Combos: Like peanut butter with jelly or macaroni with cheese, there are types of conversations that are best served alongside touch. If you employ touch while articulating worry, giving advice or information, asking for something, expressing excitement, or pleading a case, or while speaking in a deep, emotionally engrossing conversation, touch will be most natural. However, if you're listening to his words of advice, persuasion, etc., it will seem more natural for you to receive touch than to serve it up. When in doubt, you can simply remember to touch him when you want him to "feel."

Strokes of Amusement: In order to start the touch ball rolling without the awkwardness of affectionate contact, you can use playful touch. Pick up a lively game of thumb wrestling, offer kudos with high-fives, conduct a mock attack, or show off your worldwide handshake fluency. Now slipping into more sensual touching won't be so unnerving.

The fist bump is a fun way to initiate touch.

You First: The person who is the most interested will touch (or want to touch) first. Both the toucher and the touched realize this. Therefore if you can get him to "initiate" contact first, he might be surprised and encouraged by his own display of attraction. Ask him to check the clasp on your necklace or lament that you just can't get a handle on the pool cue. If he jumps in to help, you've probably just given him the touching excuse he's been looking for. Of course a slight tease with a sprinkling of almost-touches will excite him and make him want to touch you more.

Nontoxic Contact: It may be tempting to touch his shoulder, but because the shoulders are so emotive, sharing direct connections to the brain's emotional center, this could be too much, too soon. Instead opt for the back of the hand or the front of the arm. The underside of the arm is far too sensitive to touch during early stages. An attempt to touch the face or the head will likely result in flinching or rapid retreat—this is just too threatening early on.

Involuntary Connections: You might be the type of person who touches others without realizing it. You might be talking about deviled eggs, stock fluctuations, the weather . . . and touch him innocuously, as if tactile contact is a part of your everyday dealings. This makes you approachable and sends signals of interest. This is why women who are habitual touchers are often considered to be shameless flirts, even if they're not.

I touch almost everyone I speak to, and this has caused some romantic confusion in the past. I've had to remind myself, often, to only touch people to whom I want to send messages of interest. You see, especially for men, touching means interest—even if the contact is socially acceptable and seemingly habitual.

Talk as usual, but employ ever-so-slight touching. Be careful not to follow your hands with your eyes—this could make your touching seem intentional and blow your involuntary cover.

GENDER ENLIGHTENMENT: If you don't like him, don't touch him. Men have difficulty differentiating between flirting and friendliness, usually erring on the side of the sexier. For this reason, men view most touching as a sign of sexual interest.

This man views the toucher as the most interested of all the women. She's also the most likely to be romantically available because the others have deferred the center of attention to her.

The Fresh Squeeze: If you're feeling confident or if you'd like to try a bit of bold and spicy flirting while interactions with your target are still green, lay your entire hand, fingers spread, on his forearm or biceps (depending on whether he's sitting or standing), and deliver a slight squeeze and an innocuous comment like "How 'bout those Jets?" "Have you heard there's a thirteenth astrological sign?" or "What's better here—the wings or the nachos?"

Though it should not be used as an icebreaker, this type of touching is just forward enough to say *I like you* without being pushy or brimming with desperation.

Shake Him Up, Baby

Handshakes aren't tainted by taboo and they offer stellar opportunities for us to gauge another's intentions. The handshake is typically the first physical contact connection you share with another person and it can be electrifying. Make it common practice to extend your hand to every man you meet. The information that you gather will give you insight into his interest level, besides putting that all-important first touch under your belt.

A limp handshake usually indicates a lackadaisical attitude, but it can also point toward a disregard of your polite advance or a hand-necessary career like that of a pianist, surgeon, or tennis player.

If he grasps your hand willingly, places his hand higher in space than yours, or pulls you toward him as he clutches your hand, he's demonstrating dominance. Since dominant people use touch to manipulate situations, you can expect subsequent touching from him if he's interested in deeper interactions of some sort.

If his hand is on the bottom of a handshake, you've either taken the dominant role or he's showing no harm with a display of submission.

If he uses both of his hands to shake yours (one against your palm and one against the back of your hand), this is a signal of dominance and liking and he's got some serious interest boiling up for you. With this handshake, it becomes abundantly obvious that he wants to touch as much of you as a handshake will allow.

Another handshake that shows interest, even affection, is often perceived as a modified hug. If he shakes your hand with enthusiasm, gently squeezing, or makes extended contact while touching your upper arm with his other hand, he's taking this greeting opportunity to telegraph his curiosity.

Sometimes the effort he expends to get to your hand gives clues to his level of interest. If he moves his body from behind a table or other obstruction in order to come into your space, he wants to make your first touch memorable. Conversely, if he stretches his arm over objects or keeps his feet planted instead of taking a step toward you for the handshake, he's apathetic or trying to avoid showing effort. If he doesn't stand up to shake your hand, he's either suffering from etiquette ignorance or he can't justify expending the energy on someone he's not interested in.

Though sweaty palms and cold hands worry the shaker and gross out or freeze out the shaked, they matter less than the nature of the shake itself. If you're worried about sweaty palms, apply anti-perspirant or run cold water over your wrists. If your hands are cold, excuse yourself with a comment like "Cold hands, warm heart." Don't use your fingertips alone, a weak or limp hand, or a bone-crunching squeeze. A handshake should rattle his nervous system, not jostle his joints. The full arm shake is in bad taste and will be memorable for all the wrong reasons.

She's interested in the man she's extending her hand to. She's smiling with her entire face, her thumbs are in positions of power, and she's pointing to her genitals.

Left of Center: You'll remember from chapter 6 that pleas to his emotional brain should be directed to his left eye. Likewise, if you want to appeal to his memories, senses, and emotions, touch his left hand or forearm. This rule applies to the majority of the population because they are right-handed. The left-handed hunk might respond better to touches on his right side; however, the brain of a southpaw isn't as reliably split as that of a northpaw (I can say that because my children and I are all lefties). You can either choose to always default to touching on the left, or you can run a few field experiments (direct appeals to his right and his left to see which yields better results) to determine if your target is a rule-abider or a rule-breaker in the brain division department.

Is It a Bear Hug or a "Get Bare" Hug?

Your great-uncle Henry grasps your shoulders, presses his upper body against yours, and pats your back just before he stuffs you full of Slim Jims and sassafras.

At your high school reunion an old friend throws his arm around your shoulders, positions you so you're standing hip to hip with him, and asks the DJ to snap a photograph.

A man you're dancing with hugs you tight against him. His arms are low on your waist. Your pelvises and groins are separated by nothing but cotton and socially acceptable conduct.

Hugs are not created equally and you can read someone's intentions in the way that they embrace you. The three examples presented above progress from simply friendly to sexual in nature.

When two people's pelvises are kept far apart and arms and hands are high, the hug is friendly, at best. If a side hug isn't prefaced with or followed by a more intimate embrace, it is simply friendly or being used as a first, socially acceptable

High arms and the distance between the groins of this man and woman tell of friendship, not intimacy.

There are probably no romantic feelings within this group; hands and arms are high in a side hug.

Low arms and pelvic contact speak of this couple's mutual attraction.

touch. Conversely, hugs in which the arms are low on the back or around the waist and full body contact is used are more intimate and hint at intense sexual interest or established intimacy.

While hugging the hottie you're dying to touch, don't make the mistake of grabbing him and pressing your loins against his . . . unless, of course, you'd like to go from hug to hookup in record time. Instead start with an acquaintance hug and only increase intensity with his body's compliance. If his body stiffens or resists, end the embrace before you blow your chances at making him your main squeeze.

Body Watch: If you're hugging a man and he pats you on the back, you should separate faster than Emeril's eggs and move on. Just as a mother calms her crying child or a distraught friend with a pat on the back, he's attempting to calm your desire for him with a consolatory gesture.

How Touch Gets the "Jobs" Done

When two people who are attracted to each other begin touching, the sexual-destination progression that follows usually adheres to a specific formula—so says zoologist Desmond Morris. Though one or two steps may be glossed over, the completion of each leads to one or more "jobs" being completed and some serious "headway" being made.

The sequence is generally as follows:

1. Eye to body
2. Eye to eye
3. Voice to voice
4. Hand to hand
5. Arm around shoulder
6. Arm around waist
7. Mouth to mouth
8. Hand to head
9. Hand to body
10. Mouth to breast
11. Hand to genitals
12. Genitals to genitals and/or mouth to genitals

As a woman, you have a distinct advantage when using touch. Most humans have been held, cared for, and fed by mothers. Yes, fathers' roles in the raising of children are intensifying, but the mother is still, and probably always will be, the primary caretaker of infants.

When you touch a man, you hold a persuasive power that's unique to women. Researchers believe that a woman's touch profoundly affects people because it calls up memories of a mother's comforting touch. When psychologists assessed willingness to take financial risks, they found that people were more likely to gamble more or spend more freely after they'd been touched by a woman. Handshakes from women were effective, but a touch on the back elicited even more lucrative results. When men touched the participants, no effect was documented.

It seems that whether you're selling lottery tickets or time with you, a touch can go a long way in persuading him.

Controlling with touch is a valuable tool in flirting and dating. But first you must define your own intentions. If he's receptive to it, and your first order of business is to get to know him horizontally, you can steer him straight from the nightclub to the bedroom. But most of the time, controlling with touch has less to do with steering him toward the girly bits and more to do with steering him toward the romance we crave.

Powerful people touch. This is evident in social circles and in professional settings. A CEO feels free to put a hand on a receptionist's shoulder while he asks for his calls to be forwarded, but that receptionist wouldn't dare walk into the boss's office and do the same while asking for a raise. But the fact that touch signifies power doesn't mean that you have to use that power to dominate . . . you can use it subtly to send a message that you want to be dominated. In short, when you touch, you're telling him that you're not afraid of him.

> GENDER ENLIGHTENMENT: Location and context are integral parts of sending touch messages. When you extend your hand to a male business associate at a conference, you're taking professional power by making the first move. If you offer a man your hand in a social setting, you're indicating interest by throwing him for a contextual loop.

The first touch is memorable because it establishes who is experiencing the strongest feelings of attraction or who is most dominant (remember to hold eye contact while you shake his hand). The news for flirting women couldn't be better. Men rarely balk at being touched. Women generally love to touch. Perfect arrangement? At least.

Depending on your comfort level and your forward or shy nature, you can choose to deliver the first touch or to orchestrate a scenario in which you receive it.

Body Watch: Be sensitive to his comfort with touch. If you lay a hand on him and he flinches, pulls away, feels as if he's shrinking, doesn't reciprocate, or becomes rigid, assess whether other body language cues support a lack of interest, or if he's simply shy about physical contact. If he's still smiling and his body language is open, you may continue the interaction, but with a slower entry into the touching phase.

You can use touch to anchor and induce positive feelings in him by waiting until he's talking about something that brings him joy. Touch him and articulate your understanding of his happiness. This will give your touch a positive association for future interactions, giving you the power to conjure those same positive feelings in him with touch.

By the way, it works for excitement and sexual arousal, too.

A large portion of human touching is done on a subconscious level. An onlooker will recognize flirting touch, but the touchers might not even realize what's happening. This is great news for flirters and proof of how natural touch is meant to be. However, there's no harm in using cunningly placed touch to accelerate or accentuate your bonding experiences with men.

Touching can be touchy. For some it's easy and comes naturally. Others feel that without outward signs from a man, they risk their touch being rejected. Social proof helps as well. Remember that the toucher is always dominant. Even if the touch is rejected the toucher still has the "upper hand."

No matter what number on the attraction scale you have assigned to yourself, keep in mind that attractiveness isn't just about physical beauty: it's about working a room, displaying confidence, and being receptive to the advances of others. By now you should be familiar with how to read signs of interest from a man and how to determine if he'll be receptive to your touch. Use it. Shake what your momma gave you: an ability to persuade, flirt, and take seductive control with touch.

CHAPTER SIXTEEN

Mr. Right-Under-Your-Nose

THE POWER OF UNCONSCIOUS SCENT—
THE OLDEST MATCHMAKER ON EARTH

You walk into a crowded club. It seems that you can't move two feet without bumping into someone—and you're not complaining. One of your first collisions is with a gorgeous specimen: coal-black hair, piercing blue eyes, a smile that could melt even the coldest woman's heart . . . and he seems overjoyed at the surprise contact.

"Hi, I'm Matt." He extends his hand. It's warm. He holds your hand and your gaze for a few beats. He wants to dance.

After a few hours of drinks, dancing, and conversation, you and Matt exchange numbers and he promises to call you tomorrow. But as you watch him leave—tight ass, boulder shoulders, and all—you're less than enthusiastic about receiving that call. You might not even pick up the phone.

You've spent the entire evening trying to convince yourself that opportunities as good-looking as this one only come around once in a dating moon, but you just can't convince yourself that he's worth his weight in muscle. You've been suffering from a case of hookup ADD. On the dance floor, your mind wandered and your libido bottomed out.

When a man meets or exceeds all of your physical attractiveness requirements, but he's still not floating your boat, there's a lack of chemistry. You've heard it before. "There were no sparks." "The chemistry just wasn't there." "I don't understand."

Your initial feeling might be one of disappointment: you had the perfect opportunity to bag a gorgeous specimen and you just couldn't bring your appetite to the table. That reaction is a natural one; however, accepting his subsequent invitation could be detrimental.

The two of you simply aren't compatible. You'll never make a good couple. Your most primitive and reliable sense has told you so.

The human pheromone debate is raging, with professionals divided by the notion that human behavior can be altered by unconscious messages delivered by genetic chemicals to the opposite sex's olfactory brain centers.

Pheromones are chemical substances produced by animals (and humans) to stimulate varying responses in other individuals of the same species.

There are those in the scientific community who attest to the existence of human pheromones, as well as to the existence of our receptivity to them; and there are those who deny either their existence, our sensitivity to them, or both, citing a lack of hard evidence. Mice have one hundred V1R pheromone receptor genes. Humans have eight: seven that have become pseudogenes (defective because of lack of demand) and one that has remained active, named V1RL1. This gene does its work in the mucous membranes of the nose.

Discovered more than half a century ago, pheromones are known to alter the behavior of insects and mammals, that is, those creatures without problem-solving brains such as ours. But does that mean that we're not affected by them?

Could it be that our uniquely human cognitive and visual abilities have largely overridden the olfactory and pheromonal pathways that led our primitive ancestors to scent-selective copulation? I think so. Our anatomy includes a feature known as the VNO, or vomeronasal organ—a two-pitted feature located between the nose and mouth on the rear of the septum. If you were to look at a cross section of your face, you would see it directly above your upper row of teeth and directly back from the base of your nose.

This organ may shrink as a human ages, and its existence may be simply vestigial (much like the human outer ear, which no longer moves to capture sound waves and direct them into the ear canal). But just as the outer ear has been shown to aid in bolstering sound quality, the VNO probably once had the capability to detect odorless chemicals emitted by other human bodies. Even if the VNO has been deemed almost useless by evolution, there is evidence that supports our "smelling" noses' capabilities of transporting pheromones' messages to the hypothalamus. Why else would people who have been stripped of their sense of smell report a significant decline in their sex drives? Why else would blood flow to the hypothalamus increase with the inhalation of odorless human chemicals? Scientists who disabled the VNOs in mice noted that Mickey and Minnie showed no variance in sexual behavior; however, when the main olfactory pathway (the "smelling" nose) was interrupted, Mickey lost all interest in Minnie . . . like they were two young kids without a clue.

We are complicated creatures. We use every sense to choose mates. We can hold verbal and tactile exchanges, enact passion with copulatory gazes, see shapes that attract us . . . alongside our smelling abilities. Because we don't rely solely on our noses for mating, as mice and pigs do, this sense is not considered a primary channel for attraction. However, that doesn't mean it doesn't exist.

In my estimation, there's simply too much evidence, evolutionary and practical, pointing to the existence of an unconscious human pheromone detection system. Though we may not smell the chemicals with our conscious minds, or be able to recall the smells using our subconscious minds, there's plenty of evidence to suggest that our unconscious minds (the ones that drive us to do things without any cognitive intention) detect and react to human pheromones. Matt didn't flip your lid, or even rattle it. You may never know why, but possibly your unconscious mind was making decisions for you, right under your nose.

Genetic compatibility is only a sniff away. In chapter 7 we talked about how we unconsciously choose mates who aren't related to us but are similar enough to satisfy our desires to keep our faces alive in our children. Likewise our olfactory systems can determine genetic dissimilarity by reading the genetic make-ups of potential suitors. Chemical cues sent to the brain, via un-detectable MHCs, or major histocompatibility complexes, tell us if a potential partner's immune system's capabilities differ from or are similar to our own. MHCs are immune system genes that detect particular viruses and bacteria in the human body, and women's noses and brains are more astute at detecting them than men's.

The more diverse your MHCs, the broader your immunity. If your parents' MHCs differ greatly from each other, you get the benefit of that broad range, including immunity against some parasites and hepatitis. If your parents' MHCs are similar, your immunity might not be as encompassing as it could be, and you may have been born prematurely or significantly un-derweight.

Before conducting organ transplants, doctors measure the immune system compatibilities between the donor and the recipient—the more similar, the better. But unless you're looking for a kidney at the club, dissimilar is the way to go. You won't have to (nor could you) consciously detect a man's MHCs, nor will you have to ask for his health records. You need only interact with him at close range to be able to read his chemical cues.

The average long-term couple shares only a 20 percent parallel in MHCs. That means their immune systems are more different than alike. Pheromone cues unconsciously spoke to their brains during courting, drawing them together, and continue to keep them active in the sack. When couples are too similar in chemis-try, they make compatible friends, but their sexual chemistry will suffer. Some similarity is necessary for longevity in a relationship (hence the 20 percent in the average couple), but too much can be . . . well, like bunking with your brother. I can't imagine a better way to kill sex drive.

MHC cues are secreted from a man's armpits and groin, but they're undetectable to the human nose. The odor that you might notice if a man's bouquet is ripening has nothing to do with MHC and everything to do with androstenone (a testosterone derivative) being broken down by bacteria that like to dwell in dank, dark places. Body odor is a repellent, there's no doubt, and it could keep you from getting close enough to make uncon- scious compatibility decisions about him. A shame? For your would-be children, yes. For your nose, no.

Most of us can relate to the story at the beginning of the chapter: good- lookin' men sometimes don't float our canoes and we wonder why. The answer is detrimental MHC similar- ity. Matt was too much like you. Na- ture knew that your children would suffer and dictated that you allow the answering machine to take his call.

Pheromones: not to be confused with body odor.

Pheromonal Faux Pas

If you've been having bum luck on the dating scene, you might want to reevaluate the way that you handle your natural bouquet. Here are some practices that should be avoided:

Bathing in perfume
Using scented deodorants and antiperspirants
Applying heavy lipstick or scented lip gloss
Allowing body odor to overpower personal scents
Smoking

Eating garlic, onions, cumin, or curry regularly
Drinking excessively
Wearing manufactured or "natural" pheromones from a bottle
Hanging out in places that smell bad
Standing outside of your target's personal space

Not only do you need the full faculties of your senses to detect a man's genetic messages, you should also ensure that you're not screwing with your own. Remember, he's sniffing for a date, too.

GENDER ENLIGHTENMENT: Four types of testosterone-derived compounds speak to a woman's unconscious mind on behalf of the human male. Every man's chemistry is unique, and women's perceptions of chemical messages differ, but in general, here's what each is saying: Androstenone communicates aggression and dominance. Androstenol is more sociable and invites interaction. Androstenone A is a kinder and gentler pheromone, hinting at a protective nature. Androstadienone speaks of love and warm feelings.

A man's armpit is the seat of his scented magnetism. Testosterone derivatives, which can most effectively be inhaled from the male armpit, surreptitiously increase blood flow to a woman's hypothalamus. They don't do the same for a man. If you want to increase the flow to his, you'll have to use estrogen.

A woman's sense of smell is more sensitive than a man's. As with other evolutionarily built acuities, this is probably due to the fact that, throughout recorded and unrecorded history, women were the primary caregivers of children. Since the brain's olfactory cortex holds a significant connection to the emotional amygdala, women who smelled smoke, predators, or villains could easily snap into action and protect their children (this helps to explain the scent/memory connections we both enjoy and abhor in modern times).

Women can identify their babies' scent only hours after birth, and can identify their own scent 60 percent of the time, while men can only do it with 6 percent accuracy. This could help to explain why evolution has gifted men with fewer apocrine glands in their underarms: our noses are perfectly capable of detecting male hormones in only one one-hundredth of a drop of sweat.

Can't quite put your finger on that scent? Straight testosterone can be described as an olfactory trip to the zoo: musky animal with a side of goat urine. Sexy? Our hypothalamuses, along with scientists who have studied the libido-boosting qualities of a trip to the fair, think so.

Women are, on average, 7 percent shorter than men. They prefer tall men (six feet or taller), and have contributed to the growing average male stature by choosing tall ones throughout bipedal human history. This allows for a notable alignment of the female nose with the male underarm.

This underarm/nose alignment may seem awkward until you consider all of the things a pit can do for a chick. Derivatives of testosterone found in male underarm sweat elevate women's moods within a mere six minutes and keep them elevated for hours after a sniff session. They promote sexual arousal by triggering the release of ovulation hormones, which may even prompt the early release of an egg. They increase visual acuity, emotional awareness, and attentiveness. They help us to counteract sadness and to conveniently impair our own miserable memories.

As alluded to earlier, please don't confuse a man's natural underarm scent with body odor. Body odor is a result of poor hygiene or clothing that's either too tight-fitting or too heavy. On the prehistoric savannahs, winds whipped over human bodies, drying sweat quickly, before bacteria had ample opportunity to feed on the chemicals found within it and leave by-products that downright stank. To get the full effect of a man's apocrine glands doing their best work, smell him when he's just showered (preferably with an unscented soap), before he applies any type of deodorant. This is the smell of clean, untainted man.

The scent of man varies from man to man, but it also varies from sniffer to sniffer. Gender and age matter: only the brains of females who have entered puberty react to androstadienone, a product of testosterone. Time matters: high estrogen, like those levels detected in women just before ovulation, is conducive to olfactory sensitivity in the brain (for conscious, subconscious, and unconscious messages). In plain words, your sense of smell is bolstered during the days before ovulation. Additionally, genetic makeup contributes to how we perceive the scent of testosterone-derived chemicals. Some women describe the scent of androstenone as being similar to musk or urine, others liken it to vanilla, and others detect no scent at all. In a quest to uncover the reason for these differences in scent perception, researchers at Rockefeller University have isolated genetic variations that account for the differences. Participants who had inherited a copy of the gene OR7D4 from each parent smelled urine or musky sweat. Participants with a single-gene variant smelled vanilla, sweetness, or nothing. Researchers concluded that women with a prominent OR7D4 presence were disgusted by the androstenone, while others enjoyed it, could tolerate it, or were indifferent to it. This offers more evidence for the existence of scent-motivated attraction and the genetic disposition to gravitate toward high- or low-testosterone men.

Humans have more, and larger, apocrine glands in their armpits than any other primate does. This alone should be enough evidence that evolution has accounted for our sensual need for scent. If you're still not convinced, go get yourself a whiff of man and call me in the morning.

Fem-Pheromones

Just because men's sense of smell pales in comparison to ours, that doesn't mean that pheromonal messages are lost on their brains. In fact, they're powerful in both gender directions.

In order to make your genetic message more like a genetic billboard, raise your arms, toss your hair, and cross and uncross your legs to emit the natural chemicals that will speak to a man's unconscious mind. If the two of you are genetically compatible, you'll come out smellin' like a rose.

Raise your hands if you're sure you want to attract men.

Hair tossing not only looks sexy and reveals your profile; it also shows sexual interest and releases your scent into the air.

Oral contraceptives stink. At least when it comes to detecting genetic compatibility, they do. When a woman is taking the pill, she stops ovulating and the normal hormonal fluctuations that occur every month, including the one that causes the much-awaited libido surge, are eliminated. That means her elevated sense of smell before ovulation disappears, taking with it the ability to more capably detect and fall victim to androgens.

Worse, when a woman is under the influence of the pill, she's likely to choose a man who is immunologically similar to herself. As discussed earlier, women who aren't taking oral contraceptives will pass over those men who "smell" like their fathers and brothers. But with the pill . . . who knows?

This causes some major long-term compatibility problems. When the woman ditches the pill in favor of a family, her attraction to her partner could suddenly plummet—and it doesn't stop there. Any children that the couple has could suffer negative immunological effects, effectively negating the role that Mother Nature's schnoz has played in the overwhelming evolutionary success of the human race.

The first kiss is more than meets the eye (or the lips). I've alluded to Jan and Bob's first kiss. You've assumed that it happened because they eventually tied the knot, but what you may not have realized is that without the chemical communication championed by that initial smooch, our beloved couple may not have become a couple at all.

When Bob took Jan's face into his hands and touched his mouth to hers, pheromones from their upper lips were swapped, making tracks to each other's VNOs. Their brains agreed, *so far so great*. When Jan opened her lips and touched Bob's tongue with her own, spit swapping was glorified to a male/female conversation regarding immunity and biological compatibility. Their unconscious minds confirmed, *good match for hardy babies*. And it was all conducted without the conscious knowledge of two people. You see, in a kind of nature-driven intoxication, their brains were practically pickled in pleasure-inducing brain chemicals. All they felt was, *mmmmmmmm*.

Kissing is a form of human interaction that likely got its start when mothers placed food into their babies' mouths with their own. It has evolved into an incredibly sexy method for reading the genetic and immunological makeup of potential mates. Not only does a kiss between well-suited people release dopamine, endorphins, and oxytocin while reducing cortisol, it also transfers pheromones from one mouth to another. Sebum secreted from the upper lip (leftover waterproofing for our once-furry bodies) also serves to send clear messages to kissers' brains about harmonious pairing.

If a brain determines that another person's MHCs are too similar to its own, the "chemistry" of love will seem less like a concoction devised by a brilliant chemist and more like something thrown together by a mad scientist—and as you've learned, in the case of genetic chemistry, opposites really do attract.

The liking of a first kiss might seem like two people hovering on the cusp of love, but it's really a chemical reaction designed to make couplings that will result in strong, healthy babies.

Jan and Bob were certainly not thinking of parenthood while locked up in their first kiss. But that didn't matter. Nature's evolutionary motive is procreation. It has found a covert and highly effective way to decode the compatibility that's necessary to carry out its plan, and the kiss—a euphoric disguise—is a mighty clever way to package it.

A Feast Made for a Horny King

Dr. Alan Hirsch has conducted studies to determine what scents rev up human libidos. Unsurprisingly to me or you, he found that no aromas result in a male libido dip, but he did find that some hold the power to increase blood flow to the penis . . . and most of them involve food.

Going to the movies? Order black licorice, cola, and buttered popcorn. Not only will the popcorn increase arousal by 9 percent, but the combination of cola and black licorice on your breath will work as a team to make the night's climax even more exciting.

Not sure which movie theater to patronize? Choose the one that's adjacent to the mall and share a leisurely stroll before show-time. The smell of cinnamon buns from that oh-so-pungent national chain will give him a 4 percent boost, the odor wafting from the pizzeria will make a 5 percent contribution, and a sampling of vanilla or strawberry body spray from the squirter in the mall's thoroughfare will excite him.

Want to serve dessert at your place after the movie? Serve pumpkin pie while wearing the essential oil of lavender. This scent combination increases blood flow to the penis by up to 40 percent, leaving your guest like partially cured putty in your hands.

If he's still there in the morning, serve him a cream-filled doughnut with a side of leftover pumpkin pie (the scent combo will increase arousal by 20 percent), or go for that doughnut with a side of black licorice. Crazy, I know, but you'll "heighten" his libido by 32 percent. Warning: you might have to skip out on your 8 a.m. yoga class.

The easier route? Buy candles and burn them in these combinations: pumpkin pie and lavender, pumpkin pie and doughnut, doughnut and black licorice, or black licorice and cola. Or burn these single candles: cinnamon bun, vanilla, strawberry, pizza, or buttered popcorn. Yes, believe it or not, there are candle makers out there who have whipped up pizza and popcorn scents.

You'd better get cookin' (or burnin'). The king awaits.

Artificial pheromones and pheromones that claim to be authentic human varieties are advertised like car insurance, but there's a problem: how can a person expect to attract someone who's compatible if the pheromones they're wearing aren't their own, unique, genetically encoded chemical concoction? Likewise, if pheromones haven't been isolated by science, how can they make it into a bottle? Like the pill, when the spray bottle is abandoned, the attraction will soon follow.

GENDER ENLIGHTENMENT: Want to add a little scent to your own without overpowering your body's messages? Try a dab of vanilla or lavender essential oil on your neck and wrists. Middle-aged men prefer vanilla, while men with active sex lives enjoy lavender.

Copulins are the fatty acids that contribute to the bouquet in the vaginal area. As estrogen levels rise, so does the presence of copulins—along with their power over men (they cause androgen levels to rise only in males). Men who have participated in studies agree that the smell of a woman is most pleasant just before ovulation, when copulins are teeming. But even without going downtown, men will unconsciously react to rises in estrogen (which smells much like gamy sweat) and copulins (which smell similar to spoiled butter) in social settings. Men often feel more attracted to ovulating women, and when a man's mate is ovulating, he will closely guard her from other men while increasing his level of attentiveness toward her. On an unconscious level, copulins trigger a testosterone spike in males, causing them to be more dominant and competitive, leading the "have-nots" to "take a stab" at an ovulating women and compelling the "haves" to exercise their mate-keeping chops. This tells us not only that women's propensities for seeking love and for straying from current relationships increase during ovulation, but also that males' awareness of this penchant for naughtiness follows suit.

Remember, this male behavior of pursuit and guarding is conducted on an unconscious level. Seriously, what man do you know who would intentionally want to cuddle with a woman who smells of rancid dairy products?

It's time to reevaluate the importance of your nose. Scent sends messages, both detectable and undetectable, through your nose. Some human scents are obvious only to certain members of the opposite sex (due to genetic olfactory predispositions), while others are undetectable by the nose but stimulating to the sexual centers of the brain. Smell is much more than identifying stench from sweetness . . . it's about drawing the human sexes together with clandestine tactics that have been making matches for millennia.

The sense of smell is the strongest of the five, at least when it comes to triggering memories. This becomes essential when we discuss anchoring positivity to a man. A whiff of cologne, the aroma of a baking pie, or even the smell of an ocean breeze can bring old memories flooding back. That's why it's not advisable to wear commercially produced perfume while interacting with an unfamiliar man: if you're wearing the same scent used by the woman who dumped him and trampled on his heart, you'll either be incessantly compared to her or you'll bring back bad memories and he'll choose to pass on you. No one can imitate your natural scent. Nature has equipped you with the power to create anchors . . . and to avoid sinking because of the weight of someone else's.

Women's senses of smell have outperformed those of men because we are largely responsible for making sound choices in mates. Throughout history, women have been assigned to child rearing. Because they knew what lay ahead—three to five years of caretaking and nursing—the choices that they made at conception greatly impacted the quality of a generous portion of their lives. Our ancient sisters relied on their senses of smell to make those choices, and so should you. Matt wasn't a good genetic match, but a better one waits. The system is in place. Why not take advantage of the oldest and most trustworthy matchmaker on earth?

CHAPTER SEVENTEEN

Dress to Impress . . .

YOUR DATING INTENTIONS ON MEN

We've all heard the phrase "dress to impress," but this recommendation stretches far beyond Armani, Tommy, and Gucci. "Impress" also represents the use of clothing to impress certain beliefs about ourselves onto others.

The way that you dress is an integral part of the unspoken language of the body. What you wear sends signals to others about your credibility, education, personality, and status. Whether you're willing to play along or not, it's imperative that you understand that others will make judgments about you based on your appearance alone. You make those same judgments every day (even if you believe you discard them quickly in an effort to find out more). To prove this, you need only walk down any city street. You'll quickly pick up on the presence of high rollers who use their earthly possessions, including clothing, as status symbols to impress others with their success. And you'll also pick up on the messages sent by those who dress to make statements with graphic tees, Goth styles, and microskirts. You are utterly powerless against the impressions that different types of clothing make on you. We all are.

Before you go out, stand before a mirror and ask yourself,

"What are my intentions?" If you plan on heading out to the all-night bowl-o-rama for dollar tacos, then stilettos and a sequin-encrusted tube top might not be the answers (are they ever?); if you're headed out with the girls, hoping to hook up with a hottie, then tennis shoes and a turtleneck are not going to work in your favor. I know, these fashion faux pas are obvious, but others might not be so apparent.

Many women are accustomed to dressing in a certain manner, regardless of the venue or event. Their inner intentions differ—*I just want to grab coffee and get out of here; I want to talk to friends and maybe catch a guy's eye; I refuse to leave alone*—but their outer advertisements remain the same, resulting in the same outcome every time. Maybe the sexy dresser can't get out of the ShopRite without feeling like handled fruit or a side of beef. Maybe the walking libido who dresses like a librarian spends every night at home with Ben & Jerry's instead of Ben or Jerry. And maybe the businesswoman who can't seem to shake her professional attire habit can't understand why the only men who approach her are those who want to show her a wine list or grind pepper onto her salad.

It's important to understand that every time you step across your threshold and into the vast world of teeming singles, you are called upon to dress the part. But the big question is, Are you dressed for the part you're auditioning for? If you're not, it's no wonder you're having trouble landing the lead role.

Knowing the difference between work clothes, workout clothes, and working-it clothes isn't enough. Follow me into the world of clothing and accessory subtleties and you're sure to nail down the formula for looking your best and sending your intended message.

What you wear advertises why you're there. Even if those who are looking at you don't know exactly why they're getting a particular impression about you, they'll still get it. Here are some suggestions for aligning your clothing with your intentions:

Color doesn't just reflect your personal preferences; it sends messages to men about the shade of your mood, your sexual intentions, and your personal flavor. Sure, hot pink pants will send a noted message, but for a more tasteful, yet effective, implication, consider adopting the sundae rule: your bottom half should be the ice cream, the staple of your outfit. Just as you might choose vanilla ice cream for most sundaes, you should have a few principal bottoms in neutral colors that can be jazzed up with tops that convey your moods and intentions.

Here are the messages that color can send, according to anthropologist David Givens, psychotherapist and psychologist Martin Lloyd-Elliott, and Sensational Color, a website dedicated to the psychology of color:

Mimicking the cherry on that sundae, a **red** top is a blatant indicator of passionate feelings, sexy objectives, and a willing spirit that's searching to add to an already brimming feeling of excitement. Red has even been shown to increase the heart and breathing rates of those who view it.

> GENDER ENLIGHTENMENT: Men are profoundly affected by the color red, and it's purely sexual. Just as male chimps and baboons are turned on by the reddening of their ladies' rear ends during times of fertility, human males seem to be excited by the color red when it's on or around a female specimen.
>
> In a University of Rochester study, two psychologists determined that when women wore red, men were not only more attracted to those women, but also willing to spend more money on dates with them. Red did not increase the men's perceptions of the women's intelligence, compassion, or friendliness—it was all about the booty . . . ahem . . . beauty.

Yellow is the color to wear if you refuse to blend into a crowd. It will enter the room before you do, and like the other primary colors (red and blue), it brings with it a sense of urgency (that's why signs and advertisements use primary colors). Wearing this sunny shade is sure to land you in the spotlight. Pair it with black and you'll be clad in the highest attention-getting combination known to man.

When you wear **orange**, you reap the benefits of both red and yellow. You make your passionate feelings public, while drawing eyes toward you. Since orange isn't a commonly worn color, you can add "rebellious" to the storm of messages sent by this hue. Feeling particularly wild? Orange pegs you as a passionate individual who's up for experimentation.

A woman wearing **white** is generally viewed as being approachable, yet inexperienced in the sexual realm. This color proves its reputation by offering an attractive contrast to blushing cheeks. Dominant types will relish the innocence and submissiveness of a body wrapped in white, and might feel compelled to approach its wearer, thanks to a familiar, bright, and harmless connotation.

It's no surprise that **pink** is the most amicable color in the meeting, dating, and romance realms. When humans flush with sexual desire, they blush in hues of pink; sexual organs take on deep pink tones when aroused; and pink is welcoming because it makes the wearer appear to be harmless, like a child. It brings with it the passion denoted by red and the innocence symbolized by white, resulting in a nuance of virtue united with suppressed sexual desire. Pink has even been shown to slow the secretion of adrenaline.

Confidence and a cool demeanor are conveyed by **blue**. Not the color to wear if you want to seem eagerly available, it lends more of a blending quality, allowing you to disappear into a crowd, yet reemerge with a confident air if you're entertaining the idea of a first move.

Green will not attract the attention of sexually interested onlookers, but will comfort with a feeling of natural harmony. Its blue component contributes a feeling of easiness and poise, while its yellow element draws more attention than blue. Wear green if you're willing to make a first move, or if you want to appeal to the unhurried, leisure-loving portion of the male population.

Purple, particularly in deep tones, evokes feelings of melancholy and doom for most. Its hot-blooded red portion does denote sexual fervor, but that heat is suppressed by the cool blue, sending messages from purple-wearers that the sexual desires they have are deeply embedded, and are not likely to be made available to suitors. Like other secondary colors (colors created by combining primary colors), the strongest undertone (in this case, the red or the blue) determines in which direction (sexy or subdued) the purples lean. If it's a light purple, the feelings evoked will be similar to pink.

There are some people who can wear **brown** and make a statement. However, for most of us, brown, though approachable, spells b-o-r-i-n-g. Brown is not only the color of mud, it's the combination of a number of colors, which "muddies" its bearer's message. If you want to blend into a crowd, wear brown. But remember, when onlookers cannot decipher a message, their eyes will be drawn to more definitive heralds.

Black is the love of many women, thanks mostly to its talent for slimming and hiding flaws; but that also means it hides everything but a woman's face. You're less likely to stand out in a crowd wearing monochromatic black. In fact, you might go unnoticed. Unless you're sporting some bold accessories, save the black for funerals and for your staple foundation . . . the ice cream under a pop of attention-grabbing color.

Generally speaking, shades like olive, beige, brown, and gray should only be worn if everything else about you is unique enough to grab attention, if your heart has already been claimed, or if you're hiding under the veil of the witness protection program.

Vivid colors attract the attention of onlookers for a rather obvious evolutionary reason: in the distant past, those eyes that could easily pick out the bright colors of fruit served their owners well. There's no doubt that as our eyes were revolutionized to include a trichromatic color sense for survival reasons, bodies that were well nourished were healthier and therefore went on to survive and propagate. Thanks to this history, the human eye is especially sensitive to color contrast and has been conditioned to overlook those hues that don't look like food.

When you wear dark jeans, slacks, or skirts with brightly colored tops, you mimic the attention-getting factor that the peacock uses. Using color in this manner attracts eyes, which is the first step to attracting Him.

In colorful conclusion, if you want to be noticed, wear colors that will separate you from the crowd. And in allegiance to your evolutionary roots, wear colors that will make you look absolutely edible.

Can You See Your True Colors?

Cyndi Lauper, Phil Collins, and the cast of *Glee* can see your true colors, but can you? Your skin tone, hair color, and eye color determine the colors that look best on you.

You might like the message that yellow or red sends, but can you wear it well? Let's find out.

Skin tones are divided into two major categories: cool and warm. To determine what subliminal tone your skin holds, simply look at the underside of your arm in natural light. If your veins look blue and your skin has a pink or blue hue, you're cool. If your veins look green and your skin has a hint of yellow or peach, you're warm.

According to Darianne, the New York celebrity makeup artist of Darianne.com, the colors that best suit the cool complexion, or the woman with blue, green, or hazel eyes; ivory skin; and hair that is black, ash brown, ash blond, or platinum are soft blue, green, pink, lilac, plum, rosy red, or soft gray. Dark-skinned women with blue-black or red undertones look best in cool colors.

Warm complexions, usually found on ladies with brown, golden brown, or hazel eyes; olive, peach, or beige skin; and honey blond, red, or chestnut brown hair, look great in earth tones like rust, copper, gold, peach, yellow, beige, golden red, and warm plum. Women of color with yellow, brown, or gold undertones have warm complexions.

Women who can wear most any color have blue eyes, brown hair, and golden skin, which combine both warm and cool tones.

More specifically, you can divide cool tones into winter and summer complexions and warm tones into autumn and spring complexions. The prescriptions for each are as follows:

The skin of a winter woman has a blue or pink undertone beneath a dominant color of pale white, olive, or brown. Her hair and eyes are usually dark. However, Nordic women with naturally blond hair and light eyes can also be winters. If you're Asian, African, or a pale blonde, you might be a winter. Wintry women look best in black, white, navy, red, ice blue, pink, and yellow. Gold, orange, and beige are the worst colors that a winter can wear.

Summer complexions are similar to those of winter, except that they're more often accompanied by blond hair than dark. They also have blue or pink undertones, but the dominant skin color is usually pale, as are the eyes, making the contrast between hair, skin, and eyes subtle. Summers should wear pastels that aren't icy, such as brownish pink, mauve, lavender, powder blue, plum, and pale yellow. Black, orange, and vivid colors don't look good on summers—they create too much contrast between skin and clothing.

Autumn women have golden or peachy undertones. If your hair is red or brunette, you're likely an autumn. Golden blondes and some women with black hair can fall under this category, too. Often the eyes will be dark with golden hues. Autumns will look their best in olive, beige, gold, orange, brown, and gray. Like the word *autumn* suggests, the colors of changing leaves and earthy tones are perfect. Harsh, bright colors will not do the autumn woman any favors. Black, white, pastels, and blues will suck the beautiful layered color from her face.

Spring-colored women also bear golden undertones, but their overall skin color is usually light, with a peaches-and-cream quality. Hair color that ranges from golden blond to strawberry blond to auburn, along with light eye color, usually denotes a spring woman. Rosy cheeks and freckles are common in this category. Spring ladies should wear peach, salmon, golden yellows and browns, ivory, teal, green, red, and blue. They should avoid black and white and colors that are very dark. Bright is best.

Color might seem scary at first, but once you find your seasonal niche, you'll be "beautiful, like a rainbow."

Because a woman's plump facial lips mimic the texture and color of the more steamy southerly variety, they're already the focus of men's musings. But add shiny, red passion to them and *wowee* . . . you've got pure sex appeal. If pink lips look like the labia at rest, red lips mimic them in full-throttle arousal. Red lipstick is not for women who don't like sexual attention. Gwen Stefani's trademark smackers are perfect examples of how seductive a red lip can be.

Authentic red lipstick can be worn by anyone, as long as its undertone—pink, purple, or orange—doesn't clash with the hue of the wearer's skin. The only thing holding you back from going red is not having the nerve to do so.

Makeup artists recommend that if you do plan to plaster red on those lips, lay off the heavy eye makeup. Too much competition on the face will detract from the effect of this blatant sign of femininity.

Cosmetics and their recommended applications are designed to highlight the most feminine features of a woman's face, while distracting from those parts of it that could be perceived as masculine.

If you think back to when we covered the evolution of women's facial features, you'll remember that big eyes, lips, and cheeks are überfeminine, while small noses, brows, and chins are unmasculine. The effects of both high estrogen and low testosterone contribute to what we consider to be a feminine face, and properly applied makeup exacerbates the effects of these hormones.

By highlighting the eyes with shadow, liner, and mascara; simulating blushing cheeks with rouge; and drawing attention to the lips with arousal-like coloring, you emphasize the most feminine parts of the face. By evening out the skin tone (allowing the nose and chin to virtually disappear into the face) and reducing the thickness of the eyebrows, you deemphasize parts of the face that indicate masculinity (when they're large).

Jewelry does more than pull an outfit together. It speaks of your personality and your intentions. A woman who wears heart-shaped jewelry is either a born romantic (though not many buy themselves dainty, expensive jewelry), already taken, or hung up on the long-gone man who purchased the piece for her. If you're trying to look available, small heart shapes should be avoided.

Big, bold, colorful jewelry usually indicates that the wearer has a large and in-charge personality. Imagine your quietest friends wearing Wilma Flintstone's big, white rock necklace. A bad match, to say the least, right? The shy woman is more likely to feel comfortable in dainty chains, small pendants, and tiny earrings. The size of the jewelry you wear can speak of everything from power to friendliness to naïveté and vulnerability. Know your dating intentions, and wear jewelry to match.

Feminine styling contributes to sexual dimorphism. In some species, males cannot be differentiated from females without a genital examination. Cats, dogs, guinea pigs, and lizards are examples of animals that show little difference between genders. However, lions, deer, chickens, and peacocks are examples of animals that are easily discerned as male or female, even at a distance. Humans belong to the latter grouping. Women's faces are more delicate, their breasts are more prominent, their waists are (by proportion) narrower, their rear ends are more rounded, their frames are generally smaller than their male counterparts' . . . and all of these characteristics play massive roles in attracting the opposite sex.

In order to appeal to men's innate mating responses, you must dress to appear unmistakably female. Clothing that accentuates the narrowness of the waist, the fullness of the bust, the wideness of the hips, and the daintiness of the ankles are just a few examples of cuts that say, "I'm female."

There's nothing wrong with flannel shirts, overalls, and sweats, as long as you're either digging potatoes or pounding the treadmill at home. If your brother could wear it to anything other than a drag queen convention, don't wear it into the club, the coffee shop, the gym, or the market, or even to church.

Business suits are essential daily attire for many women's professions, and often we end up going for dinner or meeting friends after work without the time to change. Though proper business apparel shouldn't be revealing or overtly sexy (I don't recommend dating at work), there's no reason it can't be feminine.

Don't be tightfisted when it comes to having your suits tailored to accentuate your womanly figure. Jackets without darts to show the narrowness of the waist can be like "straitjackets" for the attention-getting portions of your day.

Forget the flats—heels, even if they're only the kitten variety, will add some meow to the roar of that suit.

Don't be afraid to choose business suits in unconventional colors. Hot pink pinstripes might not be in good taste, but shades that depart from the basic dark suit can be refreshing and attention-getting. Try a pastel suit in the springtime, or a green one during cooler months.

Accessories can turn a business suit from blah to bling. Statement jewelry, scarves, and jewel-tone or pastel silk blouses will keep you from getting bored while also marking you as unmistakably feminine.

If you can, ditch the jacket after work. The dominant messages that a jacket sends might mark you as un-approachable.

If your shoulders are broad, avoid necklines that will exacerbate the problem. Villains include boatnecks, wide V's, sabrinas, sweethearts . . .

There's no reason a business suit can't be femininely flattering, like this one.

anything that is shallow and wide. Instead choose necklines that are slender and plunging—more vertical than horizontal. Big collars add to the bulk of the shoulders (this includes turtlenecks). Tiny collars or no collars will serve you best. Shoulder pads and puffy sleeves should be avoided—why add girth? Flowing sleeves and silken, fluid fabrics will soften broad shoulders.

Embellishment around the neck and shoulders will draw attention to your problem area, while bright colors will do the same. If you have broad shoulders, try wearing darker colors on top and lighter colors on the bottom. Horizontal stripes add girth. Therefore, only narrow-shouldered women should wear them on their top halves.

Remember that sexual dimorphism suggests that male shoulders should be broad. This means, by default, that narrow shoulders are considered more feminine and will therefore contribute to opposite-sex attraction. Men of yester-millennia preferred narrowness in the shoulder region, and so do the men of today.

Narrow hips and a thick waist can throw off the ideal WHR, reducing that sexy feminine differential. In order to visually increase the width of your hips and narrow your waistline, choose skirts and dresses that flare out from the waist, use pleats to add volume, and/or have horizontal stripes below the waist. Dresses with prints that gradually become larger toward the hemline will draw the eyes to the lower half of your body, minimizing the shoulders and accentuating the hourglass figure you're creating with the A-line skirt.

Pants with pockets on the sides, at the hips, will add the illusion of hip width.

Cinch clothing at the waist and choose tailored jackets that are nipped in at the waistline. When wearing a blouse and tailored jacket, choose colors that sharply contrast with each other; the linear effect will draw eyes downward, to rest at the WHR ratio you're attempting to create.

Avoid pencil skirts; you'll look like a pencil with a big eraser on top.

Her dress increases the perceived waist-to-hip ratio by flaring out from the waist and displaying a horizontal line at the hem.

Body Watch: Not sure if your waist-to-hip ratio is in need of an A-line skirt or other help? Go to www.missfitness.com/waist. html and input your measurements. If your WHR is less than .7, you've got built-in curves that will speak for themselves. Greater than .7 and you might need a little fashion PR, in the form of clothing that narrows your waist and/or widens your hips.

Being tall with long legs is not only attractive to the opposite sex for evolutionary reasons, it's an important element of confidence. However, you don't have to be tall to look tall. You can raise the perception of your height with a few fashion tricks.

Decorating the upper portion of your body with scarves, bold jewelry, and hats will heighten your body's focal point, making you seem taller. (I am a big fan of hats of all shapes and sizes and wear them often. They remedy bad hair days and add to others' perceptions of my personality strength.)

Monochromatic outfits will make you look taller because you're not cutting the body into sections and interrupting the eye's clean sweep. However, if you do choose to segment your body, use the lighter color on top, to draw attention upward.

If your legs are short (less than half your total height), wear tops and jackets that come to rest above the hip. This will make the bottom of your body seem longer. Likewise, tucking in your shirt will pull up the waistline. If you wear a long shirt, untucked, you'll steal length from your legs.

Straight skirts will lengthen the legs, while A-lines will shorten them. Petite women should wear skirts that come above the knee, shorts that rest above the knee, or pants that fall the whole way to the shoe. Capris and Bermudas chop a body's length unnaturally and are only flattering on women who already have long legs. Jeans and pants that are straight (not flared at the bottom) add height because straight lines look longer than curved ones.

Being tall and being thin work together; therefore, if you slim yourself, you'll look taller, and if you heighten yourself, you'll look slimmer. Vertical stripes will accomplish both, while horizontal stripes will make you look shorter and wider. Since a belt is worn horizontally, it will detract from your height. If your drawers need a little support, hide the belt.

Match your shoes and socks/hose to your skirt or pants. Interruptions in color divide, making lines seem shorter. Wearing heels with high-waist pants that have hems that rest close to the floor will add some "secret" leg length.

Baggy clothing is a short person's shrink-ray. Lines elongate, and without definitive lines, you'll minimize the height you do have.

Flat hair, long hair, and wide hair make you look shorter, but hair that's worn swept up to the crown of the head will add real and perceived height (just ask fans of Bumpits).

In order to increase alleged height, wear V-shaped necklaces or V-neck collars. And don't forget the medium- to high-heeled shoe—besides adding height, it will accentuate the rest of your best assets.

It's no secret that men love breasts, and for those of you who suffer from a size AA headache, there are ways to increase the illusion of being more amply gifted in the bust department.

High necklines or those that don't scoop past medium are best. Ruffles and gathered fabrics add volume. Horizontal lines over the bust will serve to visually expand it. Combine these tactics with a cinched waist, which will make the bust seem larger in comparison.

Wear tops that are lighter than the clothing on your bottom half. Lighter colors pop, while darker colors minimize.

Wear your size. I know, it sounds elementary, but if you wear something that's two sizes too large in order to hide a portion of yourself, you'll not only hide the rest of you but also possibly spark speculation about the "baby's" due date. If you wear clothing that's too small, you could stifle any spark of speculation about what's to be discovered under the blood-pressure cuff you're calling a dress.

It's true: wearing the right size slims you. Take it from Stacy London, star of TLC's *What Not to Wear:* "Don't get hung up on the size. If you feel bad about yourself because a 12 is what fits, take a Sharpie and write '6' on the label."

The use of asymmetry will set you apart. The human body

is bilaterally uniform—therefore, incorporating an element of asymmetry into an ensemble piques the viewer's interest. Now, I'm not suggesting that you run out and purchase all the factory irregulars that you can find . . . instead learn to appreciate the interruption in drudgery that an asymmetrical neckline, a pin on the right side of your blouse, a dress that exposes one shoulder, or a T-shirt with graphics that favor one side of the body can offer. In the 1980s, mismatched earrings, unbalanced haircuts, and off-the-shoulder shaker sweaters were popular for this reason. In fact, the more "off color" the rock star, the more asymmetrical their styles (think Cyndi Lauper). Today this trend has morphed into a streak of hair color down one side of the head, and, more subtly, off-center hair parts.

Studies have shown, almost invariably, that facial symmetry and bodily symmetry are attractive to the opposite sex; however, these findings should not be confused with clothing and adornment symmetry. A symmetrical face speaks of good genes, while an asymmetrical style, no matter how subtle, can speak of a propensity to want to spread those genes (or at least have fun while going through the motions).

Eyes naturally scan the face and body in a methodical pattern. When that process is disrupted by an irregularity, excitement and an escape from the customary excite psyches and libidos.

Bai Ling is employing asymmetry with her dress and the ornament in her hair. She's also creating the illusion of an ideal WHR by cinching at the waist and adding volume to her small bustline with ruffles.

Graphics speak to our brains' visual centers. Specialized receptors enhance edges and corners, delighting our brains with lines and color delineations. In simpler terms, clothing with insignias, lines, marked color separations, banners, and geometric patterns offers feasts for human eyes. A top that boasts one of these great divides could get you the look that you're longing for.

Blue jeans just might be the most versatile article of clothing available to consumers. This would have surprised James Dean's critics decades ago, but evolutionary biologists could have seen this classic style coming from millennia past.

Our vision is supported by genes that predispose us to see three primary colors: yellow, red, and blue. This means that our eyes are especially receptive to those colors in their pure forms, such as blue jeans.

The colors of blue jeans range from light baby blue to deep, almost black. Dark jeans offer the feeling of being dressed up, while lighter shades speak of the wearer's laid-back demeanor or mood. Jeans are popular because they can be dressed up or dressed down, but there's more. They attract plenty of attention to the butt, thanks to pockets with embellishments that can't be ignored. Even plain-pocket styles employ the use of stitching that contrasts in color. The stand-out threading also runs in lines that follow the long columns of the human form, to elongate the legs. The zipper line meets the whiskering at the tops of the thighs to converge on and draw attention to your most sexual of spots, and women's jeans are cut to follow the curves of the rear end, to show off the fullness of the thighs, and to highlight the wide pelvic floor. And as if that weren't enough to convince you to pull on the Calvins, consider that jeans are constructed from cotton, a breathable fabric that allows for the circulation of pheromones.

True, jeans are not appropriate for every venue, but they can be worn with every type of shoe—heels, flats, flip-flops, boots—making them versatile for most any circumstance. When they fit and flatter your figure, they mesh perfectly with the genes that really matter—the ones that pull him in your direction.

A Pancake Butt Conversion That'll Flap His Jack

A distinctively feminine form has an ample backside, but don't fret if you've got the dreaded pancake butt—there's an easy recipe that's a quick and delicious fix.

1. Padded underwear will add the illusion of junk to that flat trunk.

2. Jeans that stretch tightly over the butt will accentuate those spanking-new curves.

3. Pockets with flaps will add some bubble to that butt.

4. Embellishments on back pockets will act like signs that declare, "Curves ahead."

5. Widely spaced pockets will add girth to your bertha.

Pancake butt isn't the only problem on the rearview menu, but it is the most challenging in the evolutionary attraction kitchen. If you feel that your butt needs work, visit www.redbookmag.com/beauty-fashion/tips-advice/best-jeans-yl to find out how you can put jeans to work for you.

Create a desire to touch with fabrics that seem irresistible. Textured weaves, satin, silk, cashmere, and suede are the types of clothing that beg to be touched. If a textile looks soft or silky, a man might feel motivated to touch and see.

Clothing with movement can be sexier than no clothing at all. That's because it exaggerates feminine motion, like the swaying of hips and the rolling of shoulders. Researchers from NYU and Texas A&M have determined that a noted sway in a woman's carriage can increase her attractiveness factor by up to 50 percent. Add an attention-grabbing extension of that sway, in the form of a flowing skirt or wide-legged linen pants, and the numbers go up from there.

Caveat: If you're extremely large-busted, flowing fabrics might not be for you. They tend to turn a little wiggle into a tsunami.

Women's shoes are dramatically different from those of men, and the reasons surrounding the great divide are more subtly sexual than many realize. Sandals, thongs, or any shoe that reveals a lot of southern skin sends messages of barefoot desires. These shoes are most appealing when they are barely there, low-cut from the ankle, when toes are showing, and when toe cleavage is exhibited.

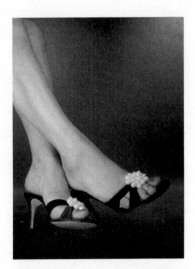

This woman is using skimpy shoes to advertise her sexy desires.

Body Watch: There is a bit of controversy surrounding the concept of toe cleavage—most likely because it mirrors the cleavage of the breasts, buttocks, and labia. Some liken it to a plumber's crack: a fashion faux pas. But the esteemed designer Manolo Blahnik claims that toe cleavage is essential to the sexuality of a shoe, and that only the first two cleavages (on the big toe's side) should be shown when closed-toe shoes are worn.

Shoes that form to the foot are also sexually appealing, but for reasons that you may not suspect. If a woman is willing to cram her foot into a stiff pump, or to stuff her foot into a strapped or buckled number that might be terribly uncomfortable, she's sending subliminal messages that she's willing to be bound and looking to get laid. This concept is not unlike ones that use rings on fingers to represent bondage, or bracelets on wrists to symbolize the willingness to be shackled. Though unhealthy for the foot, tight-fitting shoes do speak to the opposite sex about long-term relationship wishes.

High heels have long been celebrated for their body-shaping and walk-converting aptitude, and the messages they send are undeniable. Why would a woman perch herself atop five-inch heels, in which she's forced to navigate around storm grates, cobbled sidewalks, and shag carpet, unless her main intention was to advertise her sexual availability? Men sense this and jump to highly accurate conclusions about women who sacrifice foot health, comfort, and stability for sexiness.

High-heeled shoes firm calves, elongate and slim the ankles, and lengthen the look of the legs. A signal of interest, the forward lean, is exaggerated when a woman is perched on heels. And, maybe most importantly, even a modest heel holds the potential to increase the protuberance of the rear end by as much as 25 percent. That means that the rounded, feminine butt that men cherish for its baby-nourishing fat cells and its reminders of rear-entry days gone by is augmented to a delicious proportion.

The neck dimple has it all over cheek dimples . . . at least in the sexuality department. The suprasternal notch, or the concavity just above where your clavicles meet, is known affectionately as the neck dimple, and one firm press into it will leave even the hardiest sort staggering in retreat. Wearing clothing that uncovers this vulnerability sends clear messages about how open you are to the prospect of giving in to the advances of others.

A V-neck blouse works well to display this notch, but a more feminine option is a rounded neckline that shows off the length of the clavicles, as well. This gives the eye both vertical (neck) and horizontal (clavicles) lines to follow to the dimple.

Another way to draw attention to the vulnerability of the suprasternal notch is to wear a necklace that falls just below the dimple. An even stronger statement can be made with a brightly colored pendant that rests at the base of the notch.

This woman is not only displaying her neck dimple; she's also highlighting it with a pendant that rests just below it.

Shoulders should remain covered in professional scenarios, but at a party or social engagement, or in any situation where you want your feminine intentions to be noticed, they should make an appearance. When one or both shoulders are revealed, your emotional reactions will be more evident and the feminine contour (in mimicry of breasts to the male psyche) will work to mark your sexual dimorphism.

Thin, or spaghetti, straps work well to draw attention to the shoulders because the human eye naturally picks up on the linear nature of the straps and moves from shoulder to shoulder, in turn.

Tattoos and piercings aren't for everyone, and that's why they carry with them some notable taboos. Whenever people subject themselves to the needle, they are taking the same risks that tribal warriors take during rites of passage.

As long as it's original, a body decoration sends the message that its bearer does not conform to the norms of society, lending an aura of mystery. However, when a tattoo or piercing is done to become part of a social group, or if its design is uninventive, it can actually work in reverse—speaking of conformity.

Piercings and tattoos carry stigmas—I can say this because I have several. Remember that men are often both curious and sometimes intimidated by women who seem strong, or who look as though they might cause a confrontation or power struggle. Since these flesh decorations signify strength, make sure you put significant thought into what you want your billboard to display.

It seems that the majority of the population will always view people with piercings and tattoos as either different and rebellious or out to prove a point (even if the purpose is to conform). When these viewers walk away, they are, in their minds, walking away from conflict.

If you choose to tattoo, make it an original design and go with something small that can be veiled or unveiled at will. Feminine tattoos are best kept under wraps for viewing in intimate settings or for bonding purposes (like the tattooed wedding bands my husband and I share), unless you're going for the Bombshell McGee look.

No matter her inner intentions, her outer message is affected by her tattoos.

You don't have to have a personal stylist or be a fashionista in order to customize the messages that your clothing sends. You only need to gather a bit of elementary advice and to look at yourself in the mirror as if you were someone else—judge the book by its cover, so to speak, because others will certainly do the same.

There's a reason we "dress up" to go out. High status is sexy because it indicates success, and is therefore attractive. Despite the advice of mothers and mentors everywhere, books are still judged by their covers, and probably always will be. That means that your clothing does matter. It sends distinct messages about your availability, your vocation, and your sexual intentions. It can shout, it can whisper, or it can exercise a staunch gag order.

Maybe you've been committing some dressing crimes, or maybe you've been sending messages that don't align with your inner intentions.

Vow today that you will start dressing to impress—not just with designer labels and the latest in fashion trends, but with the intention to impress your purpose for the evening, or for the rest of your life, on others.

Sometimes, in order to change the outcome, all you need to do is change your wardrobe.

CHAPTER EIGHTEEN

Keep Him in Suspense . . .

WITH THE MYSTERIOUS YOU: A BESTSELLING THRILLER

A pretty young intern is sent to the file crypt. She's been charged with rummaging through a jumble of microfiche in search of a newspaper article that could hold some answers about a decades-old cold case. Her annoyance is interrupted when she pulls the naked lightbulb's cord to reveal a familiar face. It's Jack, the once-handsome northern beat reporter, lying bludgeoned next to the blood-streaked JAN–MAR 1990 filing cabinet.

Her screams pierce the newsroom, just before a clap of thunder rumbles through the building and all falls to black . . .

––––––

If you're a lover of murder mysteries and suspense novels, you're not alone. The fact that this genre is a favorite among readers comes with a side of irony, particularly when you consider the state of the world in which we live: one that thrives on instant gratification, efficient time management, and multitasking. If the identification of every perpetrator was that important, wouldn't murder mystery fans simply flip to the last chapter, disclose the bad guy, and move on to their videoconference calls, stockholders' meetings, and road-raging commutes? It seems that the allure of the question mark is alive and well, thanks in part to the escapism it provides.

Mystery is particularly stimulating for the men of the dating world. Many of them thrive on challenges and on competition—their testosterone levels and their evolutionary roles demand it. Because their early jobs included the stalking of prey, natural selection ensured that only the male brains that were best suited for conducting that job (without life loss) survived. Those men who were most compelled to get out there and hunt survived because they scored food for themselves and their children. Additionally, they lived longer because they were well fed; this provided more time to produce more little male brains with proclivities for hunting. Therefore today's man still feels the need to track and chase. When a man is teased into pursuing you, the ancient pathways in his mind are enlivened, driving him to bag you just as a caveman might bag the most elusive of prey. You could say that he's incited by a glimpse of "tail" in the distance.

Men were, and still are, enticed by the hunt.

Combine mystery with physiological arousal and you'll create a storm that just might blow him directly into a hunting frenzy. A study conducted by psychologists Donald G. Dutton and Arthur P. Aron found that when a man met a beautiful woman on a suspension bridge, as opposed to on a more stable bridge, his feelings of attraction toward her were compounded. It seems that the physiological arousal felt by being suspended over a deep ravine on a rickety bridge was enough to either emotionally confuse the men or cause their feelings of attraction to intensify. This same phenomenon is endorsed on the big screen when, after intense or life-threatening circumstances, the two most adrenaline-marinated characters fall into each other's arms (e.g., Annie and

Jack in *Speed*). I'm not suggesting that you attempt to meet men while base-jumping or cut city bus brake lines to create drama, but there's no reason you can't use mystery to re-create that feeling for the object of your desire.

He wants to hunt. He wants to feel excitement. When he does, and you're both the source and the object, you'll reap the benefits. Present a man with a mystery and you'll invite him to come along for the ride; a ride that he might be powerless to resist.

You don't have to be an award-winning novelist or screen-writer to create a mystery that could stimulate Holmes (detective Sherlock or thoroughly endowed lover John); you simply need to employ the tactics that will keep him guessing . . . and coming back.

You might feel compelled to play hard-to-get for evolution-ary reasons. Just as men's brains are built for hunting, your brain has been conditioned for you to act in an alluring manner. Ances-tral women didn't have to stalk berries or men. Instead their best efforts were made in luring. The women who were most capable of enrapturing men produced the most children, passing the femi-nine traits that worked for them to their baby girls. But that's not to say that women didn't choose whom they lured. It's likely that they were tuned in to the fact that men not only hunted venison but also hunted women; and if their behavior was anything like our hard-to-get conduct, there's probably a practical reason for it. It seems that by compelling a man to compete with other suitors, you're actually asking him to prove that he's capable of proactive fatherhood.

Researchers at the University of Bristol conducted studies using birds and determined that women who play hard-to-get are probably gauging men's willingness to work for what they want, which hints at men's eagerness to put notable effort into raising children.

But how do men feel about this plot? Not as good as advice from decades ago would have us believe. Only half of all single men are willing to pursue a woman who has expressed no initial interest in them. This median number makes perfect sense when you combine men's love of the hunt with their fears of rejection and failure.

However, if you feign a lack of interest in everyone *except* your pursuer, interested men will be doubly likely to approach, according to a five-year, early-twenty-first-century study conducted by flirting experts Paul Morris Segal and Katia Loisel-Furey.

What man wouldn't want to know that you have chosen him, and only him, while rejecting all others? This method not only incorporates an element of mystery, it also makes him feel special.

Body Watch: Make eye contact three times with the object of your desire while you participate in conversation with other men. This will make him feel special by indicating that you're willing to play hard-to-get with the general population . . . with the exception of him.

By creating temptation or a challenge, you create an obstacle for a man to hurdle. Taboos are strange creatures in that they often create more excitement than if they hadn't existed at all. If the man likes a challenge, give him one. Tell him your heart's already taken, admit that this might be a bad time for a relationship, tell him that your lifestyle contradicts typical ones, or fill him in on your intentions to join a secluded convent that's nestled in an isolated valley just south of nowhere. You'll fan his fire—if it's already been lit—and when you do submit to spending time with him, he'll feel that he's won a real prize.

GENDER ENLIGHTENMENT: In the male mind, the term *trophy wife* has more to do with winning than good looks. When men are thrown into competition with one another, testosterone levels increase. Elevated testosterone levels equate to increased sexual desire. By creating an air of competition (even if there isn't any), you're effectively increasing his desire for you.

When you're busy as a bee, your honey will be in high demand. Maybe you sit home every Friday night watching DVRs of *The Bachelor,* languishing in moth-eaten stirrup pants, foam rollers, and buckets of ice cream. Maybe your idea of a night out is grocery shopping followed by a stop at the gas pump.

No matter your schedule, it never hurts to subtly embellish your level of busyness. When your schedule is full, it tells suitors that you're in high demand and definitely worth waiting for. I witnessed this tactic taken to the extreme by a neighbor of mine. She seemed to never be home. Her schedule was filled with salon treatments, social engagements, and a rainbow of demands for her time . . . at least that's what she wanted the rest of the neighborhood to believe. She had gained a lofty level of respect from her disciples, who believed that a woman that busy had to be worth her weight in gold. However, when she wasn't home, she wasn't always slaying dragons. In fact, she was killing a portion of her time every day reading magazines and smelling Big Macs at the McDonald's in a neighboring town. She may not have had authentic social proof, but she created it for herself and reaped the benefits. In a role that was more publicized but just as convincing, Renée Zellweger played the plain, white-bread Bridget Jones in *Bridget Jones's Diary.* When her very handsome and sought-after boss takes an interest in her, she feigns a busy lifestyle, even though she spends much of her time wrapped in a comforter at home. This serves to both amplify and preserve his interest level. If she hasn't much spare time, she must be in serious social demand, right?

This approach can be equated to a business concept known as the Empty Restaurant Syndrome. If you're sporting around town, looking for a place to stop for lunch, would you patronize the establishment with an empty parking lot? Many of us don't. We would rather stick with the café that has a small line at the door, or the deli with only two or three open spaces in the lot. It's called social proof, and the same concept applies to your availability.

> **GENDER ENLIGHTENMENT:** When a gentleman (or a sexy scoundrel) asks you to dinner, respond with something like "Let me check my schedule" or "I can make it Saturday, but I won't be available until after eight."
>
> Consult your BlackBerry. Tell him you only have time for coffee tomorrow, but can schedule dinner for next week. Never jump at an invitation with a response like "I can go right now! I can always clean the hamster cage tomorrow."

An embellished day planner can be supersexy.

Do not submit to interrogation. When the chip bowl is full, partygoers will gather around it. When it's empty, they'll move away from it and toward the keg or the door. When you refuse to divulge everything about yourself, you keep the chip bowl full. Once it's empty, it's no longer interesting.

When you bridge gaps between meetings with unanswered questions, you ensure that the object of your desire will be thinking about the answers in your absence, and therefore thinking of you. He'll want to meet again to satisfy his curiosity.

Remember, dating is not a job interview. You'll be more likely to receive a call back if you divulge too little information, rather than spill the chip bowl.

If, early in the dating game, he asks you what you did today, he doesn't want to know that you took your mother to have a mole removed from her inner thigh, or that you just picked up some fungicide from the pharmacy for yourself.

Instead be selective with your responses and divide answers into three categories: full disclosure, satisfying tidbits, and downright evasion. Answer one-third of his questions honestly, and from the heart (e.g., "Yes, I was once engaged"). Answer another third with only hints at the truth (e.g., "I may or may not accept a ring again"). And as for the rest, change the subject or reverse the questions onto him (e.g., "Do I want kids? Well, I know I want a dog . . . let's order"). He should go home with a ravenous, inquiring mind (which should be your goal).

Encourage time away from you. If you can remember building a papier-mâché volcano in middle school, adding baking soda, and waiting with mounting anticipation until the teacher gave the okay to add the vinegar, you can understand the power that time can have over your love interest. The volcano is the venue. He is the baking soda. You are the vinegar. The longer that you hang out in your bottle, the more anxious he will become for the chemical reaction that he's looking forward to.

When you encourage him to pursue some interests of his own, or to submit to your busy schedule while waiting for your next date, the coupling that results will be delightfully explosive.

GENDER ENLIGHTENMENT: If your first date goes well, don't suggest meeting the next day. Instead start a conversation about what he'll be up to in the coming week, and schedule another date for next weekend. Allow him to stew about you and the results will be delicious.

Surprise him. The cerebral response to a surprise is one of defenselessness and emotional flooding. This is why military generals often choose to take the enemy by surprise: its vulnerabilities at the time of the shock make it a prime target for capture.

Innocent flirting is effective, particularly when it has nothing to do with your date. Your flirting should be subtle, but obvious enough to stimulate your date to think, *The world is her oyster. Why is she with me?*

The biggest portion of your attention should always lie with your main squeeze; however, there's no harm in being friendly to, and even mildly flirtatious with, other men. Some of your dates may be offended by this (which could be an indication of jealous tendencies), but most will find this kind of social fitness appealing.

Body Watch: Maintain eye contact with the waiter while asking him about his favorite dishes or touch the valet's arm when you tip him. Stop with one innocent interaction per individual and you will innocently help your date to recognize what a valuable social commodity you are.

Keep the girly bits cloaked. In this context, *accidentally* sexy can be much more effective than *intentionally* sexy. There's a reason that a man with an erection at a nude beach is an unusual sight. Certain venues, like those that encourage "the buff," seem to have murdered the mystery of the feminine form and have effectively stripped the skin's ability to seduce. Bodily disclosure means just that: everything has been disclosed . . . this is the culmination of discovery . . . the show's over.

However, if you were to place a man in a situation in which he could catch a glimpse of a woman undressing in a window, he would probably be tremendously aroused. Why? Because there's suspense ("Will she take it off?"), there's naughtiness ("I really shouldn't be looking at this"), and there's the building of tension ("I'll never have her").

Likewise, some religions promote modest dress to convey the understanding that desire is not built on the satisfaction of temptation, but rather on the building of sexual tension. When the prize is hidden, and even taboo, the craving for it is multiplied.

When it comes to exposition, take the cloak-and-dagger approach: keep your girly bits under cloak, and he and his dagger might be helpless to resist you.

GENDER ENLIGHTENMENT: In order to pique a man's interest, give him a glimpse, but nothing more. A blouse that shows some cleavage or a skirt with a slit that shows a bit of thigh are like movie previews. They keep him in suspense. Once he's seen the feature film, he won't "need" to watch it again. But show him the preview over and over again and you'll keep him under your spell with anticipation.

A question mark is the sexiest of all punctuation. When you create an aura of mystery, you associate yourself with its enticing, curvaceous allure. As long as that question mark is part of your essence, you will be a prize that begs to be won.

Once you've been marked as the acquired prize, the mystery will naturally wane as you reveal more of yourself (literally and figuratively) on the journey toward intimacy. However, that doesn't mean that playful, mysterious behavior should be completely abandoned. You can be mysterious enough to make each day fun and seductively exciting. If you're a hopeless neat freak, mess up your hair, prepare some sloppy food, and eat together on the floor. If you're notorious for being late, arrive early with a sexy surprise. If you're shy, suck it up and take the lead. Even when your relationship is no longer about the chase, you can still speak loudly to his primordial brain, making the thrill of the hunt a daily gift to both of you.

———————

If you've flipped to the end of this chapter in search of answers to the newsroom murder mystery, you're going to have to improvise. Just as you might speculate about who the murderer might be (a jealous female reporter, an editor who covets the sexy young intern, a conspirator in the cold case), your date will feel compelled to pin on his figurative detective's badge and dive into the mystery of you with his hungry, inquiring mind . . . if you employ the means necessary for creating that mystery.

Treat your dating experiences as murder mysteries without resolutions. Understand that if your man feels there's nothing left to discover, he'll head straight for the bookshelf—to entertain himself with a brand-new whodunit.

CHAPTER NINETEEN

The Bridge to Somewhere

ENTRUSTING YOUR LOVE LIFE TO A SOLID STRUCTURE

In the preceding chapter, we talked about how mysterious excitement lends a hand to attraction. When men stood on a suspension bridge with a woman, they were more likely to call her the next day than if they were on solid ground.

A rickety bridge might be great for increasing adrenaline and attraction, and for getting that first look, word, or phone call, but it's not great for subsequent interactions. When you're flirting with the prospect of a more concrete relationship, the bridge that you'll use to get there should be solid. You should be able to trust it with your love life.

Bridging the gap between a casual fling and a long-term thing differs little from a river crossing. You might know that you want to get to the other side—the side where enduring companionship lies—but choosing the right bridge (the right man) can mean the difference between a smooth crossing and a flailing plunge into frigid waters.

As we near the end of our time together, I think it's only fitting that I send you off with some advice for spotting the Brooklyn

Bridge (strong, reliable), the rope bridge (unpredictable, shaky), and the fallen log bridge (slippery, frightening) relationship.

A solid relationship with potential for longevity is stable, like the Brooklyn Bridge. It's safe to cross.

A questionable relationship that has qualities of both durability and instability can be compared to a rope bridge. It might support you, but there's risk involved.

A relationship with no promise for the long term is like a log fallen across a raging river. It presents significant peril.

When a short-term relationship presents a bridge—when you've been through the first five or so dates and things are going well—you'll have a decision to make: use that bridge to get to long-term territory or back away in favor of a more stable path.

With a few simple observations, you can name the type of bridge you're dealing with and take a calculated risk that you can live with.

When initial conversation flows easily, a couple is likely to continue talking . . . for a very long time. A recent study conducted by researchers at the University of Texas at Austin used audio recordings of couples on speed dates, compared the speech styles, and found that the more similar the styles of speaking were between the two, the more likely they were to move on to a more serious dating endeavor. Those couples with speaking styles that matched on above-average levels were four times more likely to pursue further contact than other, less synchronized couples.

Conversation that doesn't take a complete remanufacturing of style makes for good exchanges and the kind of communication that longevity rests upon. You've learned how to foster a flowing chat, but that doesn't mean you should try to reorganize conversation that's failing on all levels. Great initial conversation can be enhanced with preparation and good rapport-building skills, but nature plays its part, too. Most often, good basic conversation comes as a standard feature of intense attraction.

Conflict resolution is an important part of any relationship (man:woman, friend:friend, boss:employee, dog:cat), and because the early stages of dating aren't likely to present many opportunities for conflict to creep in, you can assess his willingness to come to mutually beneficial agreements by watching his interactions with others.

Does he cut the waitress some slack when she brings him blackened salmon instead of broiled cod? Is he willing to give the electrician a second chance to turn on the lights before calling the Better Business Bureau? Is he patient? Or does anger trump his reason?

By watching his interactions with others in daily life, you can determine how you will one day be treated. Of course, competition is a big part of a man's evolutionary nature, but if he turns every encounter into a battle, you might want to hang up your musket before you find yourself enlisted.

If he's not good at conflict resolution, you're taking a chance on a log rolling down the river.

Empathy is an important characteristic for supporting long-term relationships. Can you imagine how difficult heartfelt communication might be with a man whose brows are lowered, who shows no interest in your problems or your victories, and who answers your sincerest of inquiries with curt grunts and *hmmphs*? The days of grunting and whistling are long gone—as he should be if he disregards the use of empathetic verbal and nonverbal language when interacting with you.

A man will probably listen intently, with elevated brows and tilted head, touch you tenderly, and speak to you in a gentle, melodious way in the early stages of courtship. But that could be due to his intense desire to navigate your valleys and plains. If you're curious about whether this sensitive treatment will wear off—if his empathy will endure—watch his interactions with others. If he listens intently and makes efforts to understand the problems of others (especially those whom he's known for his entire life), his empathetic nature can be considered Brooklyn Bridge quality.

Fling wishes go both ways, but in general you won't find women trolling for one-night horizontal polka romps to the degree that men do. Occasionally women gather at the club with the intent of "getting some penis" or "playing hide the weeny," but for evolutionary reasons women are usually looking for the beginnings of something bigger.

Because men are often looking for soup of the day, as opposed to menu staples, it can be helpful to recognize the signals that men display when they're only interested in knowing you for one night.

If he has difficulty maintaining eye contact because he's focused on the "breast" parts of you, if he wears a sneer (as if to say "this is a joke"), if his smile isn't a genuine, face-altering one, or if he touches you in ways that push social acceptability or with timing that seems too soon, you might have a spinster (who wants to stay a spinster) on your hands. If a man's words tell you that he's interested in you but his eyes are traversing the room, he's not mirroring your actions to any degree, and he's having difficulty staying on the subject during conversation, he's not looking into the future.

This man is more than a bump on a log; he's the log that's not going to support your journey to the other side of that river.

The physical appearance of Mr. Marvelous might have everything to do with why you were drawn to him in the first place, but it has absolutely nothing to do with your long-term compatibility. If you think his tight ass walking the garbage bag to the curb is going to make everything better, after you've just endured World War III over whose turn it was to take it out, think again.

By around the fifth date, you'll likely be immersed in what Dr. Helen Fisher refers to as the second relationship stage: infatuation. During this time the brain will be releasing dopamine, phenylethylamine, serotonin, and norepinephrine—all of which contribute to feelings of exhilaration, happiness, contentedness, and invincibility. However, after about thirty months (max), those chemicals will wane. You will return to the "self" that you once were. That's why it's important to use your prefrontal cortex to determine compatibility, rather than relying solely on a chemical concoction that will eventually be outlawed by the evolutionary reproductive police.

Be objective. Know what you want in a long-term relationship and do not swerve from those criteria. There's no harm in wallowing in the pure bliss that is infatuation; in fact, I recommend it. However, I also recommend that you use your ability to make decisions, weigh the options, and choose a bridge with stability. This makes you uniquely human.

Evolution has fashioned our primal brains to make reproduction successful. It wants to make sure seeds are planted before the temporary insanity of infatuation fades. It works . . . sometimes too well. That's why it's imperative that, while looking for something more permanent than dinner and a movie, you flex the prefrontal cortex that evolution gave you.

To Walk or Not to Walk

When the sign changes to DON'T WALK, don't cross into the long term.

Imagine that every bridge (potential relationship) that you encounter is equipped with a DON'T WALK and WALK apparatus, just like the ones on every city street corner. When the WALK symbol is displayed, all signs are pointing toward setting foot on that bridge, but the moment the signal changes to DON'T WALK, you know that continuing on is a risk with dire consequence.

By baselining or norming his behavior early on, you'll be better able to recognize deviations that should halt your walk:

If signs of indifference or uninterested behavior suddenly crop up (see chapter 11), his romantic feelings could be taking a U-turn.

Take note of his resting blinking and breathing rates. If you begin to notice elevations in those rates, particularly when he's answering your questions, there could be deception or nervousness involved.

If he was staring deeply into your eyes last week, and now he seems to be more visually stimulated by passing cars and birds in trees, slow your roll.

If he normally fills his speech with junk words like *actually, like, basically,* or *um,* that's just him. But if he has gone from an articulate wordsmith to a blubbering wordiot, he's doing a poor job of addressing the elephant in the room.

If he's from a large Italian family or usually likes to use big, sweeping gestures while speaking, but he's suddenly donned an invisible straitjacket, his mind is applying the brakes to his body's movement.

If he generally looks up to the right, for example, when attempting to retrieve information from his mental bank, but loaded questions now cause him to look up to the left while thinking, he's probably being deceptive (remember not to use this method alone; use it in conjunction with others).

If hand-holding started with intertwined fingers, but he now chooses to hold your hand with closed fingers, palm to palm, his romantic feelings are weakening.

If his mouth says one thing and his body says another (for example, "Sure, we can get together on Friday," with intense ear tugging, or "I think you look great," accompanied by wandering eyes), opt for the message his body is sending.

When hugs change for the worse, his intentions are following suit. Remember that a sexually charged hug is one with pelvic contact. If he's been opting for shoulder hugs or patting you on the back to signal the end of hugging, he's cooling off.

If you've baselined him as a toucher and he's suddenly decided it's best to keep his hands to himself (not due to a slap from you), his passion is waning.

Many signs of interest decline as relationships move through time and into companion-type love. But if you haven't yet crossed the bridge into a committed relationship, and these deviations from his baseline are already cropping up, the DON'T WALK sign couldn't be brighter.

If you're terrified of crossing the Brooklyn Bridge, maybe you're just not ready for commitment. If a budding relationship has plenty of promise and all qualities point toward long-term stability and happiness, but you're still skittish about taking that first step, then stop and reevaluate your wants. It could be that you're not ready to abandon the sport of man chasing just yet.

Back away, but don't burn (or blast) that Brooklyn Bridge. Someday you might find it irresistible. For now get ready to utter those fateful words: "It's not you, it's me."

If you really want to get to the other side, but you're not willing to swing it on the rope bridge, find a better way to cross. This means that if you have doubts about entering into a particular relationship, they're probably well founded. The simple act of crossing that bridge isn't going to automatically repair its broken ropes or replace its shattered boards. Instead those flaws will only be exacerbated once you're perched above a raging river, wondering if you should turn back or forge ahead.

The rope bridge, or the man who displays both long-term and short-term characteristics, might not be worth the gamble. Move on to a new bridge, or call in the professionals to repair that rickety bridge before you set foot on it.

If a log bridge scares the stuffing out of you, your fears are justified. Pat yourself on the back for walking away while you forge on in search of a better long-term prospect. Unless you're only in the market for a slippery, adrenaline-marinated thrill, the fallen log is never a good way to get from dating shore to relationship shore. It's much better for an electrifying half-distance romp, otherwise known as the one-night stand. In the famous words of Gwen from *America's Sweethearts,* "It's not always about love; sometimes you just need to get laid."

Learning to flirt your way to steadfast connections is not about faking it or pretending to be someone you're not. In truth it's about learning to put your best self forward while using the knowledge you've amassed to interpret the signals that others are putting forth.

Demonstrate your appeal. Narrow your field. Show your interest. Interact with confidence. Then choose a bridge (a man) that is strong and reliable and suits your relationship intentions.

Some say the grass isn't always greener on the other side. But they were talking about fences, not bridges.

CHAPTER TWENTY

A Get-the-Guy Review

YOUR 10-STEP PLAN FOR PUTTING THE BODY LANGUAGE OF DATING INTO ACTION

Beneath the often-chronicled timeline of human evolution lies another, less celebrated element. It's the body language of dating, and it is vivacious and flourishing with natural energy. It has manifested itself in the human mating dance, enabling our kind to develop into the hardy, disease-resistant, long-living beings that we are today. It has worked for millennia, and is still working to better our species.

The body language of dating has been tested. It has been proven effective. Mother Nature has done her best to ensure that her fellow females are adequately equipped to perform, and we've been charged with the task of not letting her down—even if our intentions are more about hooking up with robust-looking men than producing robust children.

I'll be the first to admit that a lot of information is housed in this book—too much to strap on and exercise in one night flat. That's why I've devised some crib notes to use as quick refreshers before you head out to stun the dating world with your newfound body language fluency. I like to call them my 10-Step Get-the-Guy

Guide, but I think you'll call them indispensable at first, helpful after that, and ultimately automatic, routine, and übereffective.

If you're a true newbie to the dating scene—if you feel that you couldn't attract a fireman with your head ablaze—I suggest that you start with Step One. Move on to Step Two only when you feel that Step One is an integral part of the way you interact with dating prospects.

If you've experienced some dating success, but think that your connection:rejection ratio could use a B_{12} shot, simply review this list while you're getting ready to go out. Often a few simple reminders about how attraction works will be enough to feed a healthy hookup percentage.

The 10-Step Get-the-Guy Guide

1. **Attract with confidence.**
   a. Stand tall and hold your head high.
   b. Keep your core open for approach.
   c. Smile persistently.
   d. Make frequent and fearless eye contact.
   e. Use socially acceptable touching whenever possible.
   f. Display your thumbs proudly.
   g. Shake as many hands as possible.
   h. Speak with an average or low pitch.
   i. Slow down your speech and movements.

2. **Groom and dress appropriately.**
   a. Maintain neat fingernails and toenails.
   b. Whiten your teeth.
   c. Remain hairless in all the right places.
   d. Use cosmetics to improve facial symmetry.
   e. Highlight your eyes, cheeks, and lips with makeup, while minimizing your nose, chin, and brow.

    f. Use clothing and cosmetic colors that complement your complexion.

    g. Dress appropriately for your venue.

    h. Align your clothing style with your intentions.

    i. Wear fashions that accentuate the evolutionary features that men find attractive.

    j. Wear high heels, when appropriate, to sex up your posture.

    k. Align the messages that jewelry and tattoos send with your purpose.

3. Be conscious of the power of scent.

    a. Remember that manufactured scents will not act as biological attractants.

    b. Don't wear overpowering perfume, scented lotion, heavy lipstick, or scented lip gloss.

    c. Bathe regularly and use unscented deodorant.

    d. If you choose to wear a scent, make it lavender or vanilla.

    e. Avoid eating large amounts of garlic, onions, cumin, or curry.

    f. Don't smoke.

    g. Don't drink excessively.

    h. Avoid venues that smell bad.

    i. Toss your hair.

    j. Cross and uncross your legs.

    k. Raise your arms.

    l. Get close.

4. Show interest with your body language.

    a. Give him four or five seconds of dreamy eye contact, smile demurely, look in a downward direction, make a few more seconds of eye contact, and tilt your head to the left—in that order.

    b. Cross and uncross your legs in his direction.

    c. Dangle a shoe from your toe.

    d. Display your jugular and the underside of your wrist.

    e. Play with your hair and bat your eyelashes.

    f. Scan his entire body with your eyes.

    g. Look up at him coyly.

    h. Mirror his actions.

    i. Toss your hair around.

    j. Touch yourself.

    k. Eat seductively or use other reasons to touch your mouth, like applying lip balm with your finger.

    l. Lick your lips slowly and purposefully.

    m. Fondle your glassware.

    n. Go out of your way to walk past him.

    o. "Accidentally" brush into him or touch him.

    p. Lean toward him.

    q. Point your feet in his direction.

    r. Subtly interject yourself into his personal space.

    s. Nod while he's talking.

    t. Touch your heart.

    u. Occasionally gaze at his mouth.

    v. Always carry mints or gum.

5. **Avoid rejection.**

    a. Learn the male body language cues that point to a lack of interest and heed them.

    b. Learn the male body language cues that show interest and respond accordingly.

6. **Recognize the player.**

    a. Play along if you're up for a short-term fling.

    b. Move on if you're more interested in a long-term relationship.

    c. Use the Pick-Her-Upper's methods to increase your own social proof.

7. Provide social proof.
  a. Surround yourself with people.
  b. Place yourself in the center of groups.
  c. Engage others in lively conversation.
  d. Wield a positive attitude.
  e. Seem busy, even if you're not.
  f. Tell stories that indirectly demonstrate your popularity.

8. Become a skilled conversationalist.
  a. Listen intently.
  b. Gather details about him.
  c. Share valuable information about yourself.
  d. Thread common themes through exchanges.
  e. Watch for cues that it's your turn to speak.
  f. Use the pregnant pause to build drama.
  g. Have planned, not canned, stories ready.

9. Build rapport.
  a. Smile.
  b. Synchronize your eye movements, blink rate, gestures, posture, etc., with his.
  c. Determine if his interaction style is visual, auditory, or kinesthetic and adjust your words accordingly.
  d. Find common goals and peeves and use them as conversational springboards.
  e. Use nominalizations, or words that can easily be positive for anyone: *beautiful, relaxing, friendly, respectable, comfortable.*
  f. Exercise Yes Sets, or questions that get him in a pattern of saying "yes."
  g. Touch him when he's feeling good—to create an anchor that will conjure that same feeling when you touch him again.

   h.   Watch how your target expresses positive feelings and mirror those actions.

10. **Maintain mystery.**
   a.   Don't jump on invitations.
   b.   Slightly embellish the busyness of your life.
   c.   Don't submit to inquisition; leave some questions unanswered.
   d.   Don't give away the girly bits with clothing that's overtly sexy.

We may no longer be huddled around the mouths of caves, whipping up bat stew, stitching loincloths from animal parts, and grunting with frothy satisfaction as fine specimens of manflesh return from the fields to eat greedily, stare into the fire, and then choose their bedrock conquests. We may no longer select our men based solely on either insemination or protection, and we're certainly no longer concerned with choosing the walking genetics that will equal the best futures for our children . . . or are we?

Surely we're the most sophisticated humans to date. But most of the benefits of today's lifestyle contribute little or nothing to the effectiveness of human attraction and successful reproduction.

Long ago, man stood up. Then his brain woke up. But by the time all that happened, the essential elements of human attraction were already in full swing. We need only return to those roots and accept our own natural propensities toward animal magnetism in order to benefit from the attraction that is innate to our species.

You may remember that I opened with a conundrum: What had attracted me to my husband and him to me? Now it's all very clear to me. Whether we had met at the communal watering hole or the corner pub, it wouldn't have mattered. Nature was at work from the moment we shared that mutual eye lock. Our physical appearance, our conversation, even our smells were ensuring that Mother Nature got her way, while our prefrontal cortexes ensured that we got ours. That's the beauty that becomes evident when primal instinct meets the power of choice.

You have that power, too. But it simply can't come to fruition unless you get out there and practice it. The body language of dating is yours to use. Manipulate this gift to read his signals, send your own, and get the guy.

I wish you profound success—and when you finally find who you're looking for, tell him Mother Nature, and Tonya, sent you.

Photo Credits

CHAPTER THREE

p. 70—Photo by Valua Vitaly/shutterstock

p. 74—Photo by Pavel Sazonov/shutterstock

p. 76—Photo by Elena Kharichkina/shutterstock

p. 78—Photo by olly/shutterstock

p. 83—Photo by Serg Zastavkin/shutterstock

CHAPTER FOUR

p. 91 (top)—Photo by Helga Esteb/shutterstock

p. 91 (bottom)—Photo by Helga Esteb/shutterstock

p. 96—Photo by Shelli Jensen/shutterstock

p. 97—Photo by olly/shutterstock

p. 100 (left)—Photo by peterandersons/istockphoto

p. 100 (right)—Photo by macsmoser/istockphoto

CHAPTER FIVE

p. 107 (top)—Photo by Alberto Zornetta/shutterstock

p. 107 (bottom)—Photo by Wolfgang Schaller/shutterstock

p. 112—Photo by Tom Prokop/shutterstock

CHAPTER SIX

p. 121—Photo by Istvan Csak/shutterstock

p. 122—Photo by Diego Cervo/shutterstock

p. 128—Photo by CREATISTA/shutterstock

p. 131—Photo by prodakszyn/shutterstock

p. 134—Photo by Vladimir Wrangel/shutterstock

p. 138—Photo by dundanim/shutterstock

CHAPTER SEVEN

p. 153 (left)—Photo TonyBaggett/istockphoto

p. 153 (right)—Photo by pictore/istockphoto

p. 154—Photo by Monkey Business Images/shutterstock

CHAPTER EIGHT

p. 160 (left)—Photo by Andresr/shutterstock

p. 160 (right)—Photo by prodakszyn/shutterstock

p. 166 (left)—Photo by Vinicius Tupinamba/shutterstock

p. 166 (right)—Photo by Entertainment Press/shutterstock

CHAPTER NINE

p. 173 (top)—Photo by Power and Syred/Science Photo Library

p. 173 (bottom)—Photo by Power and Syred/Science Photo Library

p. 174—Photo by Gabi Moisa/shutterstock

p. 176—Photo by cinemafestival/shutterstock

p. 177—Photo by cinemafestival/shutterstock

p. 179—Photo by Noo/shutterstock

CHAPTER TEN

p. 183—Photo by dundanim/shutterstock

p. 184—Photo by Serg Zastavkin/shutterstock

p. 186—Photo by Piotr Marcinski/shutterstock

p. 187—Photo by Elena Yakusheva/shutterstock

p. 189 (left)—Photo by Norman Pogson/shutterstock

p. 189 (right)—Photo by DFree/shutterstock

p. 191—Photo by Squaredpixels/istockphoto

p. 192—Photo by sswartz/istockphoto

p. 196 (top)—Photo by David Lade/shutterstock

p. 196 (bottom)—Photo by Kurhan/shutterstock

p. 197 (top)—Photo by KULISH VIKTORIIA/shutterstock

p. 197 (middle)—Photo by Kzenon/shutterstock

p. 197 (bottom)—Photo by Dmitriy Shironosov/shutterstock

p. 198 (top)—Photo by Dmitriy Shironosov/shutterstock

p. 198 (middle)—Photo by Dmitriy Shironosov/shutterstock

p. 198 (bottom)—Photo by USTIN/shutterstock

p. 199 (top)—Photo by Ersler Dmitry/shutterstock

p. 199 (middle)—Photo by Dmitry Morgan/shutterstock

p. 199 (bottom)—Photo by hidesy/istockphoto

p. 200 (top)—Photo by knape/istockphoto

p. 200 (bottom)—Photo by Nikolay Mikhalchenko/shutterstock

p. 201—Photo Dmitriy Shironosov/shutterstock

CHAPTER ELEVEN

p. 206 (top left)—Photo by MaxFX/shutterstock

p. 206 (top right)—Photo by corolanty/istockphoto

p. 206 (bottom)—Photo by Tom Pennington/Stringer/Getty Images Sport/Getty Images

p. 207 (top left)—Photo by ostill/shutterstock

p. 207 (top right)—Photo by LUGO/istockphoto

p. 207 (bottom)—Photo by Pete Norton/Stringer/Getty Images Sport/Getty Images

p. 208 (top left)—Photo by Alexander Demyanenko/shutterstock

p. 208 (top right)—Photo by Ekspansio/istockphoto

p. 208 (bottom)—Photo by Sergei Bachlakov/shutterstock

p. 209 (top left)—Photo by Nickilford/istockphoto

p. 209 (top right)—Photo by dundanim/istockphoto

p. 209 (bottom)—Photo by Peyton Williams/Getty Images Sport/Getty Images

p. 210 (top left)—Photo by UrosK/shutterstock

p. 210 (top right)—Photo by JTSorrell/istockphoto

p. 210 (bottom)—Photo by The Washington Post/The Washington Post/Getty Images

p. 211 (top left)—Photo by lancelee/shutterstock

p. 211 (top right)—Photo by svbc4817/istockphoto

p. 211 (bottom)—Photo by CREATISTA/shutterstock

p. 212 (top left)—Photo by Yuri Arcurs/shutterstock

p. 212 (top right)—Photo by PhotoInc/istockphoto

p. 212 (bottom)—Photo by Helga Esteb/shutterstock

p. 217 (top)—Photo by Michelangelo Gratton/shutterstock

p. 217 (bottom)—Photo by Henri Schmit/shutterstock

p. 218 (top)—Photo by AVAVA/shutterstock

p. 218 (bottom)—Photo by Netfalls/shutterstock

p. 220—Photo by CURAphotography/shutterstock

CHAPTER FIFTEEN

p. 290—Photo by Andrey_Popov/shutterstock

p. 292—Photo by Netfalls/shutterstock

p. 294—Photo by ShutterWorx/istockphoto

p. 296—Photo by Yuri Arcurs/shutterstock

p. 297 (left)—Photo by Yuri Arcurs/shutterstock

p. 297 (right)—Photo by Tyler Olson/shutterstock

p. 298—Photo by Kurhan/shutterstock

CHAPTER SIXTEEN

p. 307—Photo by photomak/shutterstock

p. 311 (top)—Photo by OJO Images Photography/Veer

p. 311 (bottom)—Photo by bradwieland/istockphoto

CHAPTER SEVENTEEN

p. 327—Photo by dukibu/shutterstock

p. 328—Photo by Eduard Stelmakh/shutterstock

p. 331—Photo by Helga Esteb/shutterstock

p. 334—Photo by Stefan Fierros/shutterstock

p. 336—Photo by Jason Stitt/shutterstock

p. 337—Photo by Sophie Louise Phelps/shutterstock

CHAPTER EIGHTEEN

p. 340—Photo by tepic/shutterstock

p. 344—Photo by LiliGraphie/shutterstock

CHAPTER NINETEEN

p. 350 (top)—Photo by Marcel Schauer/shutterstock

p. 350 (middle)—Photo by Rachelle Burnside/shutterstock

p. 350 (bottom)—Photo by Christopher Barrett/shutterstock

p. 354—Photo by Binkski/shutterstock

Bibliography

"Achieving Facial Symmetry." *Middle Ageless.* http://www.middle-age less.com/2010/11/achieving-facial-symmetry.html (accessed April 4, 2011).

Adolphs, Ralph. "Recognizing Emotions from Facial Expressions: Psychological and Neurological Mechanisms." *Behavioral and Cognitive Neuroscience Reviews* 1, no. 1 (2002): 21–61.

Alleyne, Richard. "Women Play Hard to Get to Find Out How Helpful Men Will Be, Scientists Say." *Telegraph.* http://www.telegraph .co.uk/science/science-news/3542696/Women-play-hard-to-get-to-find-out-how-helpful-men-will-be-scientists-say.html (accessed April 5, 2011).

"American Women Suck at Flirting." *Gawker.* http://gawker.com/ 5686664/american-women-suck-at-flirting (accessed April 4, 2011).

Ashkenazy, Daniella. "A Mothering Touch." Israel Ministry of Foreign Affairs. http://www.mfa.gov.il/MFA/Israel%20beyond%20the%20 conflict/A%20Mothering%20Touch (accessed April 4, 2011).

Aubrey, Allison. "A Study to Smile About: Happiness Is Contagious." National Public Radio. http://www.npr.org/templates/story/story .php?storyId=97848789 (accessed April 4, 2011).

"Australopithecus robustus Skull SK-48 and Jaw Bone Clones BH-003 BH-003-C S-BH-003." *Bone Clones.* http://www.boneclones .com/BH-003.htm (accessed April 4, 2011).

Baker, Robin. *Sperm Wars: The Science of Sex.* New York: Basic Books, 1996.

Baxter, James C., and Richard M. Rozelle. "Nonverbal Expression as a

Function of Crowding During a Simulated Police-Citizen Encounter." *Journal of Personality and Personal Psychology* 32, no. 1 (1975): 1–54.

"Beautiful People Convey Personality Traits Better During First Impressions." *Science Daily*. http://www.sciencedaily.com/releases/2010/12/101221101830.htm (accessed April 4, 2011).

"Beyond the High Heel: Tips for Making Short Women Look Tall." *Earth Times*. http://www.earthtimes.org/articles/news/276745,beyond-the-high-heel-tips-for-making-short-women-look-tall.html# (accessed April 5, 2011).

Bielski, Zosia. "Men Can Detect When Women Are Ovulating." *Globe and Mail*. http://www.theglobeandmail.com/life/health/men-can-detect-when-women-are-ovulating/article1440287/ (accessed April 4, 2011).

Brizendine, Louann. *The Female Brain*. New York: Broadway Books, 2006.

———. *The Male Brain*. New York: Broadway Books, 2010.

Brumbaugh, Wood D. "Using Revealed Mate Preferences to Evaluate Market." National Center for Biotechnology Information. http://www.ncbi.nlm.nih.gov/pubmed/19469598 (accessed April 4, 2011).

Bush, Anne Marie. "Courtship Rules Have Changed over the Decades." *BNET*. http://findarticles.com/p/articles/mi_qn4179/is_20040208/ai_n11810411/ (accessed April 4, 2011).

Buss, David M. *The Evolution of Desire: Strategies of Human Mating*. Rev. ed. New York: Basic Books, 2003.

Carey, Bjorn. "The Rules of Attraction in the Game of Love." *LiveScience*. http://www.livescience.com/health/060213_attraction_rules.html (accessed April 4, 2011).

Carroll, Linda. "Going out of Town? Leave Your Shirt Behind." *MSNBC.com*. http://www.msnbc.msn.com/id/28528971/ns/health-behavior/ (accessed April 4, 2011).

Cheng, Jeneve. "How to Dress Broad Shoulders or Wide Shoulder Body Shapes." *Article Snatch*. www.articlesnatch.com/Article/How-to-Dress-Broad-Shoulders-or-Wide-Shoulder-Body-Shapes/1239728 (accessed April 4, 2011).

Chiodo, Keri. "The Language of Young Love: The Ways Couples Talk Can Predict Relationship Success." Association for Psychological

Science. http://www.psychologicalscience.org/index.php/news/
releases/the-language-of-young-love-the-ways-couples-talk-can-
predict-relationship-success.html (accessed April 5, 2011).

Chrisafis, Angelique. "Nicolas Sarkozy Stands Accused of Manipulating
His Height." *Guardian.* http://www.guardian.co.uk/world/2009/
sep/07/france-sarkozy-stands-accused-height (accessed April 4,
2011).

Cleland, Gary. "Another Reason Why Men Like Curves." *Telegraph.*
http://www.telegraph.co.uk/news/uknews/1569070/Another-
reason-why-men-like-curves.html (accessed April 4, 2011).

"Clues to Mysteries of Physical Attractiveness Revealed." *Science Daily.*
http://www.sciencedaily.com/releases/2007/05/070523105948
.htm (accessed April 4, 2011).

"Color Meaning, Symbolism and Psychology." *Sensational Color.*
http://www.sensationalcolor.com/color-meaning-symbolism-and-
psychology (accessed April 4, 2011).

"Color Theory: A Brief Tutorial." http://colortheory.liquisoft.com/
(accessed April 4, 2011).

"Confidence Is Key to Gauging Impressions We Make." *Science Daily.*
http://www.sciencedaily.com/releases/2010/03/100310142451.htm
(accessed April 4, 2011).

Cox, Tracey. *Superflirt.* New York: DK, 2003.

Cramb, Auslan. "Men with High Testosterone Attracted to Women
with Feminine Faces." *Telegraph.* http://www.telegraph.co.uk/
news/uknews/2964139/Men-with-high-testosterone-attracted-to-
women-with-feminine-faces.html (accessed April 4, 2011).

De Gelder, Beatrice. "Uncanny Sight in the Blind." *Scientific American,*
April 27, 2010.

Dent, Eileen. "Testosterone Emasculates the Male Immune System."
National Review of Medicine. http://www.nationalreviewofmedicine.
com/issue/2004/12_15/clinical05_23.html (accessed April 4, 2011).

"Does the Pill Keep You from Finding a Good Mate?" *Discover.* http://
blogs.discovermagazine.com/realitybase/2008/08/13/does-the-
pill-keep-you-from-finding-a-good-mate/ (accessed April 4, 2011).

"Does Weight Play a Role in Fertility?" *BabyHopes.com.* http://www.ba
byhopes.com/articles/weight-fertility.html (accessed April 4, 2011).

"Dressing Your Inverted Triangle Body Shape." *My Style Advice*. http://mystyleadvice.com/2009/11/05/dressing-the-inverted-triangle-body-shape/ (accessed April 5, 2011).

Dutton, Donald G., and Arthur P. Aron. "Some Evidence for Heightened Sexual Attraction Under Conditions of High Anxiety." *Journal of Personality and Social Psychology* 30, no. 4 (1974): 510–17.

Edwards, Lin. "Study: Men Losing Their Minds over Women." *Phys Org.com*. http://www.physorg.com/news171536828.html (accessed April 4, 2011).

Ekman, Paul. *Emotions Revealed*. New York: Henry Holt, 2003.

Etcoff, Nancy. *Survival of the Prettiest*. New York: Random House, 1999.

"Facial Attraction: Choice of Sexual Partner Shaped the Human Face." *Science Daily*. http://www.sciencedaily.com/releases/2007/08/070813095003.htm (accessed April 4, 2011).

"First Direct Recording Made of Mirror Neurons in Human Brain." *Science Daily*. http://www.sciencedaily.com/releases/2010/04/100412162112.htm (accessed April 4, 2011).

"First Impressions Count When Making Personality Judgments, New Research Shows." *Science Daily*. http://www.sciencedaily.com/releases/2009/11/091103112253.htm (accessed April 5, 2011).

Fisher, Helen E. *Anatomy of Love*. New York: Random House, 1992.

———. "Brains Do It: Lust, Attraction, and Attachment." Dana Foundation. www.dana.org/news/cerebrum/detail.aspx?id=3232 (accessed April 4, 2011).

———. *The First Sex*. New York: Random House, 1999.

———. *The Sex Contract: The Evolution of Human Behavior*. New York: Morrow, 1982.

Fitzpatrick, Kevin. "Candidates' Blink Rate Linked to Stress." National Center for Biotechnology Information. http://www.ncbi.nlm.nih.gov/pubmed/6948307 (accessed April 4, 2011).

"Five-o'Clock Shadow Tops Among Women." *Canada.com*. http://www.canada.com/ottawacitizen/news/story.html?id=cd00031a-a26f-4d95-a302-d89f10b492af (accessed April 4, 2011).

Frost, Peter. "Why Is Human Head Hair So Long?" *Evo and Proud*. http://evoandproud.blogspot.com/2008/04/why-is-human-head-hair-so-long.html (accessed April 4, 2011).

Furey, Katia, and Paul Segal. *How to Get the Man You Want: Real People—Real Answers; How to Get the Woman You Want: Real People—Real Answers.* Caulfield South, Australia: Inner Kiss, 2008.

Gangestad, Steven W., Randy Thornhill, and Christine E. Garver-Apgar. "Men's Facial Masculinity Predicts Changes in Their Female Partners' Sexual Interests Across the Ovulatory Cycle, Whereas Men's Intelligence Does Not." *Evolution and Human Behavior* 31, no. 6 (2010): 412.

Geary, David C. *Male, Female: The Evolution of Human Sex Differences.* 2nd ed. Washington, DC: American Psychological Association, 2010.

"Gender Gap in Spatial Ability Can Be Reduced Through Training." *PhysOrg.com.* http://www.physorg.com/news203744243.html (accessed April 4, 2011).

"George Clooney Effect? High-Earning Women Want Older, More Attractive Partners, Research Finds." *Science Daily.* http://www.sciencedaily.com/releases/2010/12/101210075920.htm (accessed April 4, 2011).

Geselshaft, Max. "Scientists Show How Flexibly the Brain Processes Images." *PsyPost.* http://www.psypost.org/2011/03/flexibly-brain-processes-images-4587# (accessed April 4, 2011).

"Gesturing While Talking Helps Change Your Thoughts." *Science Daily.* http://www.sciencedaily.com/releases/2011/01/110105121125.htm (accessed April 4, 2011).

Givens, David. "Feet." Center for Nonverbal Studies. http://center-for-nonverbal-studies.org:80/feet.htm (accessed April 4, 2011).

———. *Love Signals.* New York: St. Martin's Press, 2005.

Goldsmith, Belinda. "A Wiggle in the Walk Adds to Female Allure." Reuters. http://www.reuters.com/article/idUSN16265972 20070316 (accessed April 5, 2011).

"A Good Wingman." *So Suave.* http://www.sosuave.com/halloffame/hall308.htm (accessed April 4, 2011).

Greene, Robert. *The Art of Seduction.* New York: Penguin Group, 2001.

Gregory, Stanford W., Jr., and Timothy J. Gallagher. "Spectral Analysis of Candidates' Nonverbal Vocal Communication: Predicting

U.S. Presidential Election Outcomes." *Social Psychology Quarterly* 65, no. 3 (2002): 298–308.

Hatfield, Robert W. "Touch and Human Sexuality." Pacific Lutheran Theological Seminary, Berkeley, CA. http://faculty.plts.edu/ gpence/PS2010/html/Touch%20and%20Human%20Sexuality.htm (accessed April 4, 2011).

"How Running Made Us Human: Endurance Running Let Us Evolve to Look the Way We Do." *Science Daily.* http://www.sciencedaily .com/releases/2004/11/041123163757.htm (accessed April 4, 2011).

"How to Contour Your Face to Make It Look More Symmetrical and Defined." *WonderHowTo.* www.wonderhowto.com/ how-to-contour-your-face-make-look-more-symmetrical-and-defined-416627/ (accessed April 4, 2011).

"How to Dress to Enhance Small Bust." *Lady Suite.* http://www.lady suite.net/how-to-dress-to-enhance-small-bust.html (accessed April 5, 2011).

"How to Measure an Attractive Body for Men." *Correct Weight Loss* (blog). http://correct-weight-loss.net/2009/05/18/the-beautiful-body-part-3-%e2%80%93-how-science-defines-an-attractive-body-for-men/ (accessed April 4, 2011).

"Human Evolution." Faculty of Science and Engineering, University of Waikato. http://sci.waikato.ac.nz/evolution/HumanEvolution .shtml (accessed April 4, 2011).

"Human Locomotion: Development, Evolution, and Optimization." http://www.efeld.com/evolution/human_gait.html (accessed April 4, 2011).

"Human Pheromones." *Mohan: Academic Blog.* http://dmohankumar .wordpress.com/2010/12/18/human-pheromones/ (accessed April 4, 2011).

"Human Tongue." *Peace Haven.* http://12learn.blogspot.com/2006/07/ human-tongue.html (accessed April 4, 2011).

Igbigbi, Patrick S., Boniface C. Msamati, and Macfenton B. Shariff. "Arch Index as a Predictor of Pes Planus." *Journal of the American Podiatric Medical Association* 95, no. 3 (2005): 273–76.

"Is Leonardo da Vinci's Mona Lisa a Self-Portrait?" ABC News.

http://abcnews.go.com/GMA/leonardo-da-vincis-mona-lisa-self-portrait/story?id=9662394&page=2 (accessed April 4, 2011).

Johnson, L. A. "Sexy Scents: The Nose Knows the Best Sensory Stimuli." *Post-Gazette.com*. http://www.post-gazette.com/magazine/20010214scentoflove2.asp (accessed April 4, 2011).

Karson, Craig N., Karen Faith Berman, Edward F. Donnelly, Wallace B. Mendelson, Joel E. Kleinman, and Richard J. Wyatt. "Speaking, Thinking, and Blinking." National Center for Biotechnology Information. http://www.ncbi.nlm.nih.gov/pubmed/6948307 (accessed April 4, 2011).

Kin, Justine. "How to Match Colours to Your Skin Tone." *Soko*. www.thesoko.com/thesoko/article742–0.html (accessed April 4, 2011).

Kosta, Olinka. "Long Legs Mean Bigger Babies." *Mail Online*. http://www.dailymail.co.uk/health/article-176642/Long-legs-mean-bigger-babies.html (accessed April 4, 2011).

Laden, Greg. "The Evolution of Human Diet." *Evolution*. http://gregladen.com/wordpress/?p=188 (accessed April 4, 2011).

———. "The Flores Hominid and the Evolution of the Shoulder." *Greg Laden's Blog*. ScienceBlogs. http://scienceblogs.com/gregladen/2008/10/the_flores_hominid_and_the_evo_1.php (accessed April 4, 2011).

Lance, Brent, and Stacy C. Marsella. "Emotionally Expressive Head and Body Movement During Gaze Shifts." University of Southern California Information Sciences Institute. http://people.ict.usc.edu/~marsella/publications/LanceIVA07.pdf (accessed April 4, 2011).

"Learning to See Consciously: Scientists Show How Flexibly the Brain Processes Images." *Science Daily*. http://www.sciencedaily.com/releases/2011/03/110309125031.htm (accessed April 5, 2011).

"Left and Right Ears Not Created Equal as Newborns Process Sound, Finds UCLA/UA Research." *Science Daily*. http://www.sciencedaily.com/releases/2004/09/040910082553.htm (accessed April 4, 2011).

"Left Brain Helps Hear Through the Noise." *Science Daily*. http://www.sciencedaily.com/releases/2007/11/071115083707.htm (accessed April 4, 2011).

Leong, Kristie. "How to Look Feminine in a Woman's Business Suit." *eHow.* http://www.ehow.com/how_4699459_look-feminine-womans-business-suit.html (accessed April 4, 2011).

Little, Anthony, and David Perrett. "Do Women Prefer 'Manly' Faces?" *First Science.* www.firstscience.com/home/articles/humans/do-women-prefer-manly-faces-page-1–1_1326.html (accessed April 4, 2011).

Lloyd-Elliott, Martin. *Secrets of Sexual Body Language.* Berkeley, CA: Amorata Press, 2005.

Lohmus, Mare, L. Fredrik Sundstrom, and Mats Bjorklund. "Dress for Success: Human Facial Expressions Are Important Signals of Emotions." Finnish Zoological and Botanical Publishing Board. http://www.sekj.org/PDF/anz46-free/anz46–075.pdf (accessed April 4, 2011).

"Look Taller Just by Having the Right Posture and Clothes! It's All About Appearances." http://www.gainheight.com/look-taller.html (accessed April 5, 2011).

Maloney, Michael. "How Strong Are Your Fingernails?" *Bjorksten.* www.bjorksten.com/files/fingernails.pdf (accessed April 4, 2011).

Manusov, Valerie Lynn. *The Sourcebook of Nonverbal Measures: Going Beyond Words.* Mahwah, NJ: Lawrence Erlbaum, 2005.

Mapes, Diane. "When It Comes to Breasts—Three's a Crowd?" *The Body Odd.* http://bodyodd.msnbc.msn.com/_news/2008/12/22/4380023-when-it-comes-to-breasts-threes-a-crowd (accessed April 4, 2011).

"Marrying Out." Pew Research Center. http://pewsocialtrends.org/files/2010/10/755-marrying-out.pdf (accessed April 8, 2011).

Matze, Claire. "Benefits of Touch—Baby Touching and Bonding." *BabyZone.* http://www.babyzone.com/baby/nurturing/crying/article/benefits-of-touch-pg4 (accessed April 4, 2011).

"Mayo Clinic Discovers One Mechanism for Why Men and Women Differ in Immune Response." *Science Daily.* http://www.sciencedaily.com/releases/2004/11/041108015954.htm (accessed April 4, 2011).

Mayse, Kathy. "Weak Finger Nails." *Livestrong.com.* http://www.livestrong.com/article/256663-weak-finger-nails/ (accessed April 4, 2011).

"Men and Women Shown to Hear Differently." *Medscape Medical News.* http://www.medscape.com/viewarticle/412256 (accessed April 4, 2011).

"Men with Macho Faces Attractive to Fertile Women, Researchers Find." *Science Daily.* http://www.sciencedaily.com/releases/2011/01/110110154651.htm (accessed April 5, 2011).

Moir, Anne, and David Jessel. *Brain Sex.* New York: Dell, 1993.

Morosini, Piero. *The Common Glue: An Alternative Way of Transcending Differences to Unleash Competitive Performance.* Kidlington, UK: Elsevier, 2005.

Morris, Desmond. *Body Watching: A Field Guide to the Human Species.* New York: Random House, 1985.

———. *The Naked Man.* New York: Thomas Dunne Books, 2009.

———. *The Naked Woman.* New York: St. Martin's Griffin, 2004.

Morse, Jody. "10 Ways You Can Dress to Look Taller." http://www.associatedcontent.com/article/329817/10_ways_you_can_dress_to_look_taller.html?cat=69 (accessed April 5, 2011).

Mulkerrins, Jane, and Roger Dobson. "Women Seduced by 'V man' with a Matted Chest." *Times.* http://www.timesonline.co.uk/tol/news/uk/article855409.ece (accessed April 4, 2011).

Muscarella, Frank, and Michael R. Cunningham. "The Evolutionary Significance and Social Perception of Male Pattern Baldness and Facial Hair." *Ethology and Sociobiology* 17, no. 2 (1996): 99–117.

"Music in Speech Equals Empathy in Heart?" *Science Daily.* http://www.sciencedaily.com/releases/2010/01/100127085550.htm (accessed April 4, 2011).

"Need Something? Talk to My Right Ear." *Science Daily.* http://www.sciencedaily.com/releases/2009/06/090623090705.htm (accessed April 4, 2011).

"Nice Legs and Men's Attraction to Them." *Guide to Great Legs.* http://www.guide-to-great-legs.com/nice-legs.html (accessed April 4, 2011).

"Out of Mind, Out of Sight: Blinking Eyes Indicate Mind Wandering." *Science Daily.* http://www.sciencedaily.com/releases/2010/04/100429153959.htm (accessed April 4, 2011).

Ovitt, Kimberly. "Research Shows Women See Colors Better Than

Men." Arizona State University. http://www.asu.edu/news/research/womencolors_090104.htm (accessed April 4, 2011).

Patoine, Brenda. "The Chemistry of Love: In Search of Elusive Human Pheromones." Dana Foundation. http://www.dana.org/media/detail.aspx?id=19396 (accessed April 4, 2011).

Pease, Barbara, and Allan Pease. *Why Men Don't Listen and Women Can't Read Maps*. New York: Broadway Books, 1998.

"Perception of Our Heartbeat Influences Our Body Image." *Science Daily*. http://www.sciencedaily.com/releases/2011/01/110105071151.htm (accessed April 4, 2011).

Pertschuk, Michael, and Alice Trisdorfer. "Men's Bodies—The Survey." *Psychology Today*. http://www.psychologytoday.com/articles/199411/mens-bodies-the-survey (accessed April 4, 2011).

Pincott, Jena. *Do Gentlemen Really Prefer Blondes?* New York: Delta, 2008.

Pitman, Sean D. "The Evolution of the Human Eye." http://www.detectingdesign.com/humaneye.html (accessed April 4, 2011).

Platek, Steven M., and Devendra Singh. "Optimal Waist-to-Hip Ratios in Women Activate Neural Reward Centers in Men." National Center for Biotechnology Information. http://www.ncbi.nlm.nih.gov/pmc/articles/PMC2816713/ (accessed April 4, 2011).

"Red Enhances Men's Attraction to Women, Psychological Study Reveals." *Science Daily*. http://www.sciencedaily.com/releases/2008/10/081028074323.htm (accessed April 4, 2011).

"Researchers Identify Candidate Human Pheromone Receptor Gene." *Science Daily*. http://www.sciencedaily.com/releases/2000/09/000911070425.htm (accessed April 4, 2011).

Ridley, Matt. *The Red Queen*. New York: Perennial, 1993.

"Running Key to Shapely Human." *Astrobiology Magazine*. http://www.astrobio.net/pressrelease/1307/running-key-to-shapely-human (accessed April 4, 2011).

Sample, Ian. "Why Men and Women Find Longer Legs More Attractive." *Guardian*. http://www.guardian.co.uk/science/2008/jan/17/humanbehaviour.psychology (accessed April 4, 2011).

Savitz, Eric. "The Untapped Power of Smiling." *Forbes*. http://blogs

.forbes.com/ericsavitz/2011/03/22/the-untapped-power-of-smiling/ (accessed April 4, 2011).

Schwartz, John. "Evolution Throws a Helpful Curve Toward Pregnant Women." *New York Times,* December 12, 2007. http://www.ny times.com/2007/12/12/health/12iht-women.5.8719695.html?_r=1 (accessed April 4, 2011).

"Science Has Shown That Smiling Really IS Good for You." http://bipolar.about.com/cs/humor/a/000802_smile.htm (accessed April 4, 2011).

"The Sexiest Legs: 5% Longer Than Average." *Softpedia.* http://news.softpedia.com/news/The-Sexiest-Legs-5-Longer-Than-Average-76730.shtml (accessed April 4, 2011).

"Shyness Is All in Your Brain, Study Says." *MSNBC.com.* http://www.msnbc.msn.com/id/36201866/ns/health-behavior/ (accessed April 4, 2011).

Simpson, Adrian P. "Phonetic Differences Between Male and Female Speech." Wiley Online Library. http://onlinelibrary.wiley.com/doi/10.1111/j.1749–818X.2009.00125.x/full (accessed April 4, 2011).

"A Slow Smile Attracts." *PsyBlog.* http://www.spring.org.uk/2007/05/slow-smile-attracts.php (accessed April 4, 2011).

Soussignan, Robert. "Duchenne Smile, Emotional Experience, and Autonomic Reactivity: A Test of the Facial Feedback Hypothesis." *Emotion* 2, no. 1 (2002): 52–74, http://carmine.se.edu/cvonbergen/Duchenne%20Smile,%20Emotional%20Experience,%20and%20Autonomic%20Reactivity_A%20Test%20of%20the%20Facial%20Feedback%20Hypothesis.pdf (accessed April 4, 2011).

"Standing Tall Is Key for Success: 'Powerful Postures' May Trump Title and Rank." *Science Daily.* http://www.sciencedaily.com/releases/2011/01/110106145257.htm (accessed April 4, 2011).

Tan, Cheryn. "Tall People Earn More: Height, Leadership and Persuasion Abilities." *Suite101.com.* http://www.suite101.com/content/tall-people-earn-more-a141680 (accessed April 4, 2011).

"Temporal Aspects of Facial Displays in Person and Expression Perception: The Effects of Smile Dynamics, Head-Tilt, and Gender." *Journal of Nonverbal Behavior* 31 (2007): 39–56.

Than, Ker. "Symmetrical People Make Better Dancers." *LiveScience.* http://www.livescience.com/health/051221_dance_symmetry .html (accessed April 4, 2011).

Verrelli, Brian C., and Sarah A. Tishkoff. "Signatures of Selection and Gene Conversion Associated with Human Color Vision Variation." National Center for Biotechnology Information. http://www.ncbi .nlm.nih.gov/pmc/articles/PMC1182016/ (accessed April 4, 2011).

Wenner, Melinda. "Smile! It Could Make You Happier." *Scientific American.* http://www.scientificamerican.com/article.cfm?id=smile-it-could-make-you-happier (accessed April 4, 2011).

Westcott, Wayne. "Fitness Programs for Women: Strength Training for Women." *Healthy.net.* http://www.healthy.net/scr/Article .aspx?Id=322&xcntr=1 (accessed April 4, 2011).

"What Men and Women Say and Do in Choosing Romantic Partners Are Two Different Matters." *Science Daily.* http://www.sciencedaily .com/releases/2008/02/080213133337.htm (accessed April 4, 2011).

"What's Your Body Shape?" *Style Makeover HQ.* http://www.style-makeover-hq.com/body-shape.html (accessed April 5, 2011).

Wheeler, Peter. "The Evolution of Bipedality and Loss of Functional Body Hair in Hominids." *Journal of Human Evolution* 13 (1984): 91–98.

———. "The Loss of Functional Body Hair in Man: The Influence of Thermal Environment, Body Form and Bipedality." *Journal of Human Evolution* 14 (1985): 23–28.

White, Shirley A. "Effective Nonverbal Communication Cues: Your Mode of Dress Plays a Key Role." *Success Images.* http://www .successimages.com:80/articles/sw11.htm (accessed April 4, 2011).

"Why Do Humans Stink?" *Sharecare.* http://www.sharecare.com/ question/why-do-humans-stink (accessed April 4, 2011).

Widjaja, Effendi, Geok Hong Lim, and An An. "A Novel Method for Human Gender Classification Using Raman Spectroscopy of Fingernail Clippings." *Analyst* 133 (2008): 493–98.

Wirth, David A. "Climate and the Human Body." *Nature and Ecology.* http://eng.1september.ru/2003/29/1.htm (accessed April 4, 2011).

"A Woman's Touch: Physical Contact Increases Financial Risk Taking." *Science Daily.* http://www.sciencedaily.com/releases/2010/05/100511173819.htm (accessed April 4, 2011).

Wynick, David. "Why Do Women Blush More Than Men?" *Ask a Biologist.* http://www.askabiologist.org.uk/answers/viewtopic.php?id=2033 (accessed April 4, 2011).